Atlas contents

Reprinted February 2005
1st edition October 2003

Published by AA Publishing (a trading name of Automobile Association Developments Limited, whose registered office is Southwood East, Apollo Rise, Farnborough, Hampshire, GU14 0JW, UK. Registration number 1878835).

Mapping produced by the Cartography Department of The Automobile Association (A02385).

A CIP Catalogue record for this book is available from the British Library.

Printed in China.

The contents of this atlas are believed to be correct at the time of the latest revision. However, the publishers cannot be held responsible for loss occasioned to any person acting or refraining from action as a result of any material in this atlas, nor for any errors, omissions or changes in such material. This does not affect your statutory rights. The publishers would welcome information to correct any errors or omissions and to keep this atlas up to date. Please write to the Cartographic Editor, Publishing Division, The Automobile Association, Fanum House, Basing View, Basingstoke, Hampshire RG21 4EA, UK.

Map pages

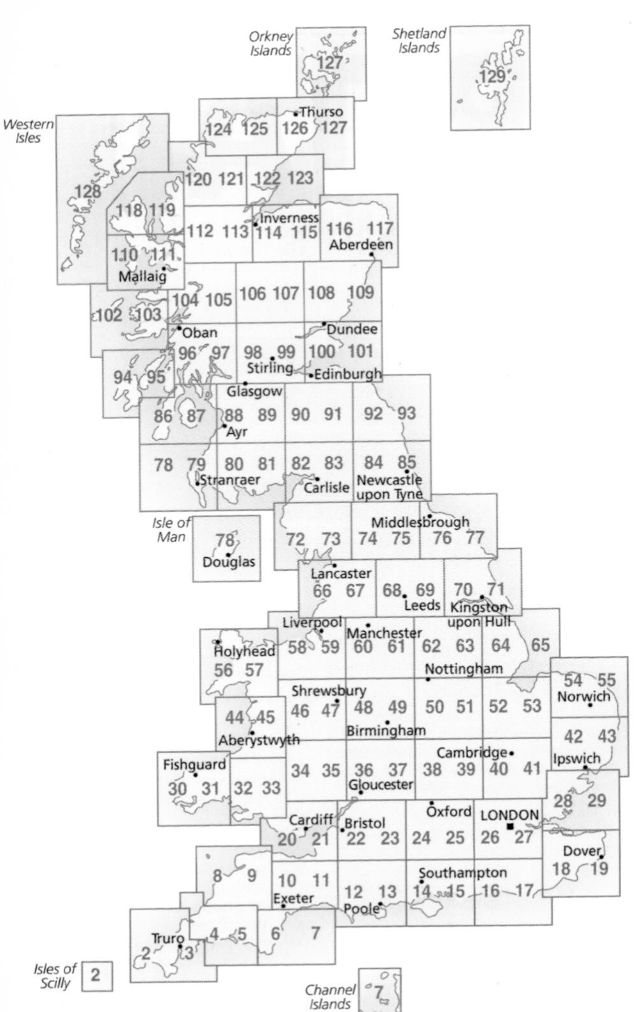

Orkney Islands
127
Shetland Islands
129
Western Isles
Thurso
124 125 126 127
120 121 122 123
128
118 119
Inverness
112 113 114 115 116 117
Aberdeen
110 111
Mallaig
104 105 106 107 108 109
102 103
Oban
Dundee
96 97 98 99 100 101
Stirling
Edinburgh
94 95
Glasgow
86 87 88 89 90 91 92 93
Ayr
78 79 80 81 82 83 84 85
Stranraer
Carlisle
Newcastle upon Tyne
Isle of Man
78
Douglas
Middlesbrough
72 73 74 75 76 77
Lancaster
66 67 68 69 70 71
Leeds
Kingston upon Hull
Liverpool
Manchester
Holyhead
58 59 60 61 62 63 64 65
56 57
Nottingham
54 55
Norwich
Shrewsbury
46 47 48 49 50 51 52 53
44 45
Aberystwyth
Birmingham
42 43
Cambridge
Ipswich
Fishguard
30 31 32 33 34 35 36 37 38 39 40 41
Gloucester
28 29
Cardiff
Bristol
Oxford
LONDON
20 21 22 23 24 25 26 27
Dover
8 9 10 11
Southampton
18 19
12 13 14 15 16 17
Exeter
Poole
Truro
2 3 4 5 6 7
Isles of Scilly
2
Channel Islands
7

Road map symbols

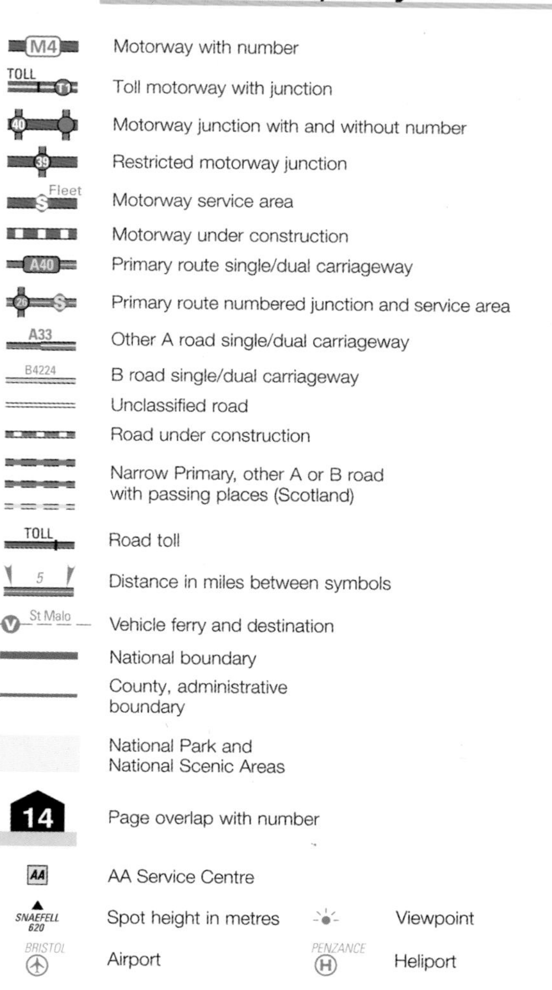
M4
Motorway with number
TOLL
T1
Toll motorway with junction
40
Motorway junction with and without number
39
Restricted motorway junction
Fleet
S
Motorway service area
Motorway under construction
A40
Primary route single/dual carriageway
26
S
Primary route numbered junction and service area
A33
Other A road single/dual carriageway
B4224
B road single/dual carriageway
Unclassified road
Road under construction
Narrow Primary, other A or B road
with passing places (Scotland)
TOLL
Road toll
5
Distance in miles between symbols
V
St Malo
Vehicle ferry and destination
National boundary
County, administrative
boundary
National Park and
National Scenic Areas
14
Page overlap with number
AA
AA Service Centre
SNAEFELL
620
Spot height in metres
Viewpoint
BRISTOL
Airport
PENZANCE
H
Heliport
8 miles to 1 inch
1: 500 000
0
5
10 miles
0
5
10
15 kilometres

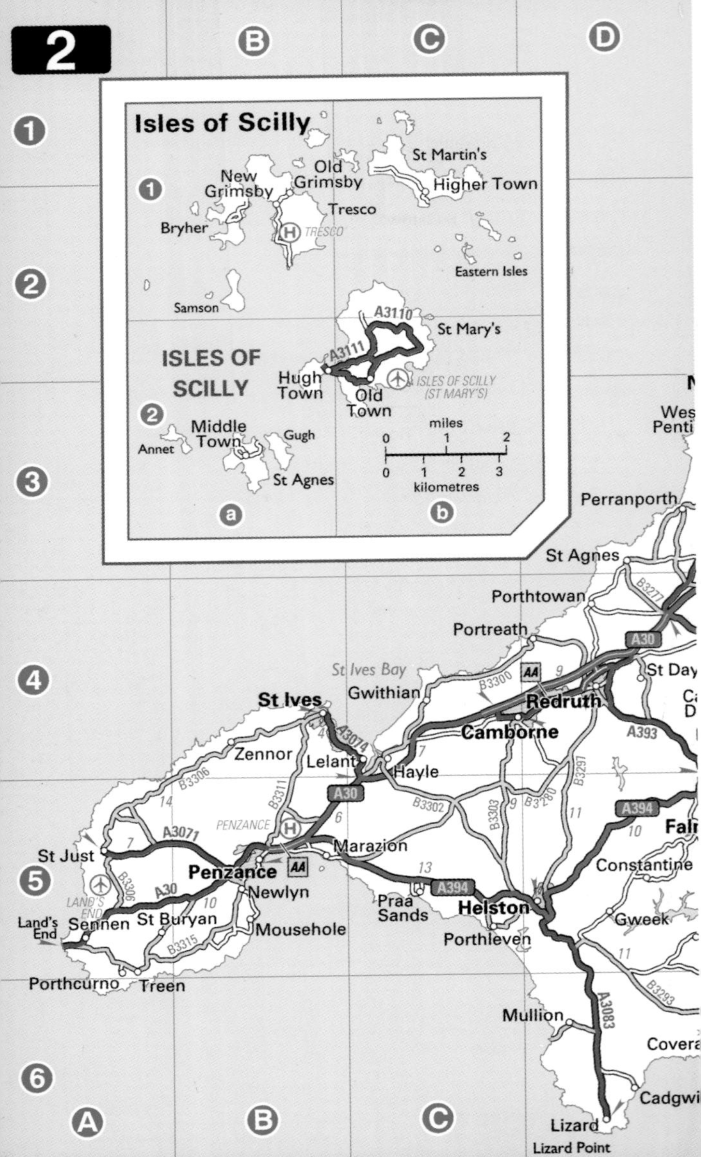
2
Isles of Scilly
St Martin's
Higher Town
Old Grimsby
New Grimsby
Tresco
Bryher
TRESCO
Eastern Isles
Samson
A3110
St Mary's
A3111
ISLES OF SCILLY
Hugh Town
Old Town
ISLES OF SCILLY (ST MARY'S)
Middle Town
Annet
Gugh
St Agnes
miles
kilometres
Perranporth
St Agnes
Porthtowan
Portreath
St Ives Bay
Gwithian
St Ives
Redruth
Camborne
St Day
Zennor
Lelant
Hayle
A30
A393
A394
A3074
A3071
A3083
B3306
B3311
B3302
B3303
B3280
B3297
B3300
B3277
B3315
B3293
PENZANCE
Marazion
St Just
Penzance
Newlyn
Praa Sands
Helston
Constantine
LAND'S END
Land's End
Sennen
St Buryan
Mousehole
Porthleven
Gweek
Porthcurno
Treen
Mullion
Cadgwith
Lizard
Lizard Point

3
E
F
G
Tintagel
Delabole
Camelford
Port Isaac
Polzeath
Pendoggett
419
BROWN WILLY
Bolventor
Harlyn
Rock
St Tudy
BODMIN MOOR
Padstow
Blisland
Porthcothan
Wadebridge
Colliford Lake
Mawgan Porth
St Mawgan
C O R N W A L L
Bodmin
Newquay
St Columb Major
Lanivet
Dobwalls
Roche
Bugle
Lostwithiel
Summercourt
St Blazey
St Austell
St Stephen
Ladock
Marazanvose
Fowey
Polruan
Grampound
Pentewan
Truro
Tregony
Mevagissey
Gorran Haven
Portloe
St Just-in-Roseland
Penryn
Portscatho
St Mawes
Pendennis Point
Mawnan Smith
Manaccan
St Keverne
A39
A30
A389
A38
A390
A391
A392
A3059
A3058
A3075
A3078
B3314
B3266
B3274
B3268
B3359
B3279
B3269
B3273
B3275
B3287
B3289
B3285
B3284
B3276
4
1
2
3
5
6
H

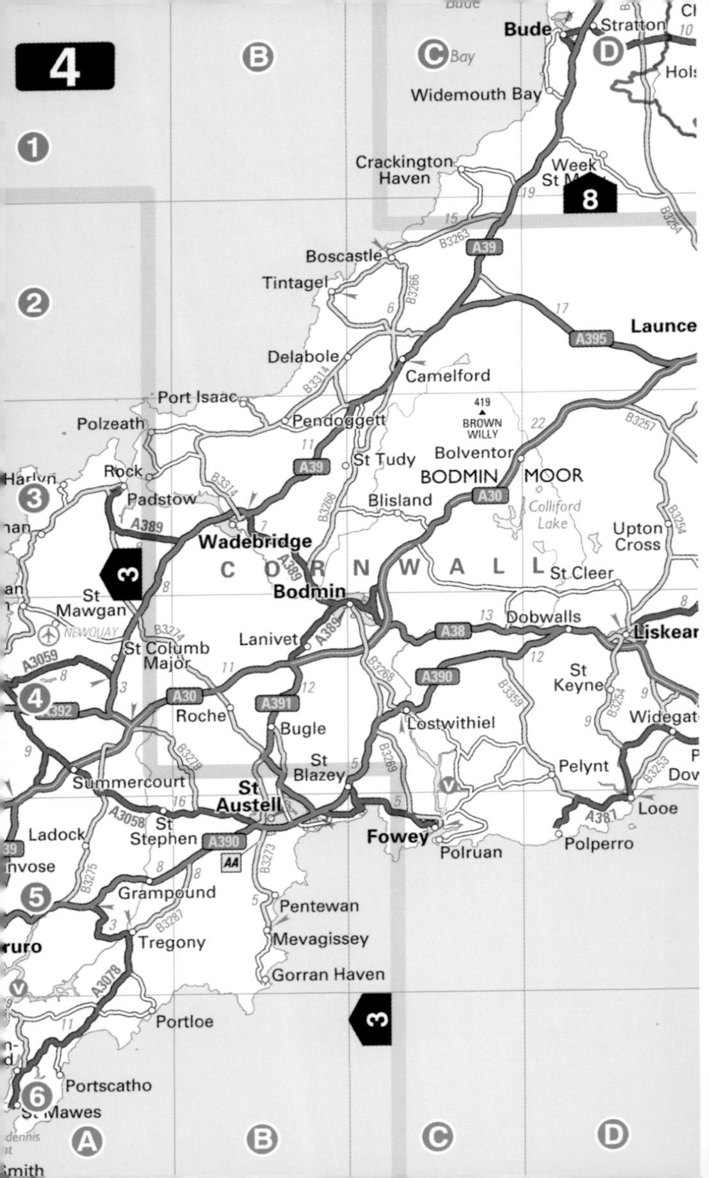
4
Bude
Stratton
Bay
Widemouth Bay
Crackington Haven
Week St Mary
8
Boscastle
Tintagel
Launceston
Delabole
Camelford
Port Isaac
Pendoggett
419 BROWN WILLY
Polzeath
St Tudy
Bolventor
Rock
BODMIN MOOR
Padstow
Blisland
Colliford Lake
Wadebridge
Upton Cross
CORNWALL
St Cleer
St Mawgan
Bodmin
NEWQUAY
Dobwalls
Liskeard
Lanivet
St Columb Major
St Keyne
Roche
Bugle
Lostwithiel
Widegates
St Blazey
Pelynt
Summercourt
St Austell
Looe
St Stephen
Ladock
Fowey
Polruan
Polperro
Grampound
Pentewan
Tregony
Mevagissey
Truro
Gorran Haven
Portloe
Portscatho
St Mawes
A39
A395
A30
A389
A38
A390
A391
A3059
A392
A3058
A3078
A387
B3263
B3266
B3314
B3274
B3268
B3359
B3254
B3257
B3279
B3269
B3273
B3275
B3287
B3253
3

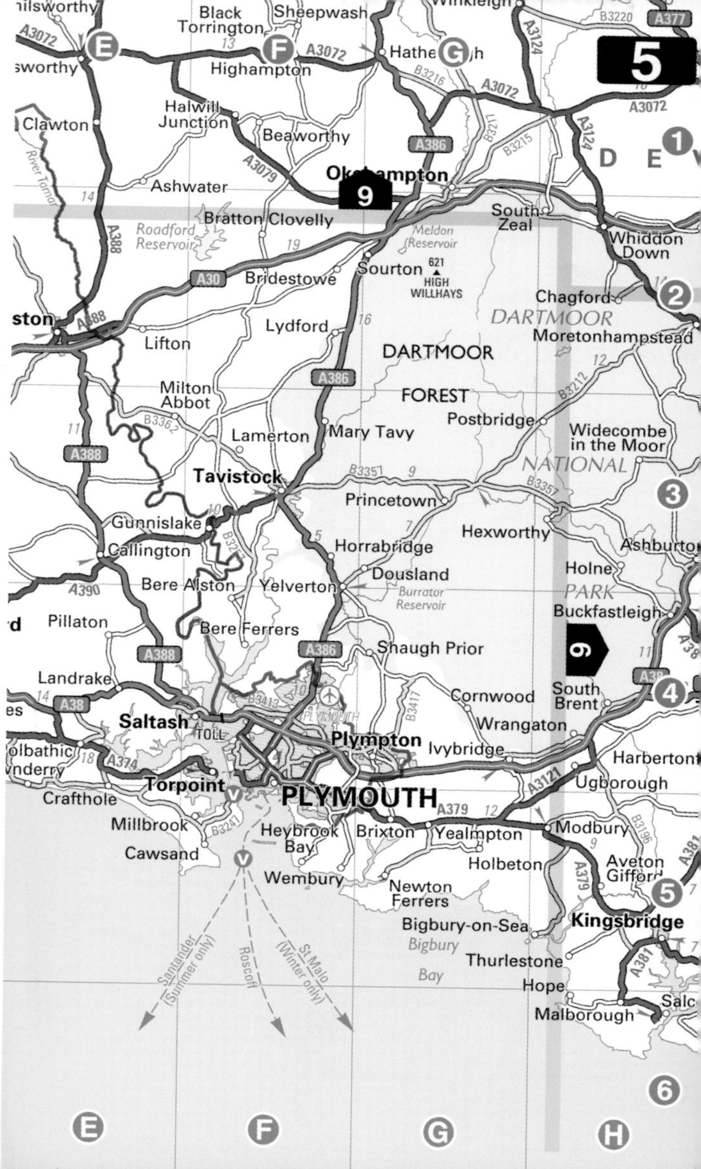
5
Black Torrington
Sheepwash
Hatherleigh
Highampton
Halwill Junction
Beaworthy
Clawton
Ashwater
Okehampton
9
Bratton Clovelly
Roadford Reservoir
South Zeal
Whiddon Down
Meldon Reservoir
Sourton
621 HIGH WILLHAYS
Bridestowe
Chagford
DARTMOOR
Moretonhampstead
Lydford
Lifton
DARTMOOR FOREST
Milton Abbot
Postbridge
Lamerton
Mary Tavy
Widecombe in the Moor
NATIONAL PARK
Tavistock
Princetown
Gunnislake
Hexworthy
Callington
Horrabridge
Ashburton
Dousland
Holne
Bere Alston
Yelverton
Burrator Reservoir
Buckfastleigh
Pillaton
Bere Ferrers
Shaugh Prior
6
Landrake
South Brent
Cornwood
Saltash
TOLL
Plymouth
Wrangaton
Plympton
Ivybridge
Harberton
Torpoint
Ugborough
Crafthole
PLYMOUTH
Millbrook
Heybrook Bay
Brixton
Yealmpton
Modbury
Cawsand
Holbeton
Aveton Gifford
Wembury
Newton Ferrers
Bigbury-on-Sea
Kingsbridge
Bigbury Bay
Thurlestone
Hope
Malborough
Santander (Summer only)
Roscoff
St Malo (Winter only)
River Tamar
A3072
A3124
A386
A3079
A388
A30
A390
A38
A374
A379
A3121
A381
A377
B3220
B3216
B3217
B3215
B3212
B3357
B3362
B3351
B3413
B3417
B3247
B3196
E
F
G
H
1
2
3
4
5
6

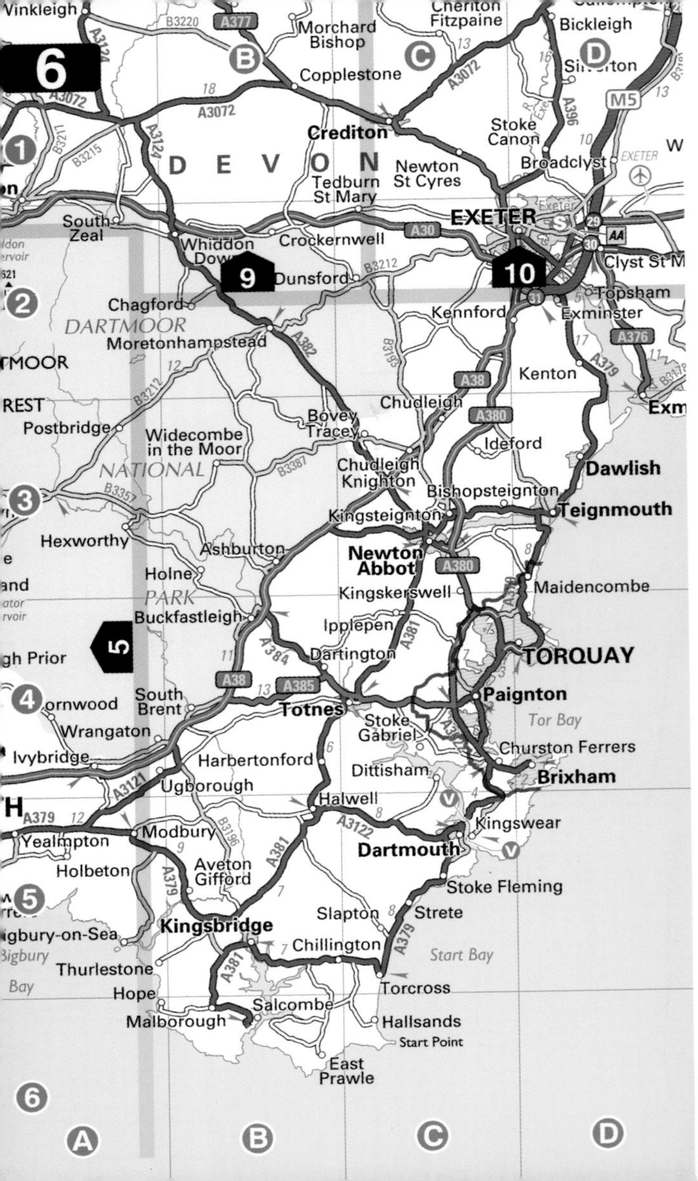
6
Winkleigh
Morchard Bishop
Copplestone
Cheriton Fitzpaine
Bickleigh
Crediton
DEVON
Newton St Cyres
Tedburn St Mary
Stoke Canon
Broadclyst
EXETER
South Zeal
Whiddon Down
Crockernwell
Dunsford
Chagford
DARTMOOR
Moretonhampstead
Kennford
Exminster
Topsham
Clyst St M
Kenton
Chudleigh
Ideford
Dawlish
Postbridge
Widecombe in the Moor
NATIONAL
Bovey Tracey
Chudleigh Knighton
Bishopsteignton
Teignmouth
Kingsteignton
Hexworthy
Ashburton
Newton Abbot
Holne
PARK
Kingskerswell
Maidencombe
Buckfastleigh
Ipplepen
Dartington
TORQUAY
South Brent
Totnes
Paignton
Tor Bay
Wrangaton
Stoke Gabriel
Churston Ferrers
Ivybridge
Harbertonford
Dittisham
Brixham
Ugborough
Halwell
Kingswear
Yealmpton
Modbury
Dartmouth
Holbeton
Aveton Gifford
Stoke Fleming
Slapton
Strete
Kingsbridge
Chillington
Start Bay
Thurlestone
Torcross
Hope
Salcombe
Malborough
Hallsands
Start Point
East Prawle
A3072
A3124
A377
A3072
A30
A38
A380
A382
A379
A376
A384
A385
A381
A3121
A3122
M5
B3220
B3212
B3387
B3357
B3193
B3196
9
10
5
A
B
C
D

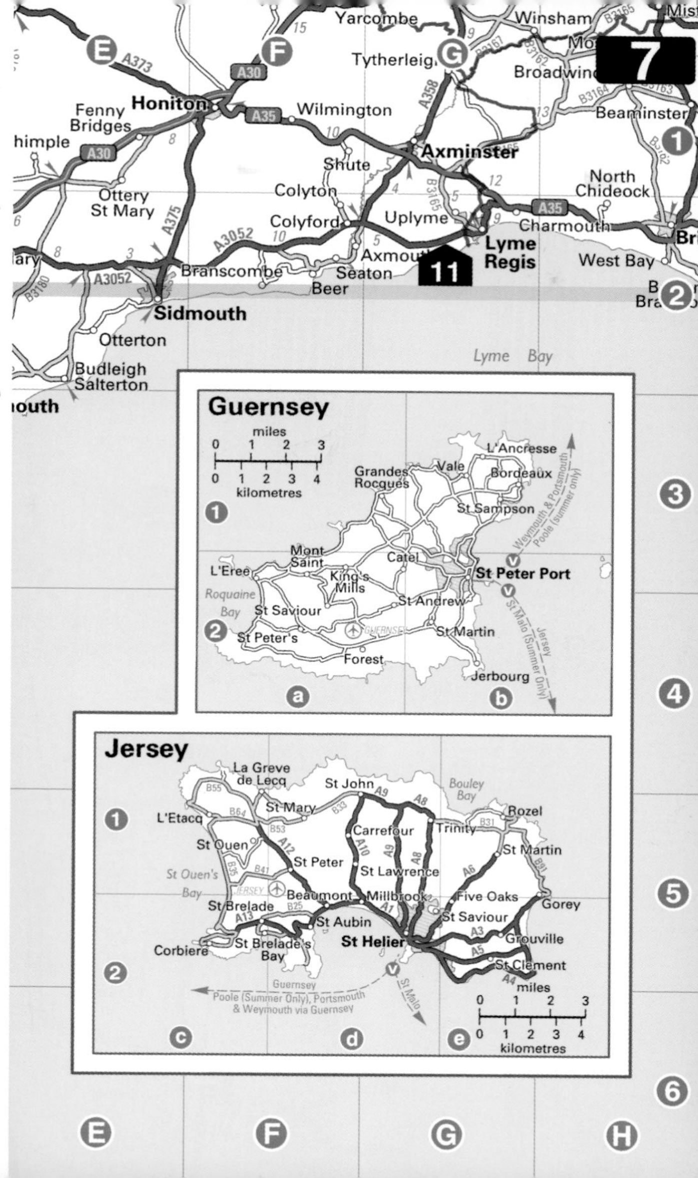

Yarcombe
Winsham
Tytherleigh
Broadwindsor
Honiton
Fenny Bridges
Wilmington
Beaminster
Axminster
Shute
North Chideock
Ottery St Mary
Colyton
Colyford
Uplyme
Charmouth
Lyme Regis
Axmouth
Seaton
West Bay
Branscombe
Beer
Sidmouth
Otterton
Budleigh Salterton
Lyme Bay
11
Guernsey
miles
kilometres
L'Ancresse
Vale
Bordeaux
Grandes Rocques
St Sampson
Weymouth & Portsmouth Poole (summer only)
Mont Saint
Catel
L'Eree
St Peter Port
King's Mills
Roquaine Bay
St Saviour
St Andrew
St Malo (Summer Only) Jersey
St Peter's
Guernsey
St Martin
Forest
Jerbourg
Jersey
La Greve de Lecq
St John
Bouley Bay
St Mary
Rozel
L'Etacq
Carrefour
Trinity
St Ouen
St Martin
St Peter
St Lawrence
St Ouen's Bay
Jersey
Beaumont
Millbrook
Five Oaks
Gorey
St Brelade
St Aubin
St Saviour
Grouville
St Helier
Corbiere
St Brelade's Bay
St Clement
Guernsey
Poole (Summer Only), Portsmouth & Weymouth via Guernsey
St Malo
miles
kilometres

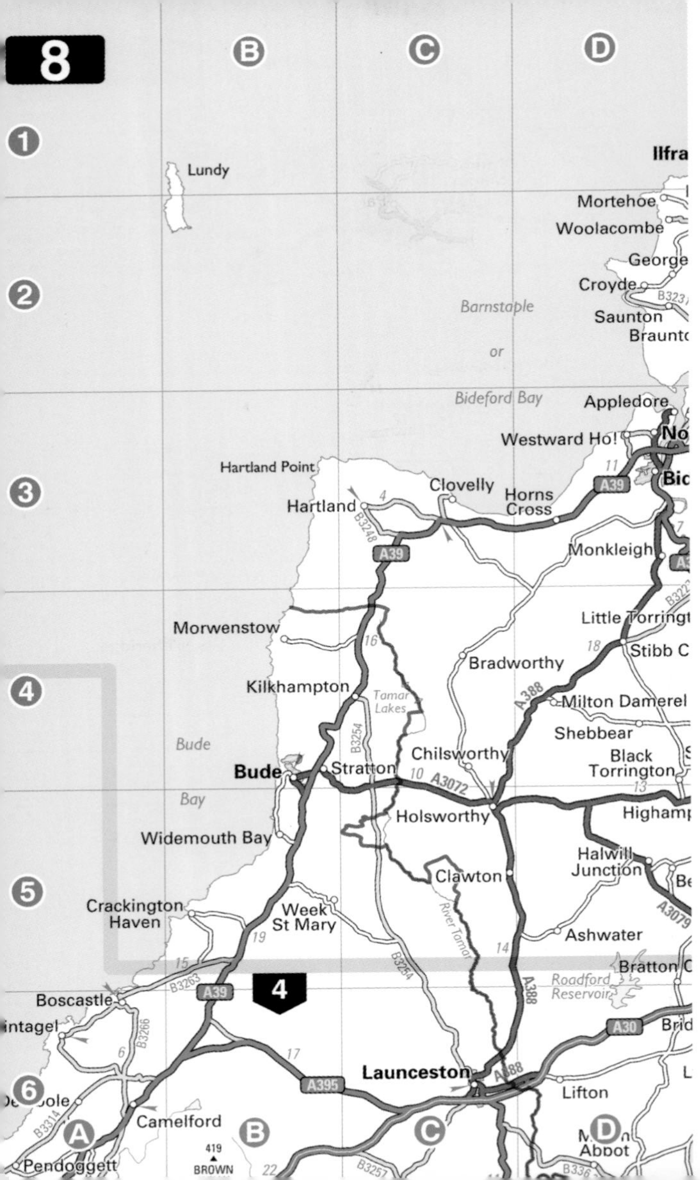
8
Lundy
Ilfra
Mortehoe
Woolacombe
George
Croyde
Barnstaple
or
Bideford Bay
Saunton
Braunt
Appledore
Westward Ho!
Hartland Point
Hartland
Clovelly
Horns Cross
A39
Monkleigh
Morwenstow
Little Torringt
Stibb C
Bradworthy
Kilkhampton
Tamar Lakes
Milton Damerel
Shebbear
A388
Bude
Bay
Bude
Stratton
Chilsworthy
Black Torrington
A3072
Holsworthy
Higham
Widemouth Bay
Halwill Junction
Clawton
Crackington Haven
Week St Mary
River Tamar
Ashwater
A3079
Bratton C
Roadford Reservoir
4
Boscastle
B3263
A39
B3266
B3254
A388
intagel
A30
Launceston
A395
Lifton
Camelford
B3314
Pendoggett
419 BROWN
B3257
B3362
Abbot
B3248
B3254
B3227

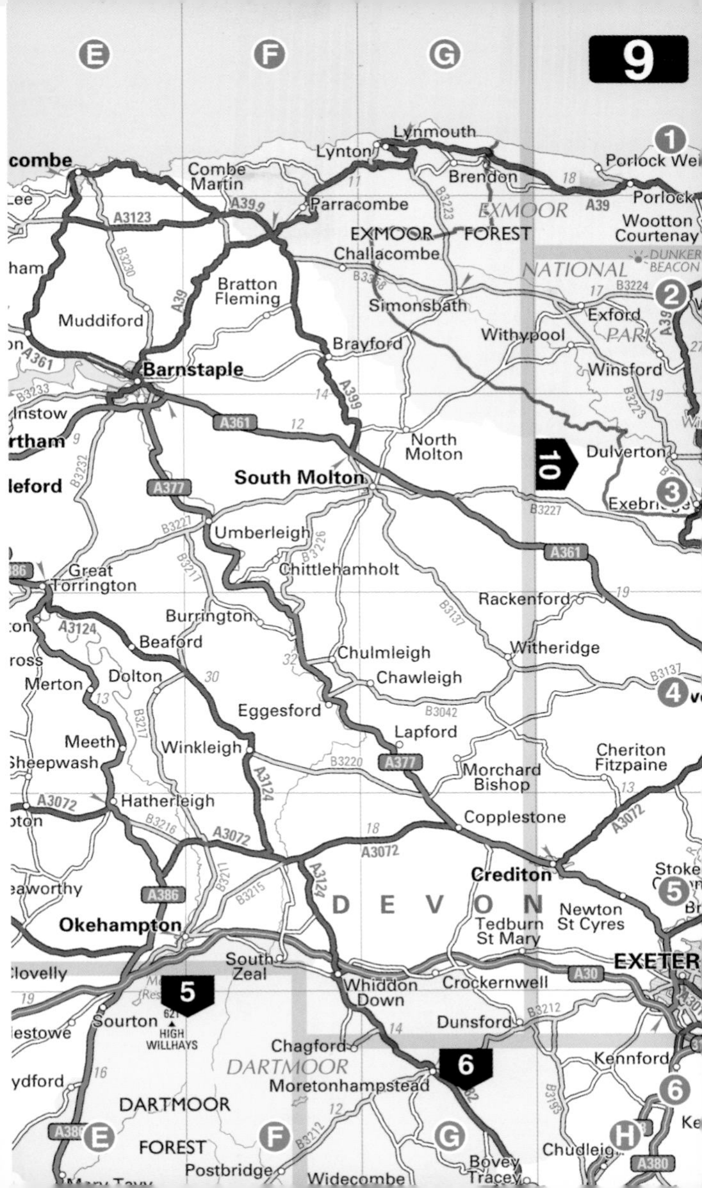
E
F
G
Lynmouth
Lynton
Porlock Weir
Porlock
Combe Martin
Brendon
EXMOOR
Parracombe
A39
A3123
EXMOOR FOREST
Wootton Courtenay
Challacombe
DUNKERY BEACON
NATIONAL PARK
B3358
B3224
B3223
B3230
Bratton Fleming
Simonsbath
Exford
Muddiford
Withypool
Brayford
Barnstaple
Winsford
A361
B3233
A399
Instow
North Molton
Dulverton
South Molton
A377
B3227
B3232
Umberleigh
Exebridge
B3226
B3217
Chittlehamholt
Great Torrington
Rackenford
B3137
A3124
Burrington
Beaford
Witheridge
Chulmleigh
Dolton
Chawleigh
Merton
B3042
Eggesford
Lapford
Meeth
Winkleigh
B3220
Cheriton Fitzpaine
Sheepwash
Morchard Bishop
A3072
Hatherleigh
B3216
Copplestone
Crediton
A386
B3215
DEVON
Newton St Cyres
Okehampton
Tedburn St Mary
South Zeal
EXETER
A30
Whiddon Down
Crockernwell
Sourton
621 HIGH WILLHAYS
B3212
Dunsford
Chagford
Kennford
DARTMOOR
Moretonhampstead
B3193
DARTMOOR FOREST
Postbridge
Widecombe
Bovey Tracey
Chudleigh
A380
H
1
2
3
4
5
6
10

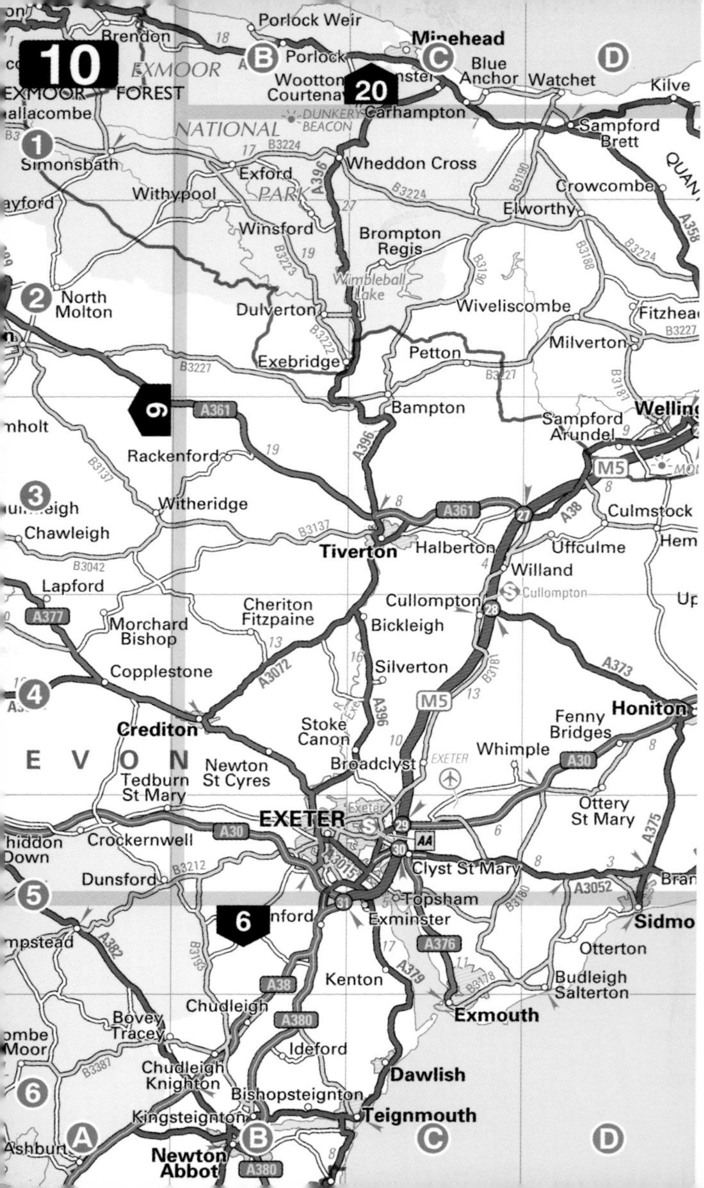

10
EXMOOR
FOREST
NATIONAL
PARK
Porlock Weir
Brendon
Porlock
Minehead
Blue Anchor
Watchet
Kilve
Wootton Courtenay
20
Carhampton
DUNKERY BEACON
Sampford Brett
Simonsbath
Exford
Wheddon Cross
Crowcombe
Withypool
Elworthy
Winsford
Brompton Regis
Wimbleball Lake
North Molton
Dulverton
Wiveliscombe
Milverton
Petton
Exebridge
Bampton
Sampford Arundel
9
Rackenford
Witheridge
Chawleigh
Tiverton
Halberton
Uffculme
Culmstock
Willand
Cullompton
Lapford
Morchard Bishop
Cheriton Fitzpaine
Bickleigh
Silverton
Copplestone
Crediton
Stoke Canon
Broadclyst
Honiton
Fenny Bridges
Whimple
D E V O N
Newton St Cyres
Tedburn St Mary
EXETER
Ottery St Mary
Crockernwell
Clyst St Mary
Dunsford
Topsham
Exminster
6
Sidmouth
Otterton
Kenton
Budleigh Salterton
Chudleigh
Exmouth
Bovey Tracey
Ideford
Dawlish
Chudleigh Knighton
Bishopsteignton
Kingsteignton
Teignmouth
Newton Abbot
A361
A396
A38
A377
A3072
A373
A30
A375
A3015
A3052
A376
A379
A380
A382
M5
B3224
B3190
B3188
B3223
B3222
B3227
B3187
B3137
B3042
B3181
B3212
B3180
B3178
B3193
B3387

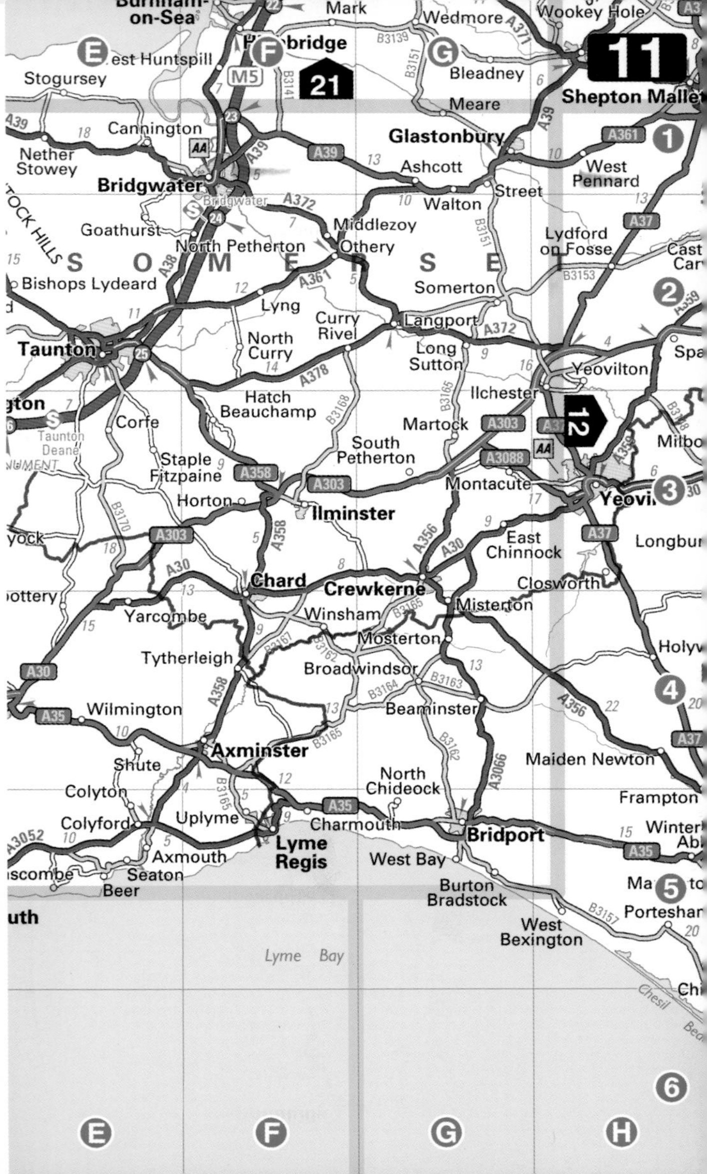

Burnham-on-Sea
Mark
Wedmore
Wookey Hole
11
West Huntspill
Highbridge
Bleadney
Stogursey
21
Meare
Shepton Mallet
Cannington
Glastonbury
Nether Stowey
Ashcott
West Pennard
Bridgwater
Walton
Street
Goathurst
Middlezoy
Lydford on Fosse
North Petherton
Othery
S O M E R S E T
Bishops Lydeard
Somerton
Lyng
Curry Rivel
Langport
Taunton
North Curry
Long Sutton
Yeovilton
Hatch Beauchamp
Ilchester
Corfe
Martock
12
South Petherton
Staple Fitzpaine
Montacute
Horton
Yeovil
Ilminster
East Chinnock
Longburton
Chard
Crewkerne
Closworth
Yarcombe
Winsham
Misterton
Mosterton
Tytherleigh
Broadwindsor
Beaminster
Wilmington
Axminster
Maiden Newton
Shute
North Chideock
Colyton
Frampton
Colyford
Uplyme
Charmouth
Bridport
Lyme Regis
Axmouth
West Bay
Seaton
Beer
Burton Bradstock
Portesham
West Bexington
Lyme Bay
E
F
G
H

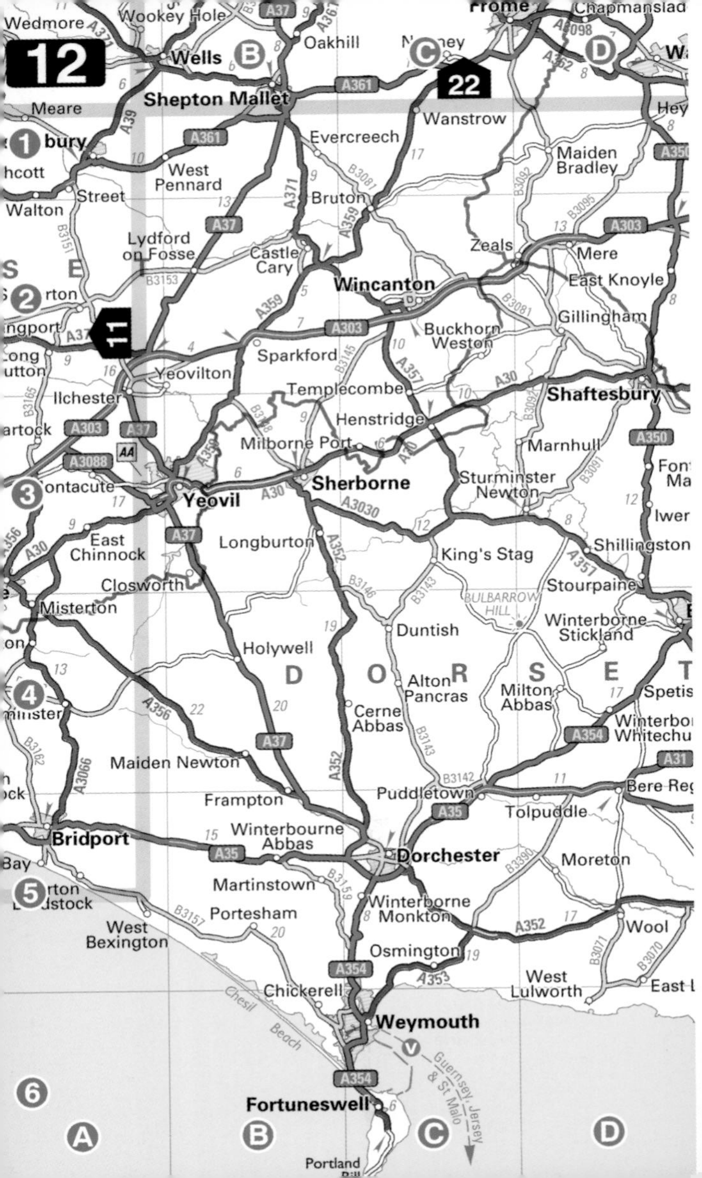

12
22
11
Wedmore
Wookey Hole
Wells
Oakhill
Frome
Chapmanslade
Shepton Mallet
Meare
Wanstrow
Evercreech
Maiden Bradley
West Pennard
Street
Walton
Bruton
Lydford on Fosse
Castle Cary
Zeals
Mere
East Knoyle
Wincanton
Gillingham
Buckhorn Weston
Sparkford
Yeovilton
Ilchester
Templecombe
Shaftesbury
Henstridge
Milborne Port
Marnhull
Sherborne
Sturminster Newton
Yeovil
East Chinnock
Longburton
King's Stag
Shillingstone
Closworth
Stourpaine
Misterton
Bulbarrow Hill
Winterborne Stickland
Duntish
Holywell
Alton Pancras
Milton Abbas
Cerne Abbas
D O R S E T
Maiden Newton
Frampton
Puddletown
Tolpuddle
Winterbourne Abbas
Bridport
Dorchester
Moreton
Martinstown
Winterborne Monkton
Portesham
West Bexington
Wool
Osmington
West Lulworth
Chickerell
Chesil Beach
Weymouth
Guernsey, Jersey & St Malo
Fortuneswell
Portland
A
B
C
D
1
2
3
4
5
6

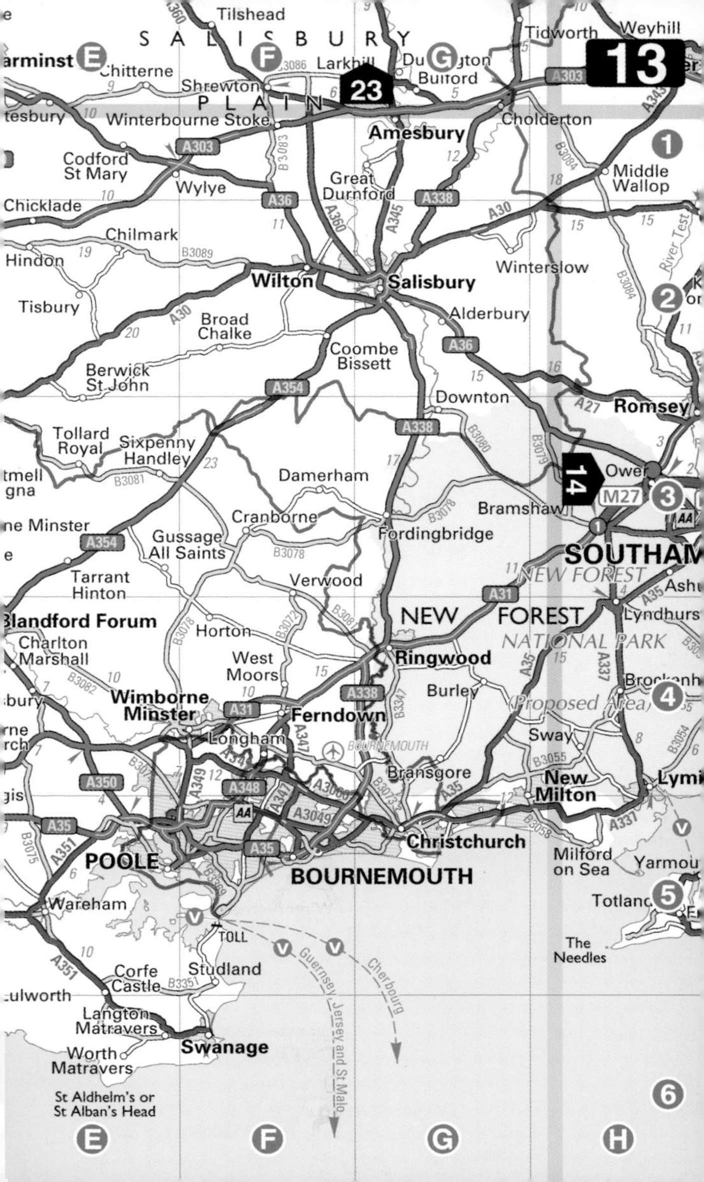

13
23
14
SALISBURY PLAIN
Salisbury
Wilton
Amesbury
Romsey
SOUTHAMPTON
NEW FOREST
NEW FOREST NATIONAL PARK
(Proposed Area)
Ringwood
Ferndown
Wimborne Minster
POOLE
BOURNEMOUTH
Christchurch
New Milton
Blandford Forum
Swanage
Wareham
The Needles
St Aldhelm's or St Alban's Head
Guernsey, Jersey and St Malo
Cherbourg
E
F
G
H

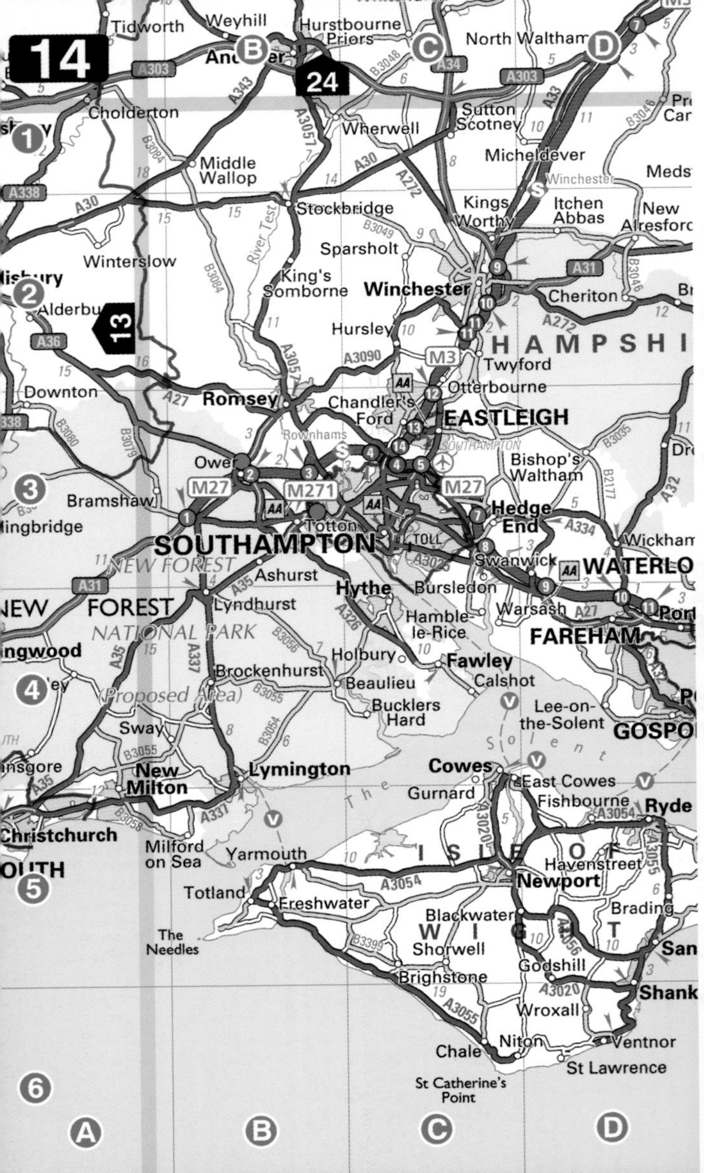
14
24
13
Tidworth
Weyhill
Hurstbourne Priors
North Waltham
Cholderton
Sutton Scotney
Wherwell
Middle Wallop
Micheldever
Winchester
Meds
Stockbridge
Kings Worthy
Itchen Abbas
New Alresford
Sparsholt
Winterslow
King's Somborne
Winchester
Cheriton
Alderbu
Hursley
HAMPSHI
Twyford
Downton
Romsey
Otterbourne
Chandler's Ford
EASTLEIGH
Rownhams
SOUTHAMPTON
Ower
Bishop's Waltham
Bramshaw
Totton
Hedge End
SOUTHAMPTON
NEW FOREST
Wickham
Ashurst
Swanwick
WATERLO
Hythe
Bursledon
FOREST
Lyndhurst
Warsash
NATIONAL PARK
Hamble-le-Rice
FAREHAM
Holbury
Fawley
Brockenhurst
Calshot
Beaulieu
(Proposed Area)
Bucklers Hard
Lee-on-the-Solent
Sway
GOSPO
Solent
New Milton
Lymington
Cowes
East Cowes
Gurnard
Fishbourne
Ryde
Christchurch
Milford on Sea
Yarmouth
ISLE OF WIGHT
Havenstreet
Newport
Totland
Freshwater
Brading
Blackwater
The Needles
Shorwell
Godshill
Brighstone
Shank
Wroxall
Niton
Ventnor
Chale
St Lawrence
St Catherine's Point
A303
A343
A3057
A34
A33
A30
A272
A338
A31
A36
A27
A3090
M3
M27
M271
A35
A337
A326
A3025
A334
A32
A3054
A3020
A3055
A3056
B3048
B3046
B3084
B3049
B3080
B3079
B3035
B2177
B3056
B3055
B3054
B3058
B3399
A B C D
1 2 3 4 5 6

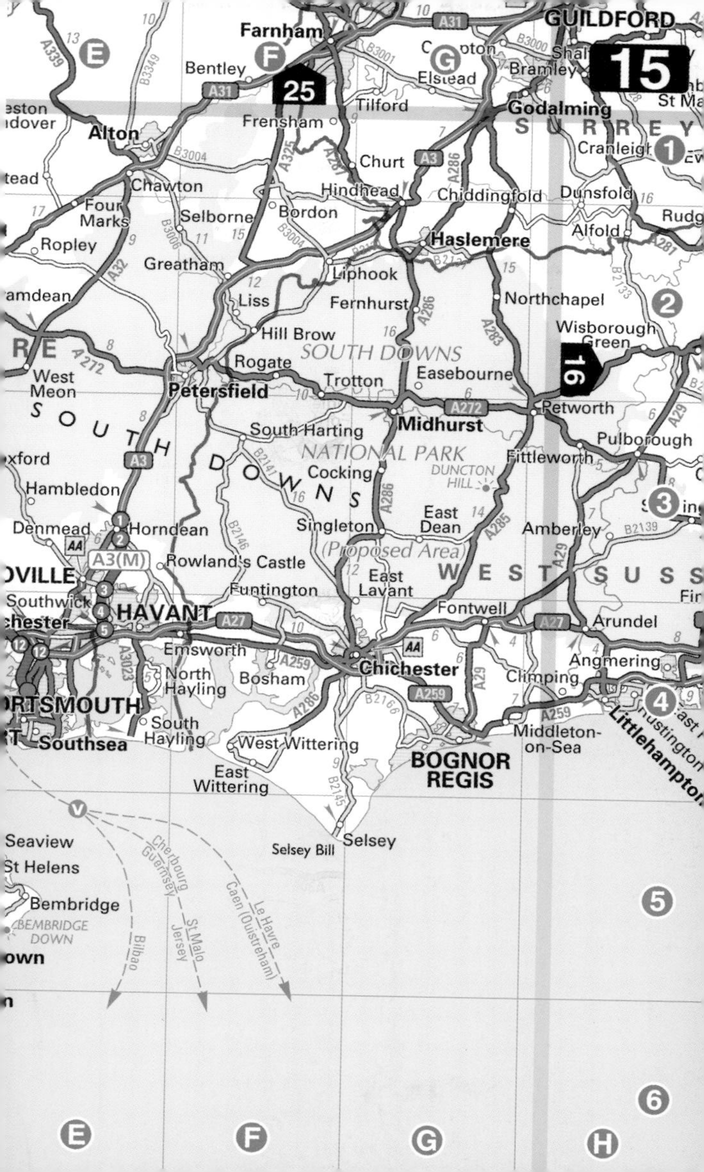

GUILDFORD
15
25
16
Farnham
Bentley
Alton
Frensham
Tilford
Elstead
Bramley
Godalming
SURREY
Cranleigh
Churt
Hindhead
Chiddingfold
Dunsfold
Alfold
Chawton
Four Marks
Selborne
Bordon
Ropley
Greatham
Haslemere
Liphook
Liss
Fernhurst
Northchapel
Hill Brow
Wisborough Green
SOUTH DOWNS
Rogate
Trotton
Easebourne
West Meon
Petersfield
Midhurst
Petworth
South Harting
Pulborough
NATIONAL PARK
Fittleworth
Cocking
DUNCTON HILL
Hambledon
Denmead
Horndean
Singleton
East Dean
Amberley
(Proposed Area)
Rowland's Castle
WEST SUSSEX
Southwick
HAVANT
Funtington
East Lavant
Fontwell
Arundel
Emsworth
Chichester
Angmering
North Hayling
Bosham
Climping
PORTSMOUTH
South Hayling
Southsea
West Wittering
Middleton-on-Sea
Littlehampton
East Wittering
BOGNOR REGIS
Selsey
Selsey Bill
Seaview
St Helens
Bembridge
BEMBRIDGE DOWN
Cherbourg
Guernsey
St Malo
Jersey
Le Havre
Caen (Ouistreham)
Bilbao
A31
A3
A286
A272
A283
A29
A285
A27
A259
A3(M)
A32
A325
A287
A339
A3023
A281
B3000
B3001
B3004
B3006
B3349
B2141
B2146
B2145
B2166
B2133
B2139
B2131
E
F
G
H
1
2
3
4
5
6

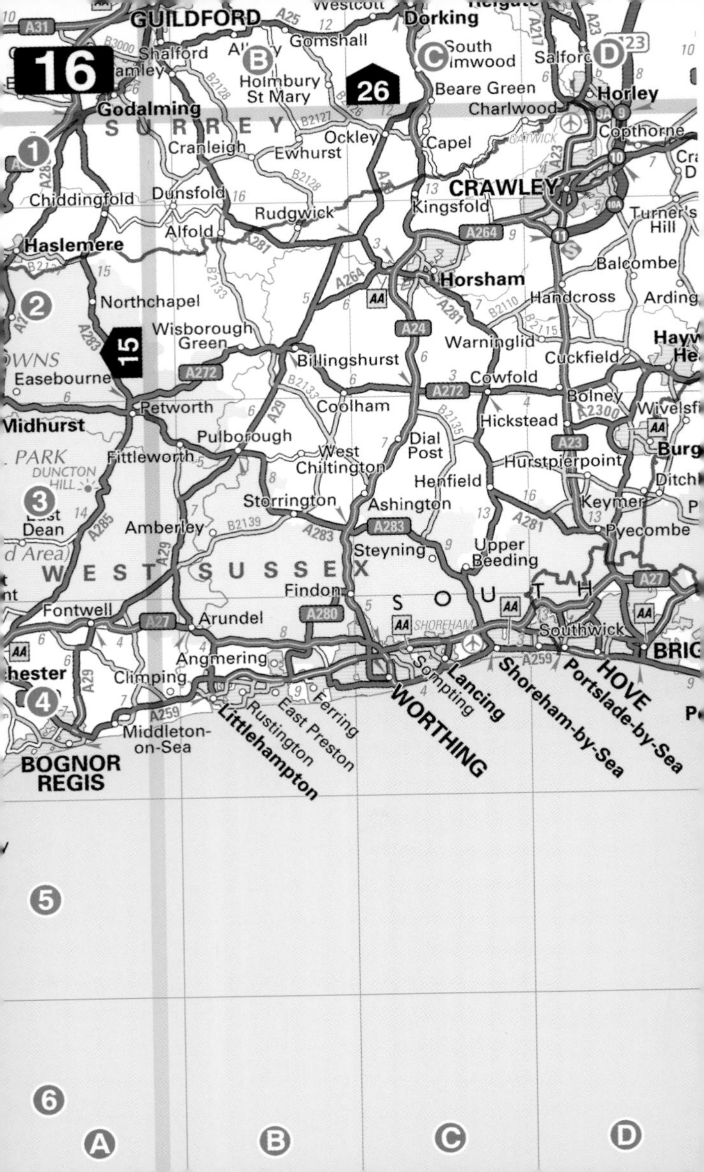
16
GUILDFORD
Dorking
Gomshall
Shalford
Holmbury St Mary
South Holmwood
Salfords
26
Beare Green
Charlwood
Horley
Godalming
SURREY
Ockley
Capel
Cranleigh
Ewhurst
Copthorne
Chiddingfold
Dunsfold
CRAWLEY
Kingsfold
Rudgwick
Turner's Hill
Alfold
Haslemere
Horsham
Balcombe
Northchapel
Handcross
Wisborough Green
Warninglid
15
Billingshurst
Cuckfield
Easebourne
Cowfold
Bolney
Petworth
Coolham
Hickstead
Midhurst
Pulborough
Dial Post
Fittleworth
West Chiltington
Hurstpierpoint
DUNCTON HILL
Henfield
Storrington
Keymer
Ashington
East Dean
Amberley
Pyecombe
Steyning
Upper Beeding
WEST SUSSEX
Findon
SOUTH
Fontwell
Arundel
Southwick
Angmering
HOVE
Climping
Sompting
Lancing
Shoreham-by-Sea
Portslade-by-Sea
Ferring
Middleton-on-Sea
East Preston
WORTHING
Rustington
Littlehampton
BOGNOR REGIS
A
B
C
D
1
2
3
4
5
6

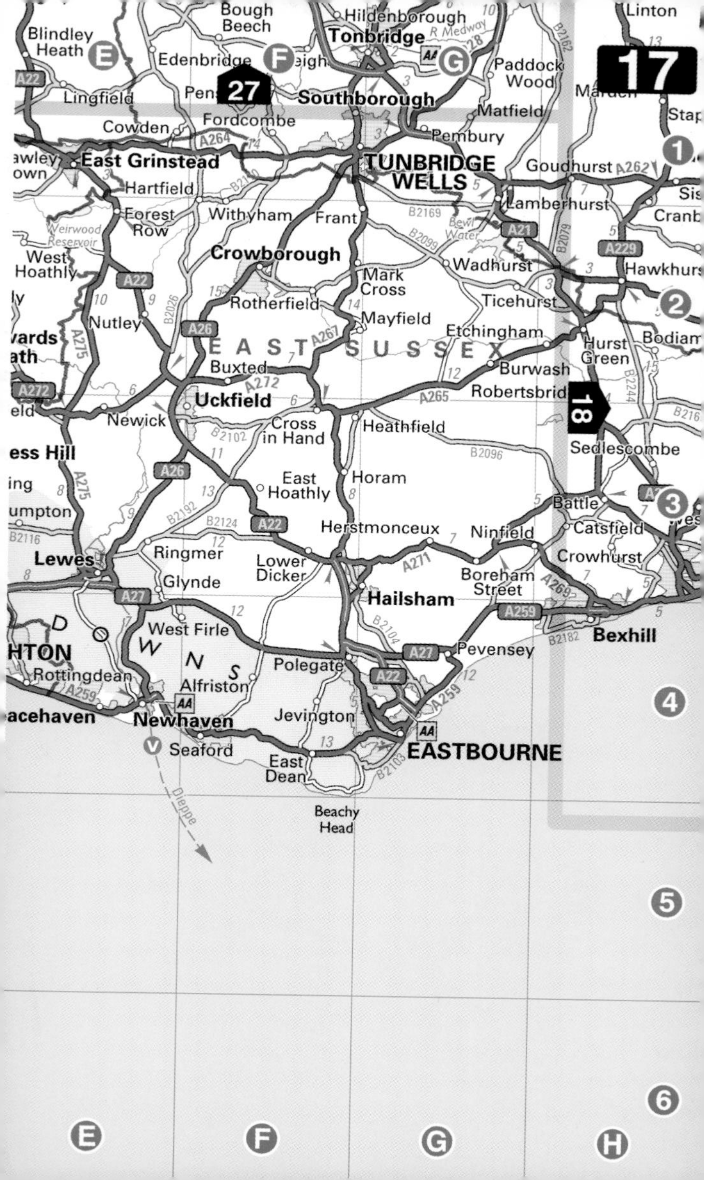

17
27
18
Tonbridge
Southborough
TUNBRIDGE
WELLS
East Grinstead
Crowborough
Uckfield
Lewes
Hailsham
Bexhill
Newhaven
EASTBOURNE
E A S T S U S S E X
Hildenborough
Bough
Beech
Blindley
Heath
Edenbridge
Lingfield
Cowden
Fordcombe
Paddock
Wood
Matfield
Pembury
Goudhurst
Lamberhurst
Hartfield
Forest
Row
Withyham
Frant
Weirwood
Reservoir
West
Hoathly
Wadhurst
Mark
Cross
Rotherfield
Mayfield
Ticehurst
Etchingham
Hurst
Green
Bodiam
Hawkhurst
Nutley
Buxted
Burwash
Robertsbridge
Newick
Cross
in Hand
Heathfield
Sedlescombe
East
Hoathly
Horam
Battle
Catsfield
Herstmonceux
Ninfield
Crowhurst
Ringmer
Lower
Dicker
Boreham
Street
Glynde
West Firle
Pevensey
Polegate
Rottingdean
Alfriston
Jevington
Seaford
East
Dean
Beachy
Head
Dieppe
Bewl
Water
R Medway
D O W N S

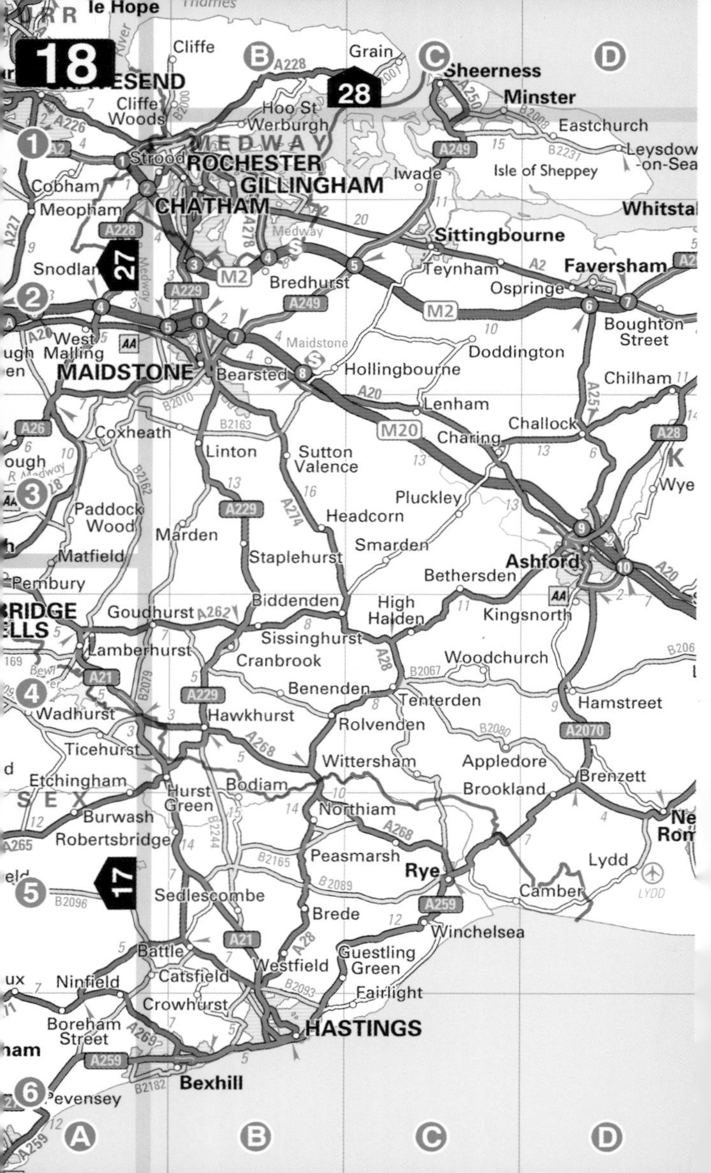

18
28
27
17
Cliffe
Grain
Sheerness
Minster
Eastchurch
Leysdown-on-Sea
Isle of Sheppey
Cliffe Woods
Hoo St Werburgh
MEDWAY
Strood
ROCHESTER
GILLINGHAM
CHATHAM
Cobham
Meopham
Iwade
Whitstable
Sittingbourne
Teynham
Faversham
Ospringe
Boughton Street
Snodland
Bredhurst
West Malling
MAIDSTONE
Bearsted
Hollingbourne
Doddington
Chilham
Lenham
Challock
Charing
Coxheath
Linton
Sutton Valence
Pluckley
Wye
Paddock Wood
Marden
Headcorn
Smarden
Matfield
Staplehurst
Ashford
Pembury
Bethersden
Biddenden
High Halden
Kingsnorth
Goudhurst
Sissinghurst
Lamberhurst
Cranbrook
Woodchurch
Benenden
Tenterden
Hamstreet
Wadhurst
Hawkhurst
Rolvenden
Ticehurst
Wittersham
Appledore
Etchingham
Brenzett
Hurst Green
Bodiam
Brookland
Burwash
Northiam
Robertsbridge
Peasmarsh
Lydd
Rye
Camber
Sedlescombe
Brede
Winchelsea
Battle
Guestling Green
Westfield
Catsfield
Ninfield
Fairlight
Crowhurst
Boreham Street
HASTINGS
Bexhill
Pevensey
A
B
C
D
1
2
3
4
5
6

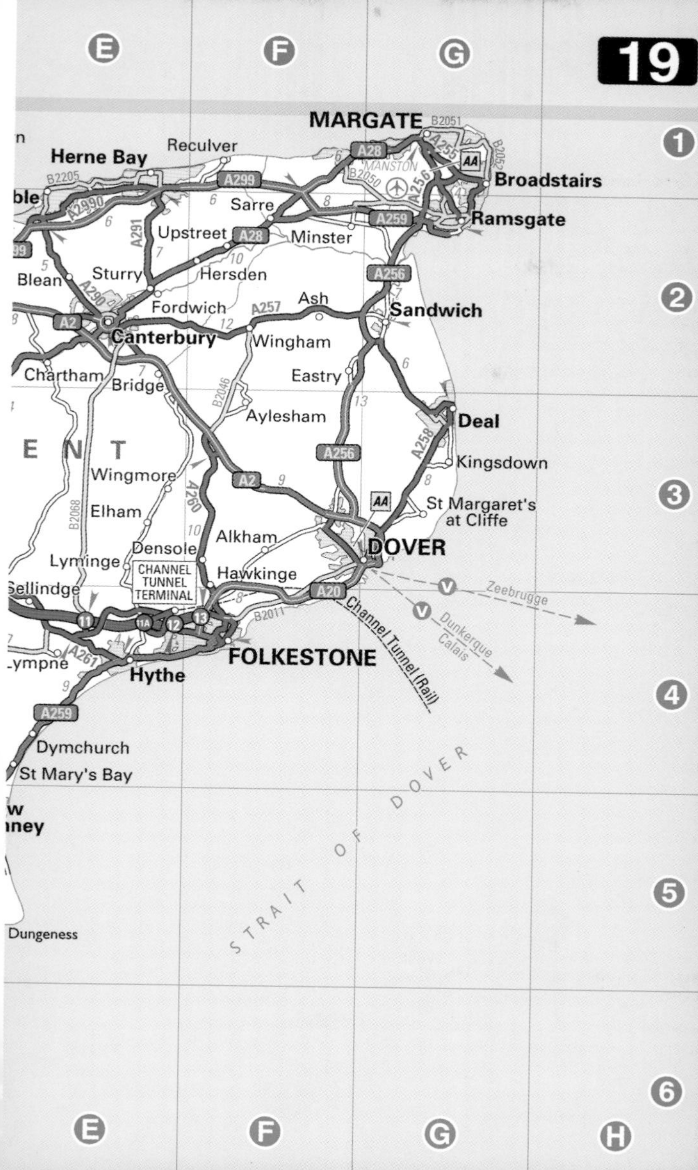

E
F
G
MARGATE
Herne Bay
Reculver
Broadstairs
Ramsgate
MANSTON
Sarre
Upstreet
Minster
Hersden
Blean
Sturry
Fordwich
Ash
Sandwich
Canterbury
Wingham
Chartham
Bridge
Eastry
Aylesham
Deal
K E N T
Kingsdown
Wingmore
Elham
St Margaret's at Cliffe
Alkham
DOVER
Densole
Lyminge
CHANNEL TUNNEL TERMINAL
Hawkinge
Sellindge
Zeebrugge
Dunkerque
Calais
FOLKESTONE
Channel Tunnel (Rail)
Lympne
Hythe
Dymchurch
St Mary's Bay
Dungeness
STRAIT OF DOVER
A28
A255
A299
A256
A2990
A259
A291
A290
A2
A257
A258
A260
A20
A261
B2051
B2052
B2050
B2205
B2046
B2068
B2011
1
2
3
4
5
6
H

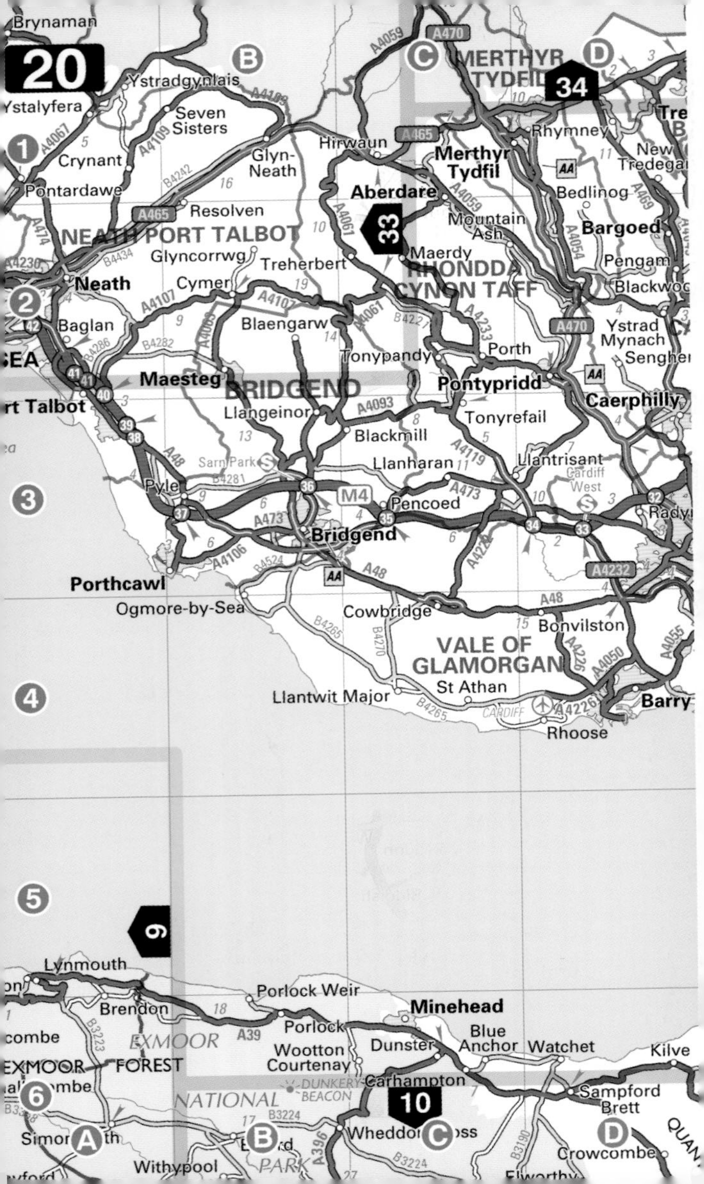
20
Brynaman
B
C
D
A470
A4059
MERTHYR TYDFIL
34
Ystradgynlais
A4109
Ystalyfera
Seven Sisters
1
A4067
Crynant
A4109
Glyn-Neath
Hirwaun
A465
Merthyr Tydfil
Rhymney
New Tredegar
Pontardawe
B4242
Resolven
A465
Aberdare
A4059
Mountain Ash
Bedlinog
A469
A4061
33
A4054
Bargoed
A474
NEATH PORT TALBOT
Glyncorrwg
Treherbert
Maerdy
RHONDDA CYNON TAFF
Pengam
Blackwood
A4230
B4434
Neath
Cymer
A4107
A4107
A4061
B4227
A4233
A470
Ystrad Mynach
Senghenydd
2
Baglan
Blaengarw
A4063
B4286
B4282
Tonypandy
Porth
SEA
Maesteg
BRIDGEND
Pontypridd
Caerphilly
Port Talbot
Llangeinor
A4093
Tonyrefail
Blackmill
A48
A4119
Llantrisant
Llanharan
Sarn Park
B4281
Cardiff West
3
Pyle
M4
A473
Pencoed
Radyr
A473
Bridgend
A4222
A4106
B4524
A48
A4232
Porthcawl
Ogmore-by-Sea
A48
Cowbridge
Bonvilston
B4265
B4270
VALE OF GLAMORGAN
A4226
A4050
A4055
4
Llantwit Major
St Athan
B4265
CARDIFF
A4226
Barry
Rhoose
5
9
Lynmouth
Porlock Weir
Minehead
Brendon
Porlock
A39
EXMOOR
Blue Anchor
Watchet
Kilve
Wootton Courtenay
Dunster
EXMOOR FOREST
B3223
Carhampton
DUNKERY BEACON
6
NATIONAL
10
Sampford Brett
B3224
A
B
C
D
A396
Wheddon Cross
B3190
B3224
Withypool
PARK
Crowcombe
QUANTOCK

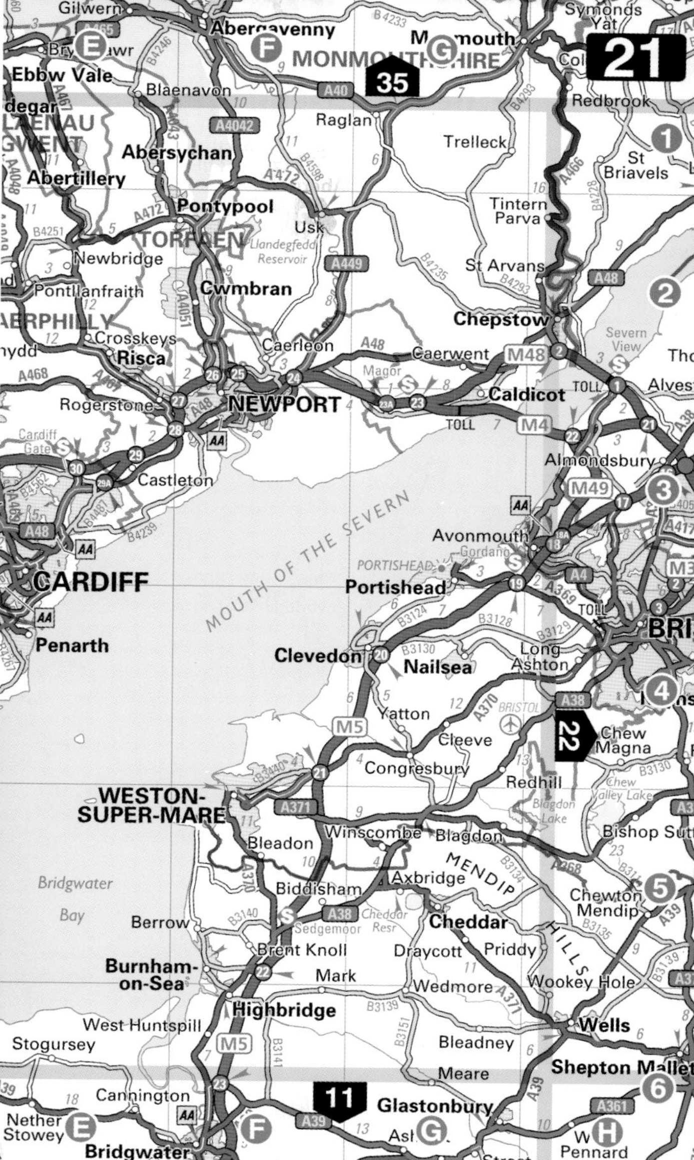
Gilwern
A465
Abergavenny
B4233
Monmouth
Symonds Yat
Ebbw Vale
Blaenavon
MONMOUTHSHIRE
35
A40
Redbrook
A4042
Raglan
Trelleck
Abersychan
St Briavels
Abertillery
A466
Tintern Parva
Pontypool
Usk
A472
TORFAEN
Llandegfedd Reservoir
Newbridge
A449
St Arvans
Cwmbran
A48
Pontllanfraith
B4235
B4293
Chepstow
Crosskeys
Caerleon
Severn View
Risca
A48
Caerwent
M48
Magor
A468
NEWPORT
Caldicot
Alveston
Rogerstone
TOLL
M4
Cardiff Gate
Almondsbury
Castleton
M49
AA
MOUTH OF THE SEVERN
Avonmouth
Gordano
A48
A4
CARDIFF
PORTISHEAD
Portishead
A369
TOLL
BRIS
B3124
B3128
B3129
Penarth
Clevedon
B3130
Nailsea
Long Ashton
A38
BRISTOL
A370
Yatton
M5
Cleeve
22
Chew Magna
Congresbury
B3130
Chew Valley Lake
Redhill
B3440
WESTON-SUPER-MARE
A371
Blagdon Lake
Bleadon
Winscombe
Blagdon
Bishop Sutt
MENDIP
A368
B3134
Bridgwater Bay
Axbridge
Biddisham
Chewton Mendip
A38
Cheddar Resr
Berrow
B3140
Sedgemoor
Cheddar
HILLS
B3135
A39
Brent Knoll
Draycott
Priddy
Burnham-on-Sea
Mark
Wedmore
Wookey Hole
A371
Highbridge
B3139
B3151
Wells
West Huntspill
Stogursey
M5
B3141
Bleadney
Shepton Mallet
Meare
Cannington
11
Glastonbury
A361
A39
Nether Stowey
Ash
W Pennard
Bridgwater
Street

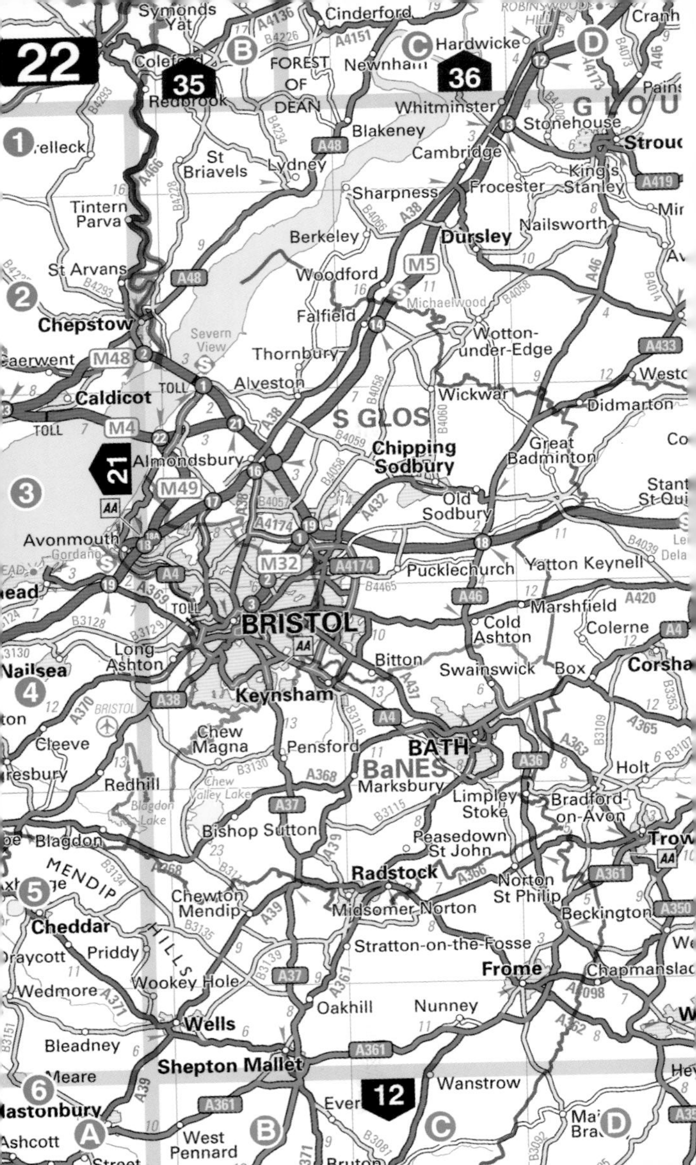

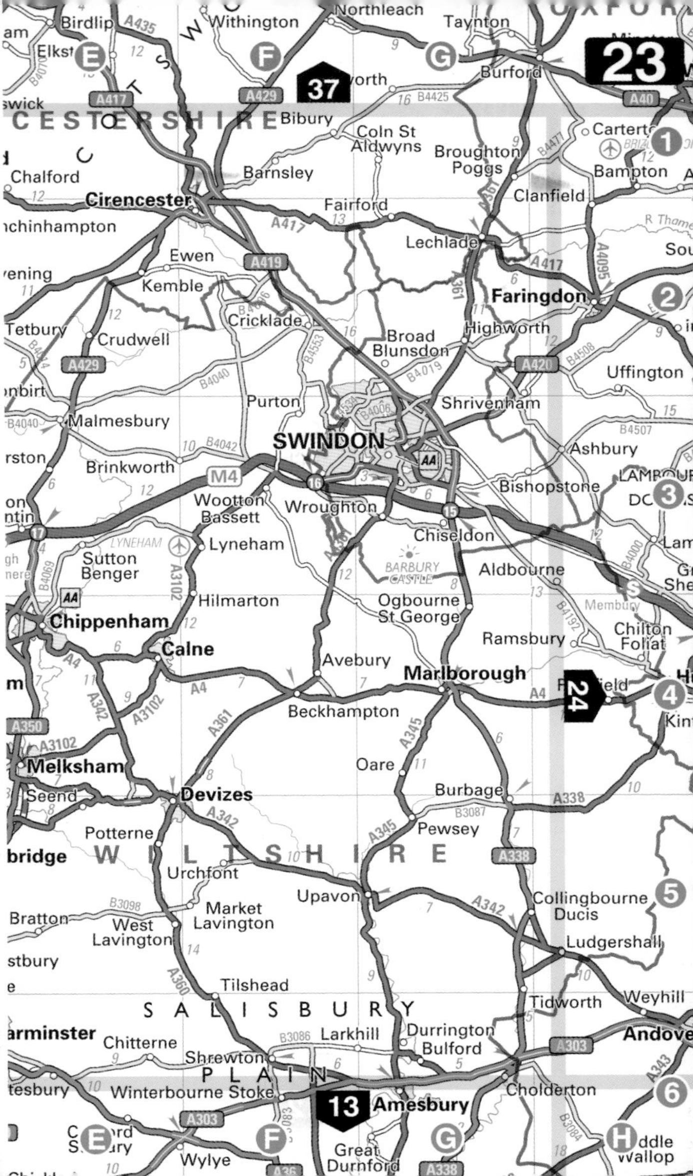

23
37
24
13
Northleach
Withington
Birdlip
Taynton
Burford
Bibury
Coln St Aldwyns
Broughton Poggs
Carterton
Bampton
Clanfield
Chalford
Cirencester
Barnsley
Fairford
Lechlade
Ewen
Kemble
Cricklade
Faringdon
Tetbury
Crudwell
Broad Blunsdon
Highworth
Uffington
Purton
Shrivenham
Malmesbury
SWINDON
Ashbury
Brinkworth
Bishopstone
Wootton Bassett
Wroughton
Chiseldon
Lyneham
Sutton Benger
Barbury Castle
Aldbourne
Hilmarton
Ogbourne St George
Membury
Chippenham
Chilton Foliat
Ramsbury
Calne
Avebury
Marlborough
Beckhampton
Oare
Melksham
Seend
Devizes
Burbage
Pewsey
Potterne
WILTSHIRE
Urchfont
Upavon
Collingbourne Ducis
Market Lavington
Bratton
West Lavington
Ludgershall
Tilshead
Tidworth
Weyhill
SALISBURY PLAIN
Chitterne
Larkhill
Durrington
Bulford
Andover
Shrewton
Winterbourne Stoke
Amesbury
Cholderton
Wylye
Great Durnford
Wallop
M4
A417
A429
A419
A420
A4
A361
A342
A345
A338
A350
A3102
A360
A303
A40
A4095
A435
A36
A343
B4425
B4040
B4042
B4019
B4553
B4508
B4507
B4192
B4069
B3087
B3098
B3086
B3083
B3084
B4000

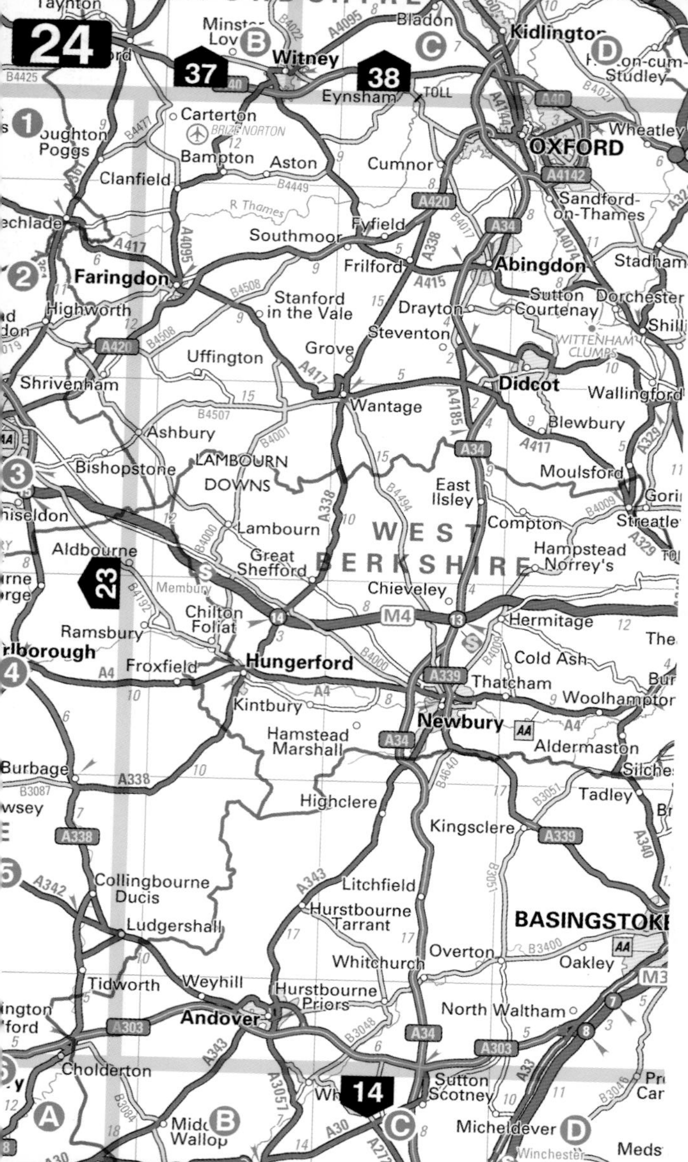

24
37
38
23
14
OXFORD
Witney
Kidlington
Abingdon
Didcot
Wantage
Faringdon
Hungerford
Newbury
Andover
BASINGSTOKE
WEST
BERKSHIRE
LAMBOURN
DOWNS
M4
A34
A4
A338
A339
A303
A420
A417
A343
Carterton
Bampton
Clanfield
Eynsham
Cumnor
Fyfield
Frilford
Drayton
Steventon
Grove
Uffington
Shrivenham
Highworth
Ashbury
Bishopstone
Lambourn
Aldbourne
Ramsbury
Froxfield
Kintbury
Thatcham
Hermitage
Cold Ash
Chieveley
Compton
East Ilsley
Blewbury
Moulsford
Wallingford
Sutton Courtenay
Dorchester
Highclere
Kingsclere
Tadley
Aldermaston
Litchfield
Whitchurch
Overton
Oakley
North Waltham
Ludgershall
Tidworth
Weyhill
Cholderton
Micheldever
Sutton Scotney

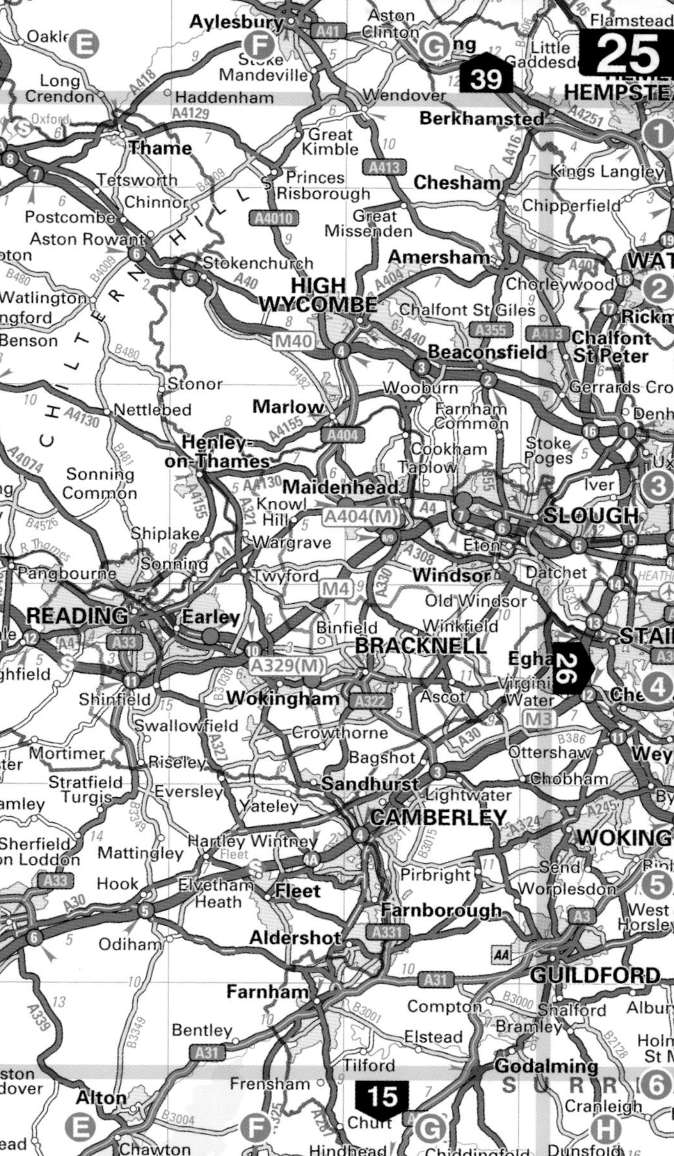

25
39
26
15
Aylesbury
Stoke Mandeville
Aston Clinton
Wendover
Berkhamsted
Flamstead
Little Gaddesden
Oakley
Long Crendon
Haddenham
Thame
Great Kimble
Princes Risborough
Chesham
Kings Langley
Chipperfield
Tetsworth
Chinnor
Postcombe
Aston Rowant
Great Missenden
Amersham
Stokenchurch
HIGH WYCOMBE
Chorleywood
Watlington
Benson
Chalfont St Giles
Chalfont St Peter
Beaconsfield
Stonor
Wooburn
Gerrards Cross
Marlow
Nettlebed
Farnham Common
Henley-on-Thames
Cookham
Stoke Poges
Taplow
Sonning Common
Maidenhead
Iver
Knowl Hill
SLOUGH
Shiplake
Wargrave
Eton
Sonning
Datchet
Pangbourne
Twyford
Windsor
Old Windsor
READING
Earley
Binfield
Winkfield
BRACKNELL
Shinfield
Wokingham
Ascot
Virginia Water
Swallowfield
Crowthorne
Mortimer
Riseley
Bagshot
Ottershaw
Stratfield Turgis
Eversley
Sandhurst
Lightwater
Chobham
Yateley
CAMBERLEY
WOKING
Sherfield on Loddon
Mattingley
Hartley Wintney
Fleet
Hook
Elvetham Heath
Pirbright
Send
Worplesdon
West Horsley
Farnborough
Odiham
Aldershot
GUILDFORD
Farnham
Compton
Shalford
Albury
Bentley
Elstead
Bramley
Tilford
Godalming
Frensham
Alton
Cranleigh
Churt
Chawton
Hindhead
Chiddingfold
Dunsfold
SURREY
CHILTERN HILLS
R. Thames
M40
M4
M3
A41
A418
A4129
A413
A4010
A40
A404
A355
A4130
A4155
A4074
A321
A4
A404(M)
A308
A330
A33
A329(M)
A322
A327
A30
A3
A331
A31
A339
A245
A324
A416
A4251
B4009
B480
B481
B482
B4526
B3030
B3349
B3015
B311
B386
B3000
B3001
B2128
B3004
HEATHROW

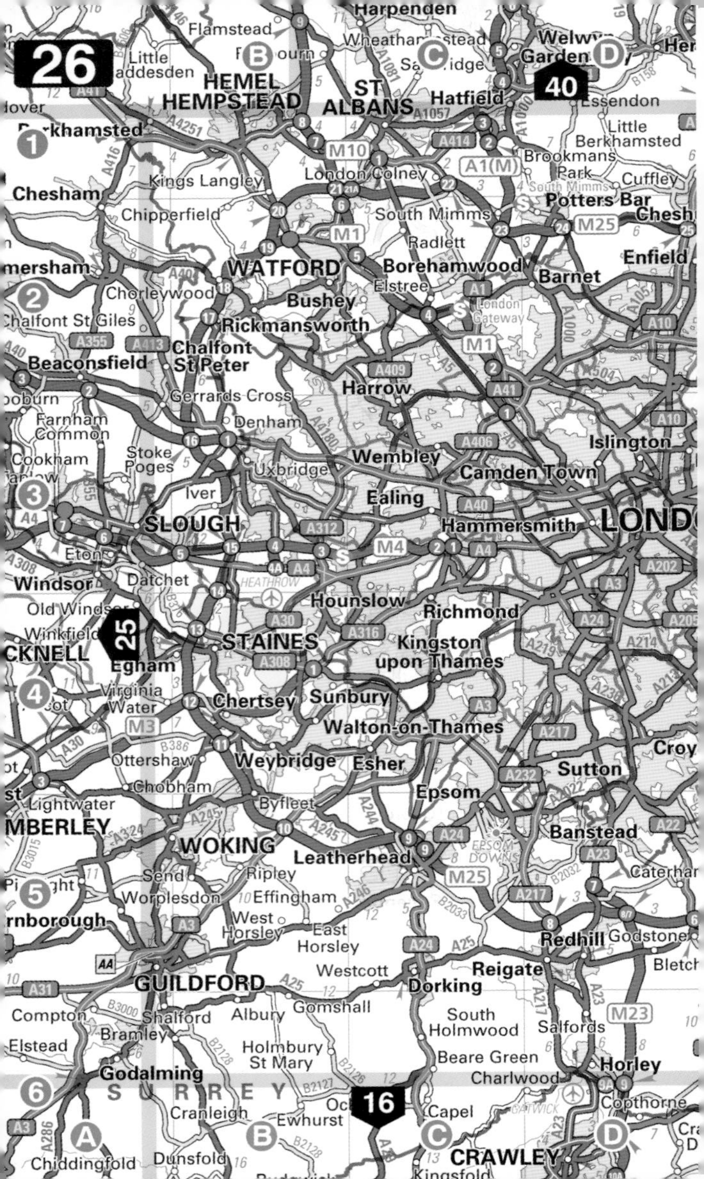
26
Harpenden
Flamstead
Wheathampstead
Welwyn Garden City
Little Gaddesden
HEMEL HEMPSTEAD
ST ALBANS
Hatfield
40
Essendon
Berkhamsted
Little Berkhamsted
Brookmans Park
South Mimms
Cuffley
Potters Bar
Kings Langley
London Colney
Chesham
Chipperfield
South Mimms
Radlett
Enfield
Amersham
WATFORD
Borehamwood
Barnet
Chorleywood
Elstree
Bushey
London Gateway
Chalfont St Giles
Rickmansworth
Chalfont St Peter
Beaconsfield
Harrow
Gerrards Cross
Farnham Common
Denham
Islington
Cookham
Stoke Poges
Wembley
Camden Town
Uxbridge
Iver
Ealing
SLOUGH
Hammersmith
LONDON
Eton
Windsor
Datchet
HEATHROW
Hounslow
Richmond
Old Windsor
Winkfield
25
STAINES
Kingston upon Thames
Egham
Virginia Water
Chertsey
Sunbury
Walton-on-Thames
Ottershaw
Weybridge
Esher
Sutton
Chobham
Epsom
Lightwater
Byfleet
CAMBERLEY
Banstead
WOKING
EPSOM DOWNS
Leatherhead
Send
Ripley
Caterham
Worplesdon
Effingham
Farnborough
West Horsley
East Horsley
Redhill
Godstone
Reigate
Westcott
Bletchingley
GUILDFORD
Dorking
Compton
Shalford
Albury
Gomshall
South Holmwood
Salfords
Bramley
Elstead
Holmbury St Mary
Beare Green
Horley
Godalming
Charlwood
S U R R E Y
16
Cranleigh
Ewhurst
Capel
GATWICK
Copthorne
Chiddingfold
Dunsfold
CRAWLEY
Kingsfold
M1
M3
M4
M10
M23
M25
A1(M)
A1
A3
A4
A5
A10
A24
A25
A30
A40
A41
A217
A232
A308
A312
A316
A355
A406
A409
A413
A414
A1000
A1057
A4251

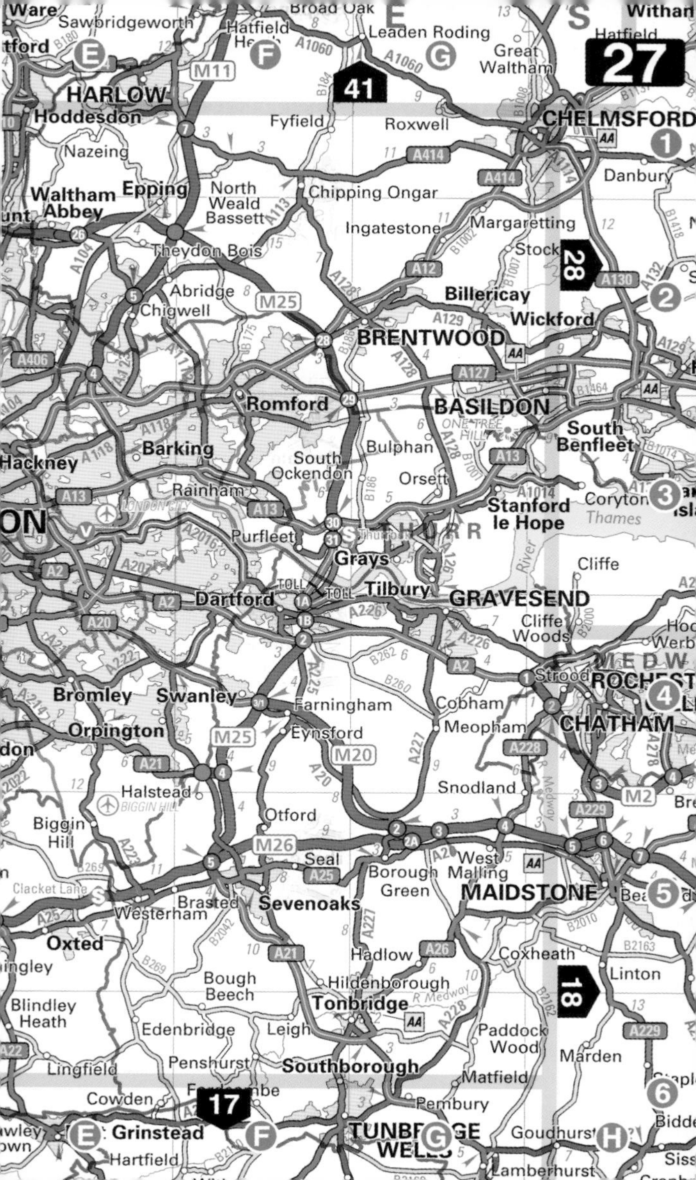

27
41
28
18
17
HARLOW
Hoddesdon
Nazeing
Waltham Abbey
Epping
North Weald Bassett
Chipping Ongar
Fyfield
Roxwell
Leaden Roding
Great Waltham
CHELMSFORD
Danbury
Margaretting
Ingatestone
Stock
Theydon Bois
Abridge
Chigwell
Billericay
Wickford
BRENTWOOD
Romford
BASILDON
South Benfleet
Barking
Hackney
Bulphan
Orsett
South Ockendon
Rainham
Stanford le Hope
Coryton
Thames
Purfleet
Grays
Tilbury
GRAVESEND
Cliffe
Cliffe Woods
Dartford
Strood
ROCHESTER
CHATHAM
Bromley
Swanley
Farningham
Eynsford
Cobham
Meopham
Orpington
Halstead
Snodland
Biggin Hill
Otford
Seal
Borough Green
West Malling
MAIDSTONE
Westerham
Brasted
Sevenoaks
Oxted
Hadlow
Coxheath
Linton
Hildenborough
Bough Beech
Tonbridge
Blindley Heath
Edenbridge
Leigh
Paddock Wood
Marden
Penshurst
Southborough
Lingfield
Matfield
Cowden
Pembury
Grinstead
TUNBRIDGE WELLS
Goudhurst
Hartfield
Lamberhurst
Sawbridgeworth
Hatfield Heath
Broad Oak
Ware
M11
M25
M20
M26
M2
A1060
A414
A12
A130
A129
A127
A13
A1014
A128
A126
A2
A226
A20
A21
A25
A26
A227
A228
A229
A406
A118
A104
A113
A225
A22
B1002
B1007
B186
B175
B262
B260
B2000
B2010
B2163
B2162
B2042
B269
LONDON CITY
BIGGIN HILL
ONE TREE HILL
THURROCK
Clacket Lane
R Medway
River
TOLL

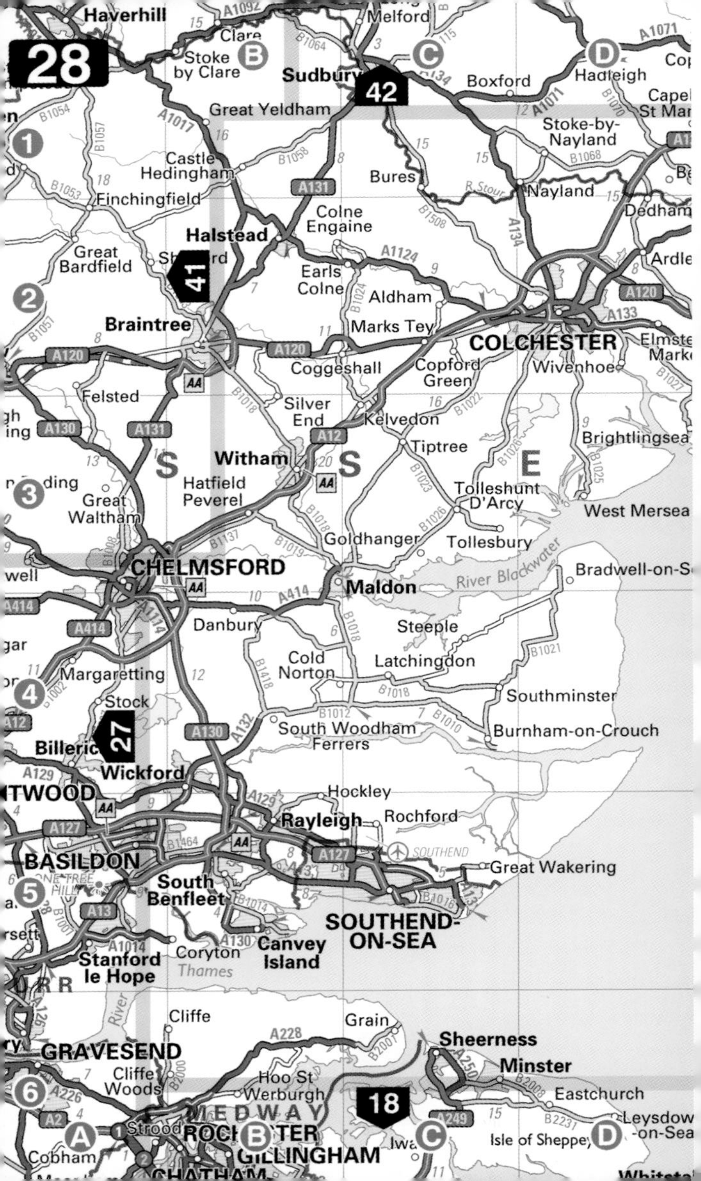
28
42
41
27
18
Haverhill
Melford
Clare
Stoke by Clare
Sudbury
Boxford
Hadleigh
Great Yeldham
Stoke-by-Nayland
Castle Hedingham
Bures
Nayland
Finchingfield
Dedham
Halstead
Colne Engaine
Great Bardfield
Earls Colne
Aldham
Braintree
Marks Tey
COLCHESTER
Coggeshall
Copford Green
Wivenhoe
Felsted
Silver End
Kelvedon
Tiptree
Brightlingsea
Witham
Hatfield Peverel
Great Waltham
Tolleshunt D'Arcy
West Mersea
Goldhanger
Tollesbury
CHELMSFORD
Maldon
River Blackwater
Danbury
Steeple
Cold Norton
Latchingdon
Margaretting
Stock
Southminster
South Woodham Ferrers
Burnham-on-Crouch
Wickford
Hockley
Rayleigh
Rochford
BASILDON
SOUTHEND
Great Wakering
South Benfleet
SOUTHEND-ON-SEA
Canvey Island
Coryton
Stanford le Hope
Thames
Cliffe
Grain
Sheerness
GRAVESEND
Minster
Cliffe Woods
Hoo St Werburgh
Eastchurch
MEDWAY
Strood
Isle of Sheppey
Cobham
GILLINGHAM
CHATHAM

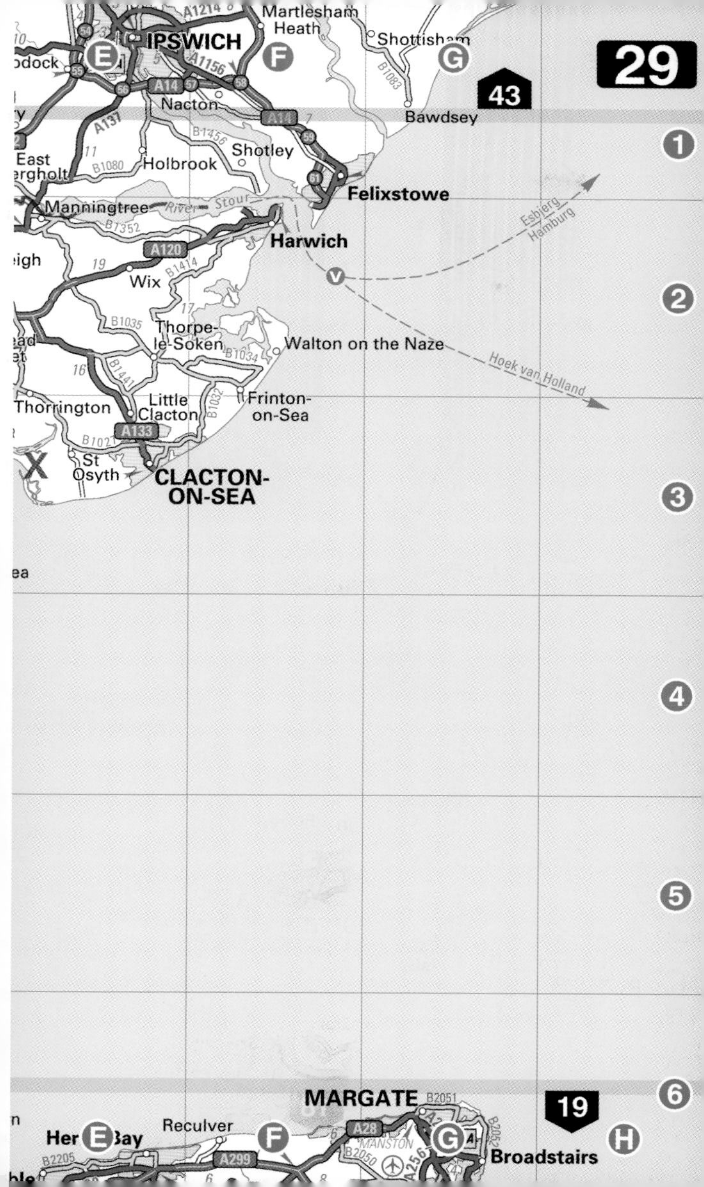
29
43
19
IPSWICH
Martlesham Heath
Shottisham
Nacton
Bawdsey
East Bergholt
Holbrook
Shotley
Felixstowe
Manningtree
River Stour
Harwich
Esbjerg
Hamburg
Wix
Thorpe-le-Soken
Walton on the Naze
Hoek van Holland
Thorrington
Little Clacton
Frinton-on-Sea
St Osyth
CLACTON-ON-SEA
MARGATE
Reculver
Herne Bay
MANSTON
Broadstairs
A14
A137
A120
A133
A1156
A1214
A28
A299
B1080
B1456
B1083
B1352
B1414
B1035
B1034
B1441
B1032
B1027
B2205
B2050
B2051
1
2
3
4
5
6
E
F
G
H

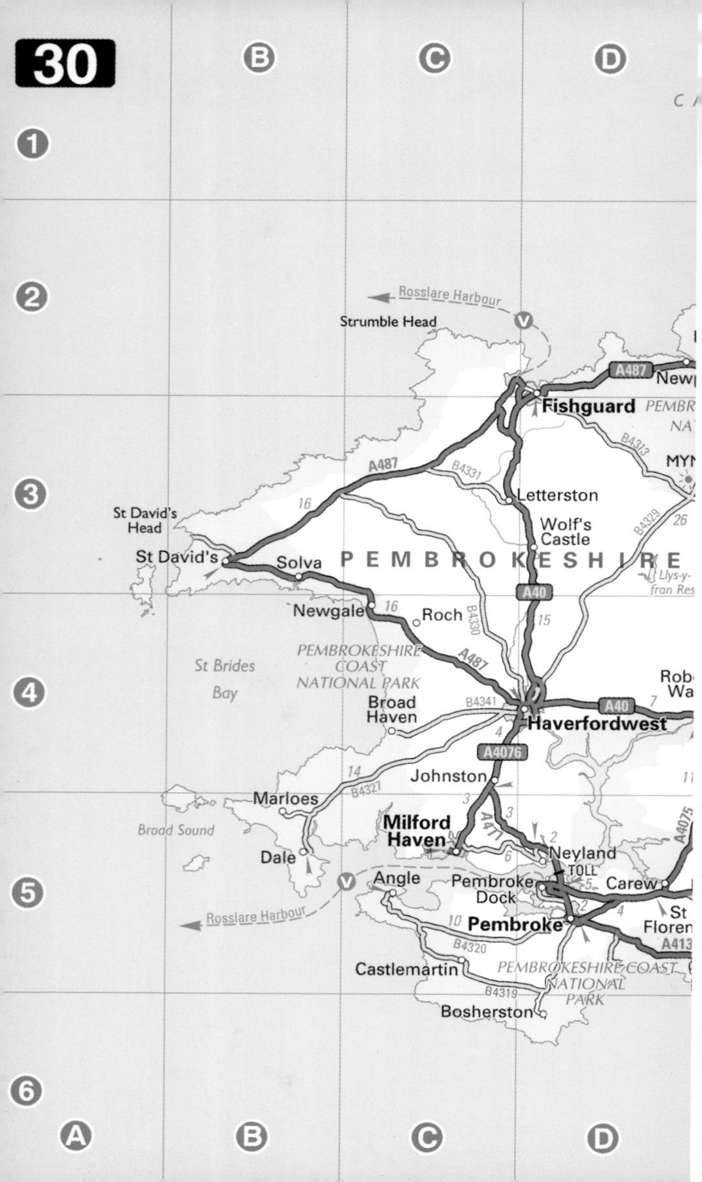
B
C
D
1
2
3
4
5
6
A
B
C
D
Rosslare Harbour
Strumble Head
A487
Fishguard
A487
B4331
Letterston
B4313
St David's Head
16
Wolf's Castle
B4329
26
St David's
Solva
PEMBROKESHIRE
Llys-y-fran Res
A40
Newgale
16
Roch
B4330
15
PEMBROKESHIRE COAST NATIONAL PARK
A487
St Brides Bay
Broad Haven
B4341
A40
7
Haverfordwest
4
A4076
14
Johnston
B4327
Marloes
3
3
A477
Broad Sound
Milford Haven
2
A4075
Dale
6
Neyland
TOLL
Angle
Pembroke Dock
5
Carew
Rosslare Harbour
2
4
St
10
Pembroke
B4320
Castlemartin
PEMBROKESHIRE COAST NATIONAL PARK
B4319
Bosherston

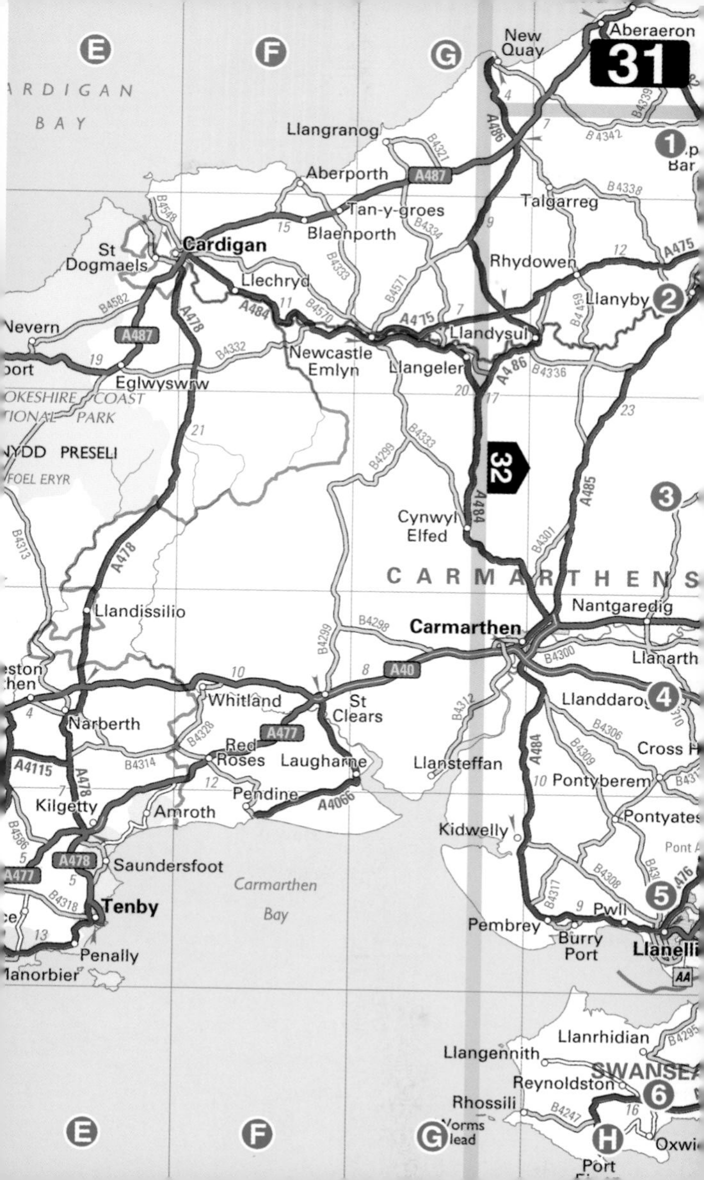

31
32
Aberaeron
New Quay
Llangranog
Aberporth
Tan-y-groes
Blaenporth
Cardigan
St Dogmaels
Llechryd
Newcastle Emlyn
Llangeler
Llandysul
Rhydowen
Talgarreg
Llanyby
Nevern
Eglwyswrw
PRESELI
Cynwyl Elfed
Carmarthen
Nantgaredig
Llanarth
Llandissilio
Whitland
St Clears
Narberth
Red Roses
Laugharne
Llansteffan
Llanddarog
Cross H
Pontyberem
Pontyates
Kilgetty
Amroth
Pendine
Kidwelly
Saundersfoot
Tenby
Penally
Carmarthen Bay
Pembrey
Burry Port
Pwll
Llanelli
Llanrhidian
Llangennith
Reynoldston
Rhossili
Oxwi
Port
CARMARTHENS
SWANSEA

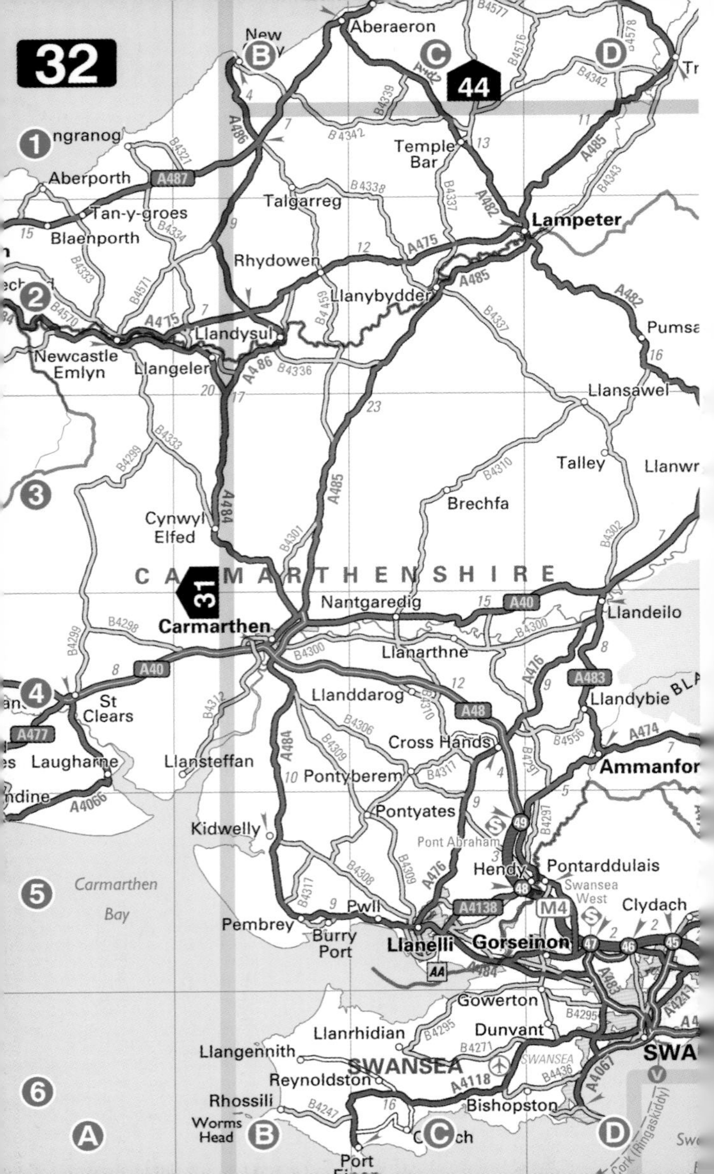
Aberaeron
New Quay
Llangranog
Aberporth
Tan-y-groes
Blaenporth
Talgarreg
Temple Bar
Lampeter
Rhydowen
Llanybydder
Newcastle Emlyn
Llangeler
Llandysul
Pumsaint
Llansawel
Talley
Brechfa
Cynwyl Elfed
CARMARTHENSHIRE
Carmarthen
Nantgaredig
Llandeilo
Llanarthne
Llanddarog
Llandybie
St Clears
Laugharne
Llansteffan
Cross Hands
Ammanford
Pontyberem
Pontyates
Kidwelly
Pont Abraham
Hendy
Pontarddulais
Swansea West
Carmarthen Bay
Pembrey
Pwll
Burry Port
Llanelli
Gorseinon
Clydach
Gowerton
Llanrhidian
Dunvant
Llangennith
SWANSEA
Reynoldston
Rhossili
Bishopston
Worms Head
Port Eynon
Oxwich
Pendine
SWANSEA
Cork (Ringaskiddy)
A487
A486
A475
A485
A482
A484
A40
A477
A4066
A476
A483
A48
A474
A4138
A4118
A4067
M4
B4342
B4339
B4338
B4337
B4334
B4333
B4321
B4571
B4570
B4336
B4459
B4310
B4302
B4301
B4299
B4298
B4300
B4312
B4306
B4309
B4317
B4308
B4297
B4556
B4295
B4271
B4436
B4247
B4577
B4576
B4578
B4343
44
31
1
2
3
4
5
6
A
B
C
D
49
48
47
46
45

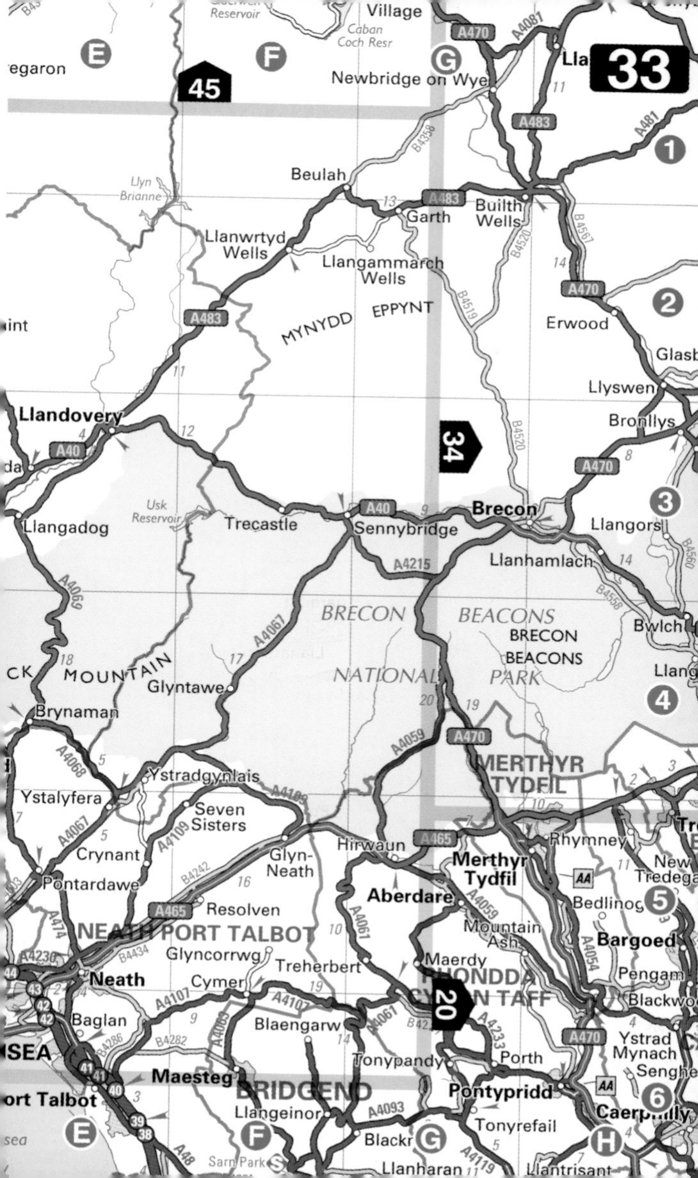

Reservoir
Village
Caban Coch Resr
E
F
G
egaron
45
33
A470
A4081
Lla
Newbridge on Wye
11
A483
A481
1
B4358
Beulah
Llyn Brianne
A483
13
Garth
Builth Wells
B4520
B4567
Llanwrtyd Wells
Llangammarch Wells
14
A470
2
Erwood
A483
MYNYDD EPPYNT
B4519
int
Glasb
11
Llyswen
Llandovery
4
12
Bronllys
A40
34
B4520
8
A470
da
Usk Reservoir
3
Trecastle
A40
9
Brecon
Llangors
Llangadog
Sennybridge
A4215
Llanhamlach
14
B4560
A4069
B4558
BRECON
BEACONS
BRECON
BEACONS
Bwlch
A4067
18
17
CK
MOUNTAIN
NATIONAL
PARK
Llang
Glyntawe
20
19
4
Brynaman
A470
A4059
A4068
5
MERTHYR TYDFIL
3
Ystradgynlais
2
A4109
Ystalyfera
10
Seven Sisters
A4067
5
Rhymney
A4109
A465
Crynant
Hirwaun
Glyn-Neath
Merthyr Tydfil
New Tredega
AA
11
Pontardawe
B4242
16
Aberdare
A4059
5
A474
A465
Resolven
Bedlinog
A4061
10
Mountain Ash
NEATH PORT TALBOT
A4054
Bargoed
A4230
B4434
Glyncorrwg
Maerdy
44
Treherbert
Pengam
Neath
RHONDDA CYNON TAFF
43
Cymer
19
Blackwo
42
A4107
20
A4107
42
9
A4061
A4063
Baglan
Blaengarw
B42
A4233
4
B4286
B4282
14
A470
Ystrad Mynach
SEA
Porth
41
41
Tonypandy
Senghe
Maesteg
40
BRIDGEND
Pontypridd
AA
ort Talbot
3
6
39
Llangeinor
A4093
Caerphilly
38
Tonyrefail
sea
E
F
G
H
Blackr
5
A48
A4119
4
Sarn Park
Llanharan
11
7
Llantrisant

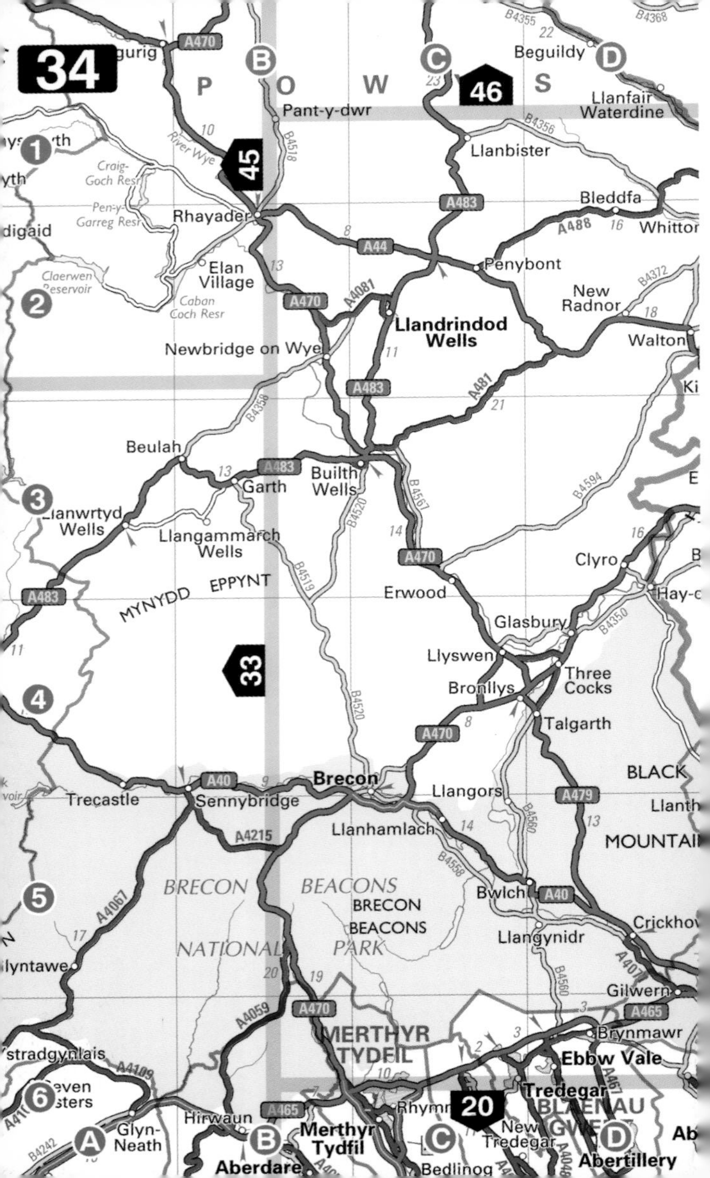

34
45
46
33
20
A
B
C
D
1
2
3
4
5
6
POWYS
Pant-y-dwr
Beguildy
Llanfair Waterdine
Llanbister
Bleddfa
Whitton
Penybont
New Radnor
Walton
Rhayader
Craig-Goch Resr
Pen-y-Garreg Resr
Claerwen Reservoir
Elan Village
Caban Coch Resr
River Wye
Llandrindod Wells
Newbridge on Wye
Beulah
Garth
Builth Wells
Llanwrtyd Wells
Llangammarch Wells
MYNYDD EPPYNT
Erwood
Clyro
Glasbury
Llyswen
Bronllys
Three Cocks
Talgarth
BLACK MOUNTAINS
Trecastle
Sennybridge
Brecon
Llangors
Llanhamlach
Bwlch
Llangynidr
Crickhowell
Gilwern
BRECON BEACONS NATIONAL PARK
BRECON BEACONS
MERTHYR TYDFIL
Brynmawr
Ebbw Vale
Tredegar
BLAENAU GWENT
Rhymney
New Tredegar
Abertillery
Bedlinog
Merthyr Tydfil
Aberdare
Hirwaun
Glyn-Neath
Seven Sisters
Ystradgynlais
Ystradgynlais
A470
A483
A44
A4081
A481
A488
A40
A4215
A4067
A4059
A465
A479
A4077
A4109
B4355
B4368
B4356
B4518
B4372
B4358
B4520
B4567
B4594
B4519
B4350
B4560
B4558
B4242

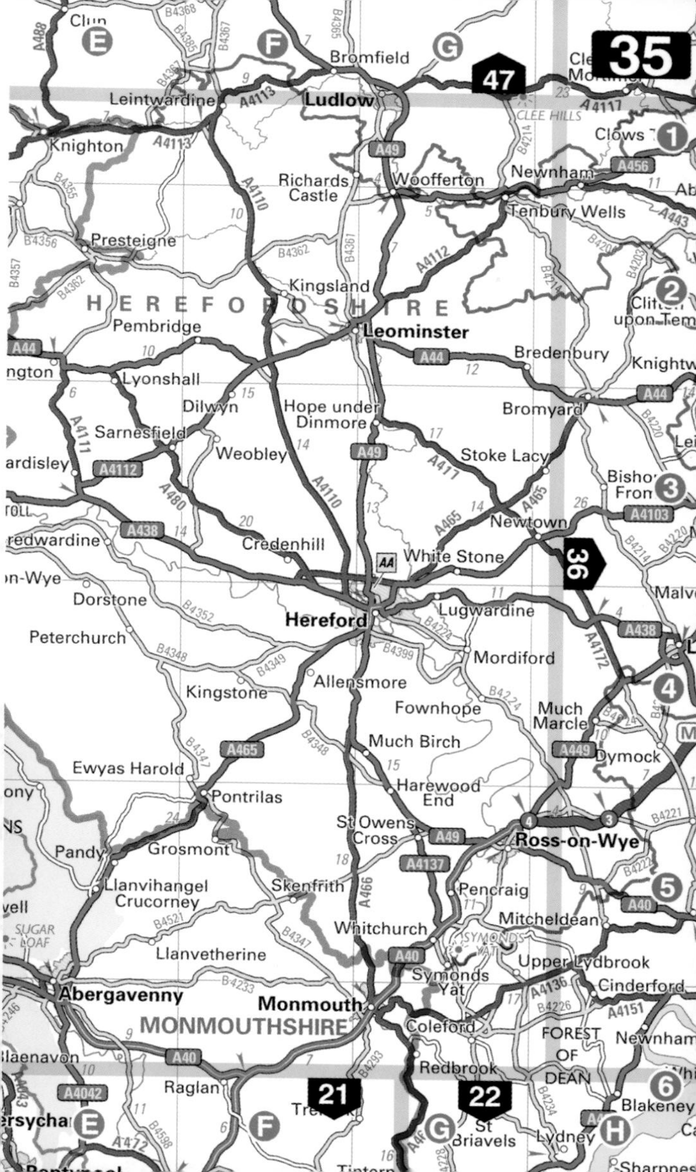

35
47
36
21
22
Clun
Bromfield
Leintwardine
Ludlow
Knighton
Richards Castle
Woofferton
Newnham
Tenbury Wells
Presteigne
HEREFORDSHIRE
Kingsland
Pembridge
Leominster
Bredenbury
Lyonshall
Dilwyn
Hope under Dinmore
Bromyard
Sarnesfield
Weobley
Stoke Lacy
Newtown
Credenhill
White Stone
Dorstone
Hereford
Lugwardine
Peterchurch
Mordiford
Allensmore
Kingstone
Fownhope
Much Marcle
Much Birch
Dymock
Ewyas Harold
Harewood End
Pontrilas
St Owens Cross
Ross-on-Wye
Pandy
Grosmont
Llanvihangel Crucorney
Skenfrith
Pencraig
Mitcheldean
Whitchurch
Llanvetherine
Symonds Yat
Upper Lydbrook
Abergavenny
Cinderford
Monmouth
MONMOUTHSHIRE
Coleford
FOREST OF DEAN
Redbrook
Raglan
Blakeney
St Briavels
Lydney
CLEE HILLS
SUGAR LOAF

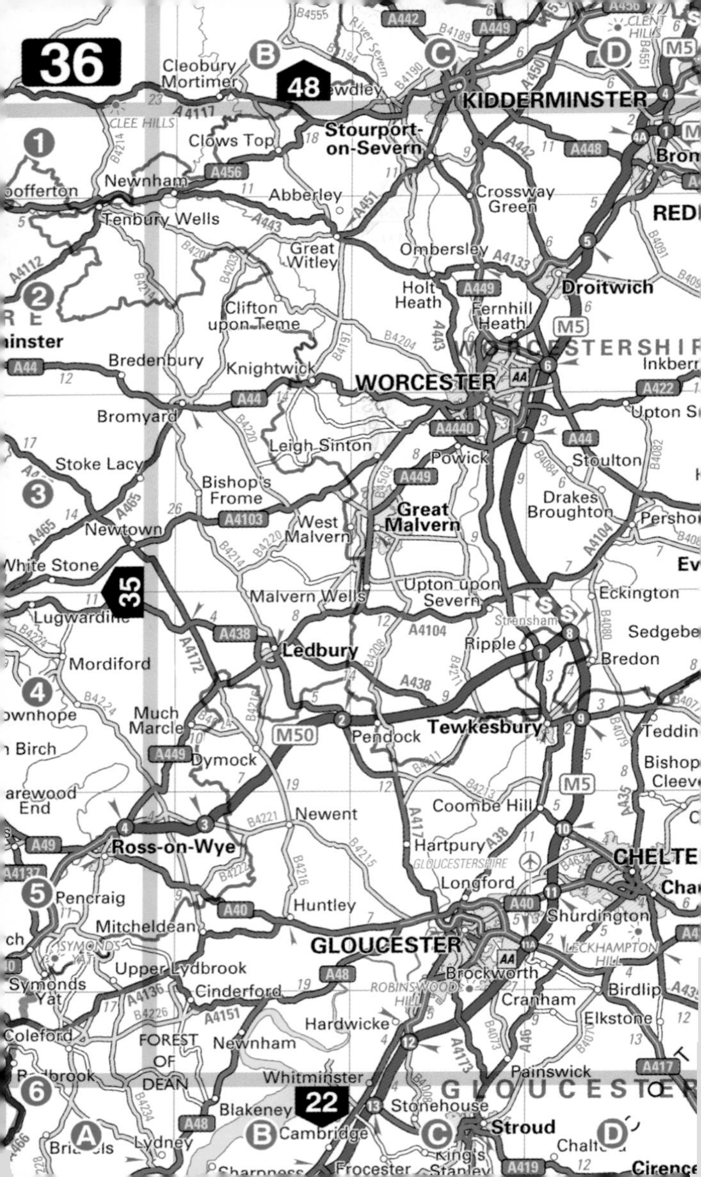
36
48
35
22
A
B
C
D
1
2
3
4
5
6
KIDDERMINSTER
Stourport-on-Severn
Cleobury Mortimer
Bewdley
CLEE HILLS
CLENT HILLS
Clows Top
Newnham
Tenbury Wells
Abberley
Great Witley
Crossway Green
Ombersley
Holt Heath
Droitwich
Fernhill Heath
Clifton upon Teme
Knightwick
WORCESTER
WORCESTERSHIRE
Inkberrow
Bredenbury
Bromyard
Leigh Sinton
Powick
Stoulton
Stoke Lacy
Bishop's Frome
Great Malvern
West Malvern
Drakes Broughton
Pershore
Newtown
White Stone
Upton upon Severn
Eckington
Malvern Wells
Lugwardine
Strensham
Ripple
Sedgeberrow
Mordiford
Ledbury
Bredon
Much Marcle
Tewkesbury
Pendock
Teddington
Dymock
Bishop's Cleeve
Newent
Coombe Hill
Hartpury
GLOUCESTERSHIRE
Ross-on-Wye
CHELTENHAM
Pencraig
Longford
Huntley
Shurdington
Mitcheldean
GLOUCESTER
LECKHAMPTON HILL
SYMONDS YAT
Symonds Yat
Upper Lydbrook
Brockworth
Cinderford
ROBINSWOOD HILL
Cranham
Birdlip
Coleford
FOREST OF DEAN
Newnham
Hardwicke
Elkstone
Whitminster
Painswick
GLOUCESTER
Blakeney
Stonehouse
Stroud
Cambridge
Lydney
Chalford
King's Stanley
Frocester
Cirencester
M5
M50
A442
A449
A456
A4117
A443
A451
A4133
A448
A44
A4440
A422
A4103
A438
A4104
A4172
A417
A38
A49
A40
A48
A4136
A4151
A4173
A46
A419
A435
A465
A4112
B4555
B4194
B4189
B4190
B4214
B4204
B4203
B4197
B4220
B4084
B4082
B4080
B4079
B4211
B4208
B4216
B4215
B4221
B4213
B4634
B4226
B4234
B4008
B4073
B4070
B4091

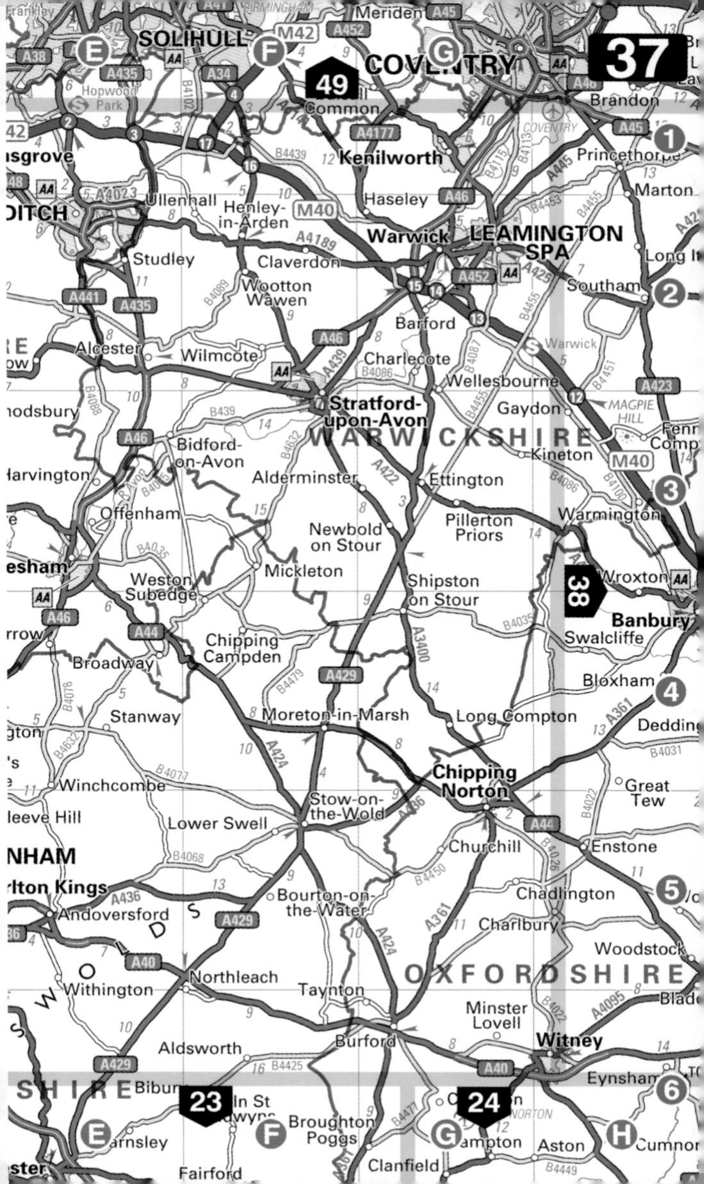
37
49
38
23
24
SOLIHULL
COVENTRY
Meriden
Common
Kenilworth
Haseley
Warwick
LEAMINGTON SPA
Princethorpe
Marton
Brandon
Southam
Hopwood Park
Ullenhall
Henley-in-Arden
Studley
Claverdon
Wootton Wawen
Barford
Charlecote
Wellesbourne
Alcester
Wilmcote
Stratford-upon-Avon
WARWICKSHIRE
Gaydon
Kineton
Bidford-on-Avon
Alderminster
Ettington
Harvington
Offenham
Newbold on Stour
Pillerton Priors
Warmington
Mickleton
Weston Subedge
Shipston on Stour
Wroxton
Banbury
Swalcliffe
Chipping Campden
Broadway
Bloxham
Stanway
Moreton-in-Marsh
Long Compton
Winchcombe
Chipping Norton
Great Tew
Stow-on-the-Wold
Lower Swell
Churchill
Enstone
Chadlington
Bourton-on-the-Water
Andoversford
Charlbury
Woodstock
Withington
Northleach
Taynton
OXFORDSHIRE
Minster Lovell
Burford
Witney
Aldsworth
Eynsham
Broughton Poggs
Clanfield
Aston
Fairford
Magpie Hill
Warwick
Coventry
M40
M42
A46
A44
A40
A429
A424
A361
A422
A3400
A439
A435
A441
A423
A452
A4177
A4189
A45
A436
A4095
B4439
B4035
B4450
B4425
B4068
B4632
B4078
B4077
B4088
B4089
B4086
B4087
B4455
B4451
B4100
B4031
B4022
B4026
B4449
B4479
B4102
B4453

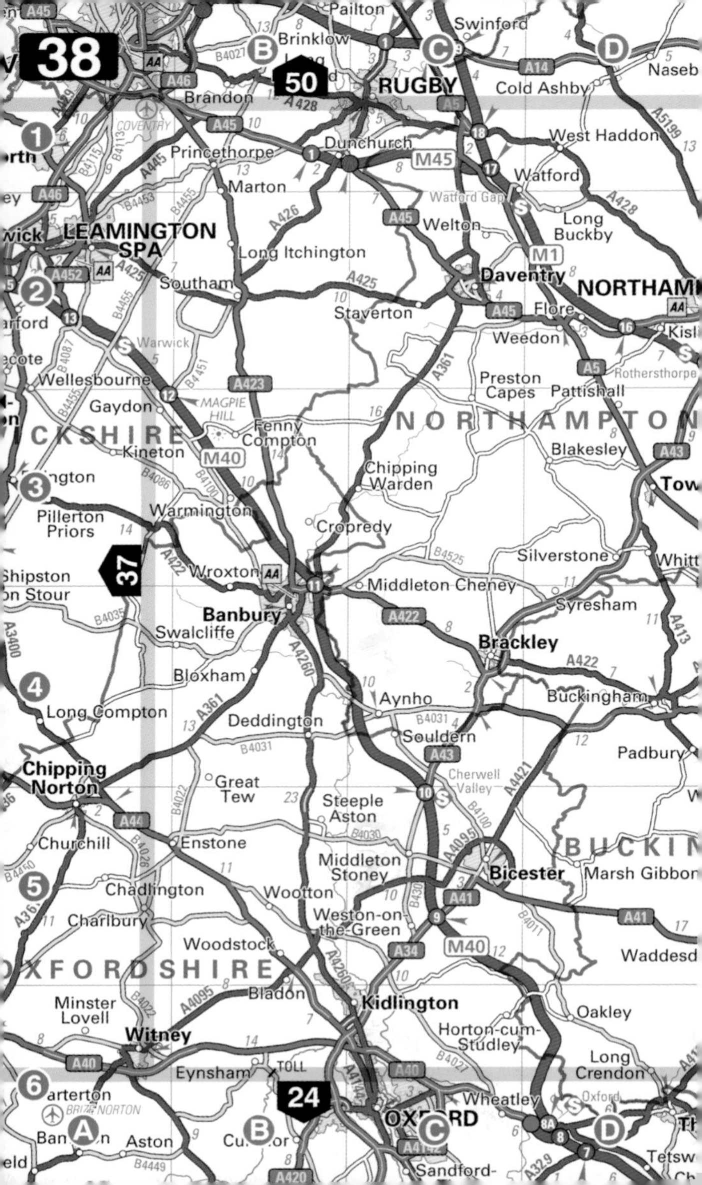

38
50
37
24
Pailton
Swinford
Brinklow
RUGBY
Naseby
Cold Ashby
Brandon
COVENTRY
A45
A46
A14
A5
A428
M45
A445
A426
A5199
B4027
B4113
B4115
B4453
B4455
Princethorpe
Dunchurch
West Haddon
Marton
Watford
Watford Gap
Long Buckby
LEAMINGTON SPA
Welton
Long Itchington
M1
Daventry
NORTHAMPTON
Southam
A425
A452
Staverton
Flore
Weedon
Kislingbury
Warwick
Rothersthorpe
Wellesbourne
B4087
B4451
A423
A361
Preston Capes
Pattishall
Gaydon
MAGPIE HILL
Fenny Compton
NORTHAMPTON
Kineton
M40
Blakesley
A43
Chipping Warden
Towcester
B4086
B4100
Pillerton Priors
Warmington
Cropredy
Silverstone
Shipston on Stour
A422
Wroxton
Middleton Cheney
B4525
Whittlebury
Syresham
Banbury
B4035
Swalcliffe
A3400
Brackley
A413
Bloxham
A4260
Aynho
Buckingham
Long Compton
Deddington
B4031
Souldern
Padbury
Chipping Norton
Great Tew
Steeple Aston
Cherwell Valley
A44
B4022
B4026
B4030
A4421
Churchill
Enstone
Middleton Stoney
A4095
Bicester
Marsh Gibbon
BUCKINGHAMSHIRE
Chadlington
Wootton
A41
Charlbury
Weston-on-the-Green
B4011
Woodstock
A34
OXFORDSHIRE
Waddesdon
Bladon
Minster Lovell
Kidlington
Oakley
Witney
Horton-cum-Studley
A40
Eynsham
TOLL
Long Crendon
A4144
Carterton
Wheatley
Oxford
BRIZE NORTON
OXFORD
Bampton
Aston
Cumnor
B4449
A4142
A420
A329
Tetsworth
Sandford-

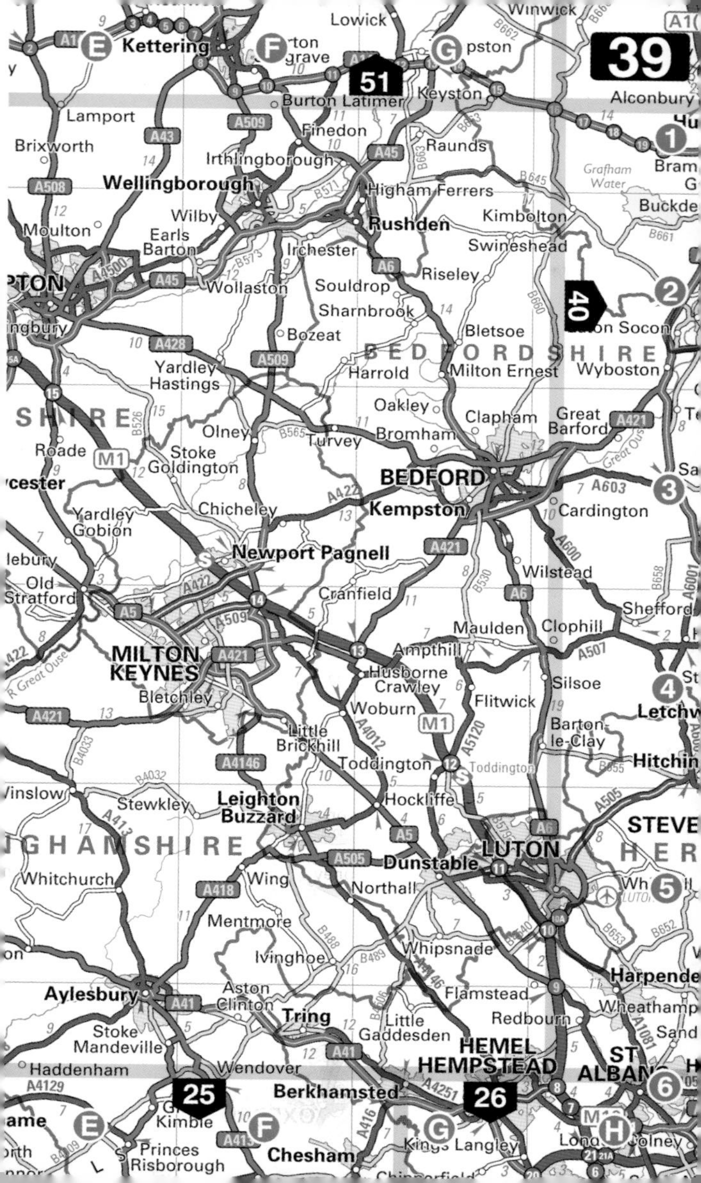
39
51
40
25
26
Kettering
Lowick
Winwick
Keyston
Burton Latimer
Alconbury
Lamport
Finedon
Raunds
Brixworth
Irthlingborough
Wellingborough
Higham Ferrers
Grafham Water
Wilby
Rushden
Kimbolton
Buckden
Moulton
Earls Barton
Irchester
Swineshead
Riseley
Wollaston
Souldrop
Sharnbrook
Bozeat
Bletsoe
BEDFORDSHIRE
Harrold
Milton Ernest
Wyboston
Yardley Hastings
Oakley
Clapham
Great Barford
Olney
Turvey
Bromham
Roade
Stoke Goldington
BEDFORD
Chicheley
Kempston
Cardington
Yardley Gobion
Newport Pagnell
Wilstead
Old Stratford
Cranfield
Shefford
Maulden
Clophill
MILTON KEYNES
Ampthill
Husborne Crawley
Silsoe
Bletchley
Flitwick
Woburn
Barton-le-Clay
Little Brickhill
Toddington
Hitchin
Winslow
Stewkley
Hockliffe
Leighton Buzzard
LUTON
Dunstable
Whitchurch
Wing
Northall
Mentmore
Ivinghoe
Whipsnade
Harpenden
Aylesbury
Aston Clinton
Flamstead
Wheathampstead
Tring
Redbourn
Stoke Mandeville
Little Gaddesden
HEMEL HEMPSTEAD
Haddenham
Wendover
Berkhamsted
ST ALBANS
Kimble
Chesham
Kings Langley
Princes Risborough
M1
A1
A5
A6
A41
A43
A45
A418
A421
A422
A428
A505
A507
A509
A600
A603
A4146
A5120

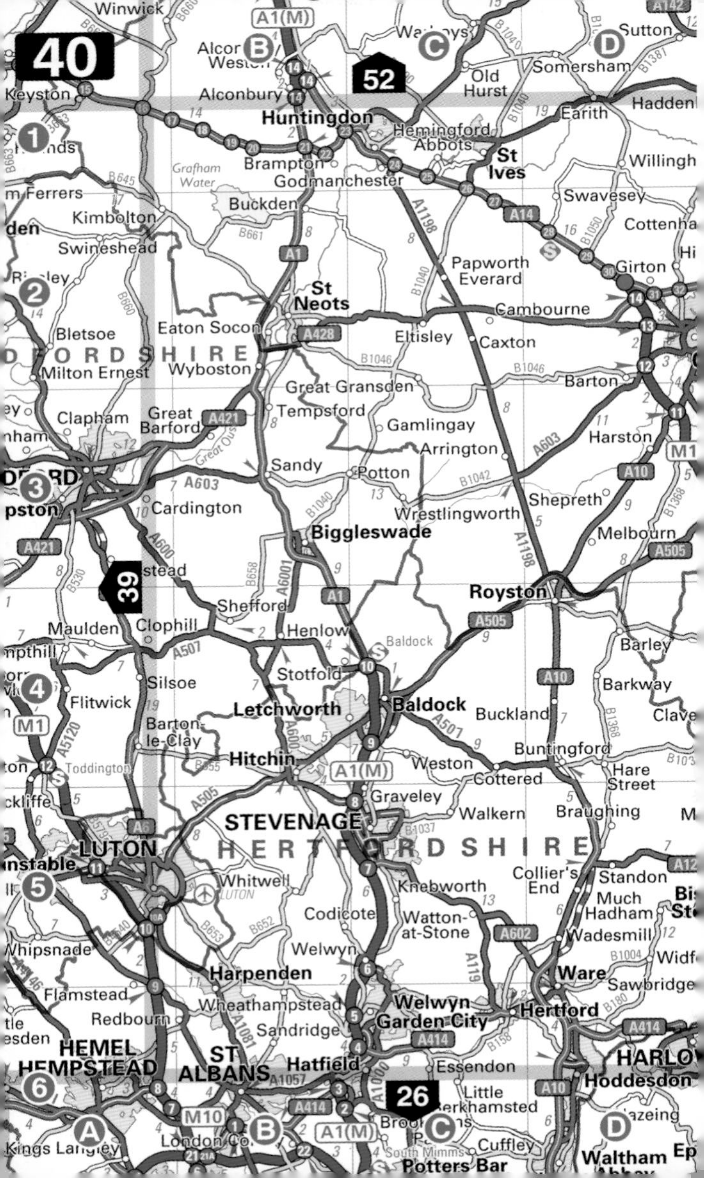
40
52
39
26
Huntingdon
St Ives
St Neots
Biggleswade
Royston
Letchworth
Baldock
Hitchin
STEVENAGE
LUTON
Harpenden
Welwyn Garden City
Hertford
Ware
HEMEL HEMPSTEAD
ST ALBANS
Hatfield
Potters Bar
Hoddesdon
Waltham Abbey
BEDFORDSHIRE
HERTFORDSHIRE
Alconbury
Brampton
Godmanchester
Hemingford Abbots
Somersham
Earith
Buckden
Kimbolton
Swineshead
Bletsoe
Milton Ernest
Eaton Socon
Wyboston
Papworth Everard
Cambourne
Eltisley
Caxton
Great Gransden
Barton
Tempsford
Gamlingay
Clapham
Great Barford
Sandy
Potton
Arrington
Harston
Cardington
Wrestlingworth
Shepreth
Melbourn
Shefford
Clophill
Maulden
Henlow
Stotfold
Silsoe
Flitwick
Barton-le-Clay
Toddington
Barley
Barkway
Buckland
Buntingford
Weston
Cottered
Graveley
Walkern
Braughing
Hare Street
Whitwell
Knebworth
Codicote
Watton-at-Stone
Collier's End
Standon
Much Hadham
Wadesmill
Welwyn
Whipsnade
Flamstead
Redbourn
Wheathampstead
Sandridge
Essendon
Little Berkhamsted
Cuffley
Kings Langley
London Colney
South Mimms
Swavesey
Girton
Grafham Water
Keyston
Winwick
A1(M)
A14
A1
A428
A421
A603
A600
A6001
A505
A507
A10
A1198
A602
A414
A1057
A1000
M1
M10
A5120
A6

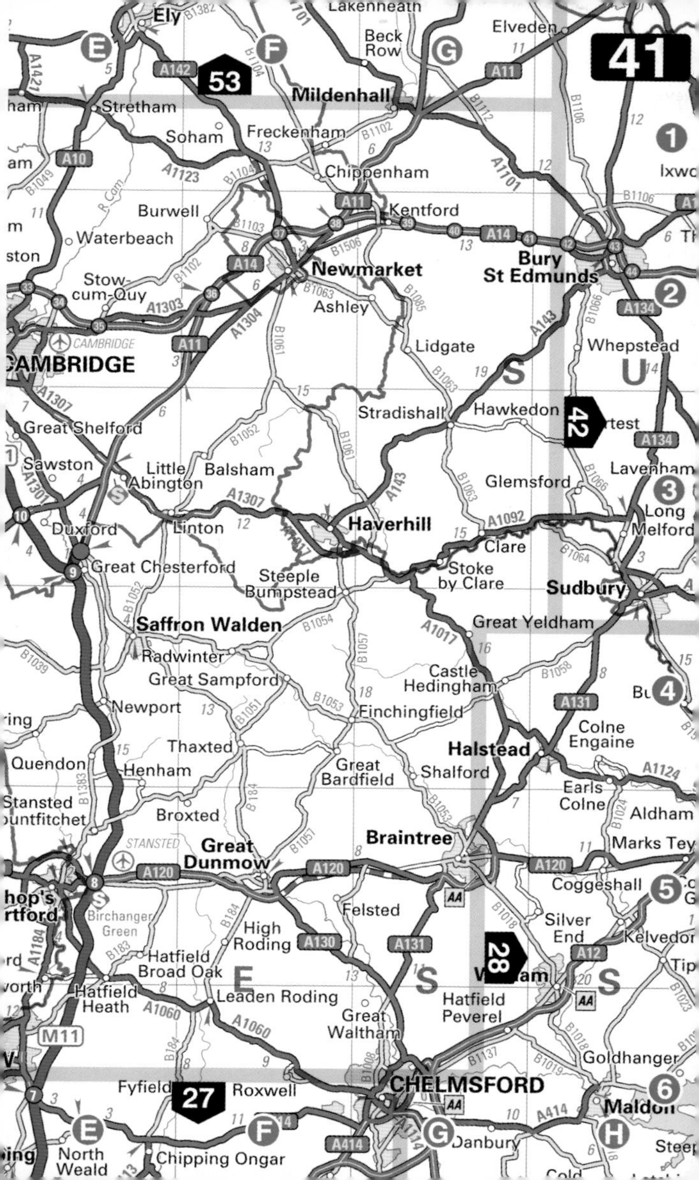

41
53
42
28
27
Ely
Lakenheath
Beck Row
Elveden
Mildenhall
Stretham
Soham
Freckenham
Chippenham
Burwell
Kentford
Waterbeach
Newmarket
Bury St Edmunds
Stow-cum-Quy
Ashley
CAMBRIDGE
Lidgate
Whepstead
Great Shelford
Stradishall
Hawkedon
Sawston
Little Abington
Balsham
Glemsford
Lavenham
Duxford
Linton
Haverhill
Clare
Long Melford
Great Chesterford
Steeple Bumpstead
Stoke by Clare
Sudbury
Saffron Walden
Great Yeldham
Radwinter
Great Sampford
Castle Hedingham
Newport
Finchingfield
Thaxted
Halstead
Colne Engaine
Quendon
Henham
Great Bardfield
Shalford
Earls Colne
Stansted Mountfitchet
Broxted
Aldham
Great Dunmow
Braintree
Marks Tey
STANSTED
Coggeshall
Birchanger Green
Felsted
Silver End
High Roding
Kelvedon
Hatfield Broad Oak
Hatfield Heath
Leaden Roding
Hatfield Peverel
Great Waltham
Goldhanger
Fyfield
Roxwell
CHELMSFORD
Maldon
North Weald
Chipping Ongar
Danbury

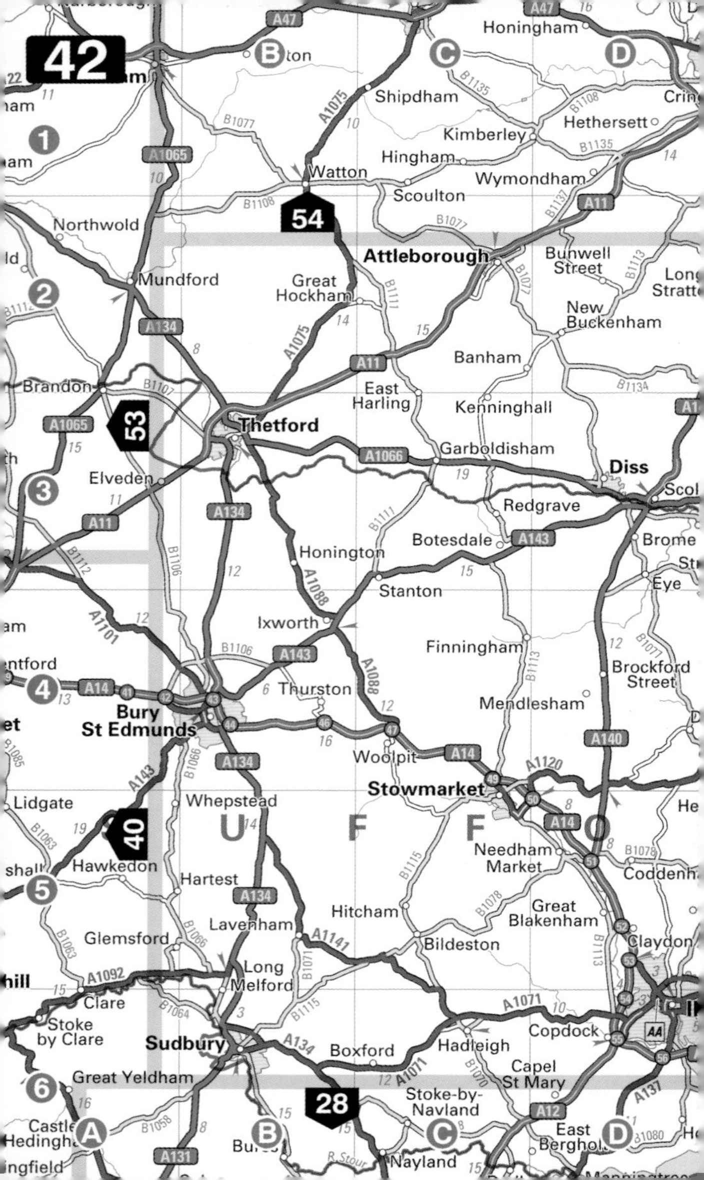

42
54
53
40
28
Honingham
Shipdham
Hethersett
Kimberley
Hingham
Watton
Scoulton
Wymondham
Northwold
Attleborough
Bunwell Street
Mundford
Great Hockham
New Buckenham
Banham
Brandon
East Harling
Kenninghall
Thetford
Garboldisham
Diss
Elveden
Redgrave
Botesdale
Brome
Honington
Eye
Stanton
Ixworth
Finningham
Brockford Street
Thurston
Mendlesham
Bury St Edmunds
Woolpit
Stowmarket
Lidgate
Whepstead
Needham Market
Hawkedon
Hartest
Coddenham
Hitcham
Great Blakenham
Lavenham
Glemsford
Bildeston
Claydon
Long Melford
Clare
Stoke by Clare
Copdock
Sudbury
Hadleigh
Boxford
Great Yeldham
Capel St Mary
Stoke-by-Navland
East Bergholt
Nayland
R. Stour
U
F
F
O

Thorpe End
Walsham
Acle
Filby
Caister-on-Sea
NORWICH
Brundall
THE BROADS
Burgh Castle
GREAT YARMOUTH
Caistor St Edmund
Yelverton
Belton
Reedham
Hopton on Sea
Brooke
Loddon
Hales
Fritton
Corton
55
Haddiscoe
LOWESTOFT
Hempnall
Ellingham
Gillingham
Bungay
Earsham
Beccles
Pulham St Mary
Homersfield
Henstead
Kessingland
Wrentham
Metfield
Brockdish
Halesworth
Southwold
Fressingfield
Walberswick
Laxfield
Bramfield
Darsham
Dunwich
Peasenhall
Yoxford
Dennington
Theberton
Framlingham
Leiston
Saxmundham
Stratford St Andrew
Thorpeness
Easton
Snape
Aldeburgh
Wickham Market
Tunstall
Butley
Orford
Woodbridge
Martlesham Heath
Shottisham
Bawdsey
29
Felixstowe
A47
A146
A140
A12
A1064
A144
A145
A1095
A1120
A1094
A1152
A1214
A1156
A14
B1140
B1332
B1136
B1074
B1527
B1062
B1127
B1124
B1126
B1123
B1118
B1116
B1117
B1125
B1122
B1119
B1121
B1069
B1078
B1079
B1084
B1083
B1456
E
F
G
H
K
1
2
3
4
5
6

Abersoch
56
Llanbe
Dyffryn Ardudwy
Tal-y-bont
A496
Barmouth
Fairbourne
A493
Llwyngwril
Bryncrug
Tywyn
Penn
A493
Aberdyfi
A487
B4353
Borth
Tal-y
Llandre
B4572
A4159
Aberystwyth
Capel
Bangor
Llanfarian
Llanilar
B4340
B4575
A487
B4576
Llanrhystud
A485
31
B4337
Llansantffraid
C E R E D I G
Aberarth
B4577
Aberaeron
B4578
New
Quay
B4576
A482
B4342
B4339
A486
32
Temple
A485
Abe porth
A487
B4321
Talgarreg
B4338

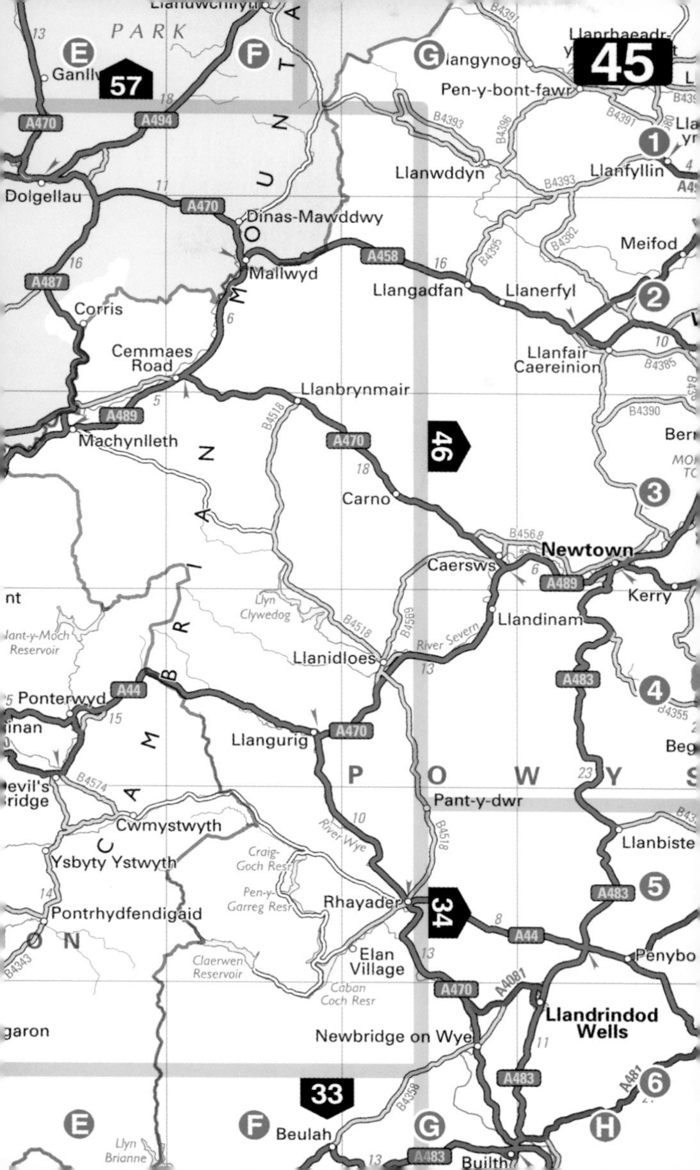

45
57
46
34
33
Dolgellau
Dinas-Mawddwy
Mallwyd
Corris
Cemmaes Road
Machynlleth
Llanbrynmair
Carno
Newtown
Caersws
Llandinam
Llanidloes
Llangurig
Rhayader
Pant-y-dwr
Llanwddyn
Llanfyllin
Pen-y-bont-fawr
Meifod
Llangadfan
Llanerfyl
Llanfair Caereinion
Kerry
Llanbiste
Penybont
Llandrindod Wells
Newbridge on Wye
Elan Village
Beulah
Ponterwyd
Cwmystwyth
Ysbyty Ystwyth
Pontrhydfendigaid
Llyn Clywedog
River Severn
River Wye
Craig-Goch Resr
Pen-y-Garreg Resr
Claerwen Reservoir
Caban Coch Resr
Llyn Brianne
POWYS
CAMBRIAN MOUNTAINS

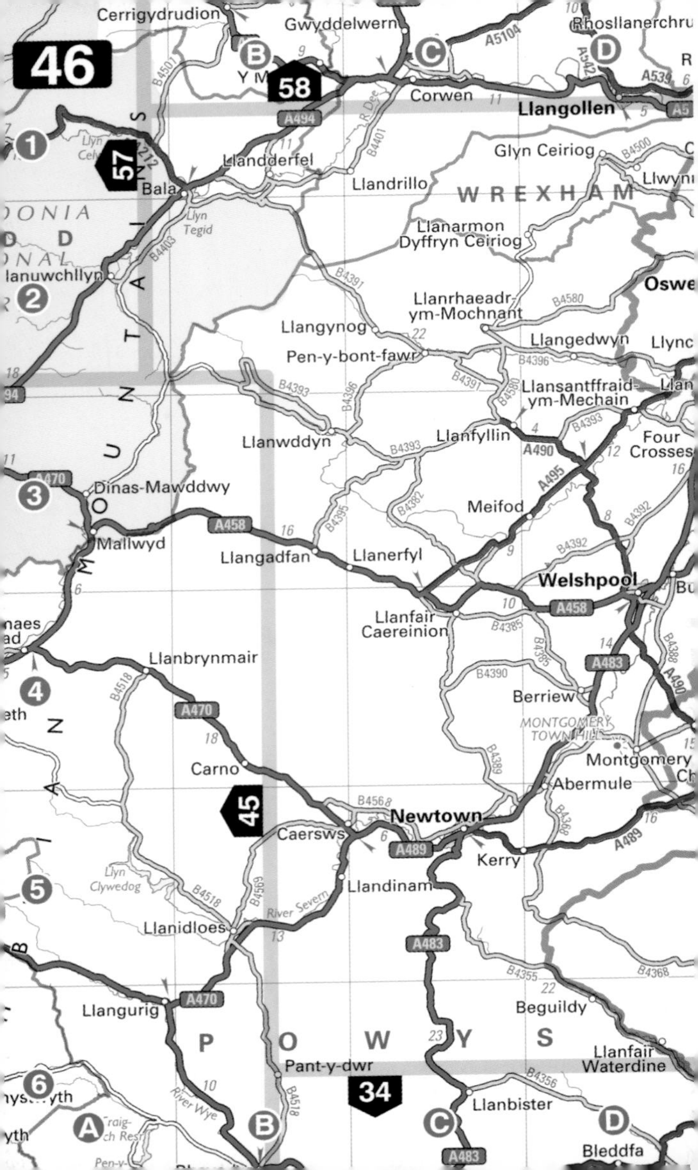

46
58
57
45
34
Cerrigydrudion
Gwyddelwern
Rhosllanerchrugog
Corwen
Llangollen
Glyn Ceiriog
Llandderfel
Llandrillo
Bala
Llyn Tegid
WREXHAM
Llanarmon Dyffryn Ceiriog
Llanuwchllyn
Oswestry
Llanrhaeadr-ym-Mochnant
Llangynog
Pen-y-bont-fawr
Llangedwyn
Llansantffraid-ym-Mechain
Llanwddyn
Llanfyllin
Four Crosses
Dinas-Mawddwy
Meifod
Mallwyd
Llangadfan
Llanerfyl
Welshpool
Llanfair Caereinion
Llanbrynmair
Berriew
MONTGOMERY TOWN HILL
Montgomery
Carno
Abermule
Newtown
Caersws
Kerry
Llandinam
Llyn Clywedog
River Severn
Llanidloes
Beguildy
Llangurig
POWYS
Llanfair Waterdine
Pant-y-dwr
Llanbister
River Wye
Bleddfa
SNOWDONIA NATIONAL PARK
CAMBRIAN MOUNTAINS
A5104
A542
A539
A494
A470
A458
A495
A490
A483
A489
B4501
B4401
B4391
B4402
B4403
B4500
B4580
B4396
B4393
B4382
B4395
B4392
B4385
B4390
B4388
B4389
B4368
B4518
B4569
B4355
B4356

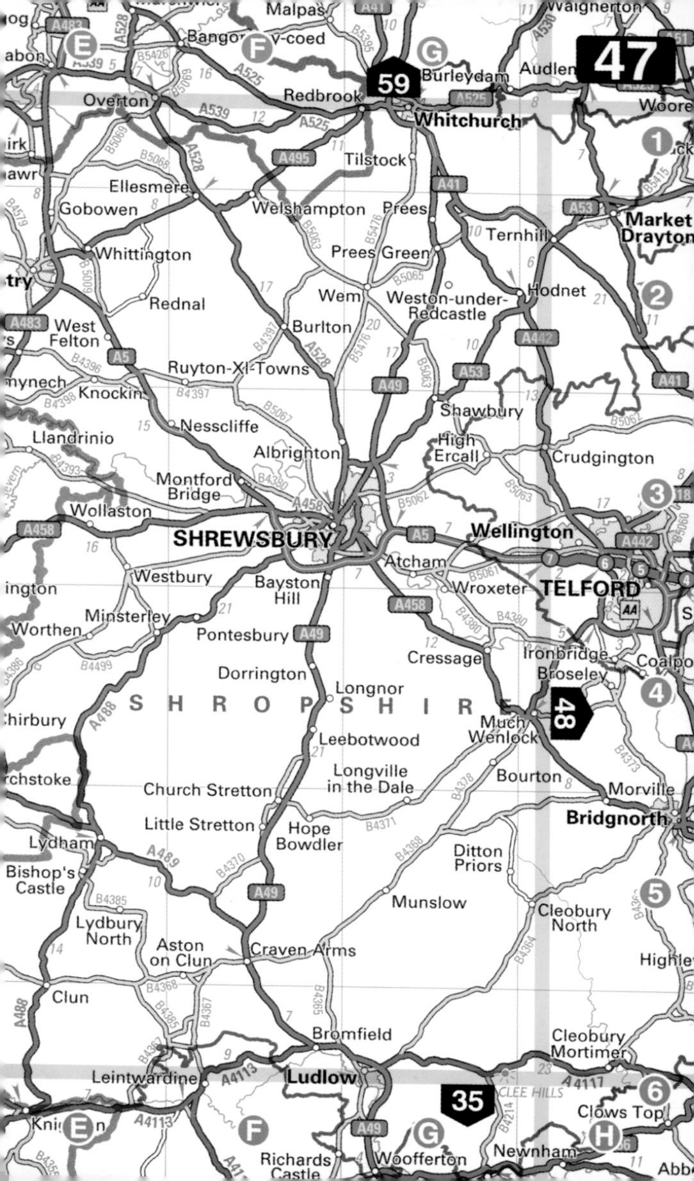

Malpas
A41
A483
A528
E
Bangor
F
A539
G
B5395
59
Burleydam
Audlem
47
A525
B5426
B5069
Overton
A539
Redbrook
Whitchurch
Woore
A525
A528
B5068
B5069
A495
Tilstock
1
B5415
A41
Ellesmere
Gobowen
Welshampton
Prees
A53
Market Drayton
B4579
B5063
B5476
Ternhill
Whittington
Prees Green
B5009
B5065
Hodnet
Wem
Weston-under-Redcastle
2
Rednal
A483
West Felton
Burlton
B4397
A528
B5476
A442
A5
B4396
Ruyton-XI-Towns
B5063
A53
A49
A41
Knockin
B4398
B4397
B5067
Shawbury
Nesscliffe
B5062
Llandrinio
Albrighton
High Ercall
Crudgington
B4393
Montford Bridge
B4380
B5063
3
A458
B5062
Wollaston
A458
SHREWSBURY
A5
Wellington
A442
B5060
Atcham
7
6
5
4
Westbury
Bayston Hill
B5061
Wroxeter
TELFORD
A458
Minsterley
B4380
Worthen
Pontesbury
A49
Cressage
Ironbridge
B4499
Broseley
Coalport
Dorrington
4
Longnor
SHROPSHIRE
48
A488
Much Wenlock
Leebotwood
B4373
Longville in the Dale
Bourton
B4378
Church Stretton
Morville
Bridgnorth
Little Stretton
Hope Bowdler
B4371
Lydham
A489
B4368
Ditton Priors
Bishop's Castle
B4370
5
A49
B4385
Munslow
Cleobury North
Lydbury North
B4364
Aston on Clun
Craven Arms
Clun
B4368
B4385
B4367
B4365
A488
Bromfield
Cleobury Mortimer
Leintwardine
A4113
Ludlow
A4117
CLEE HILLS
35
6
Clows Top
A4113
A49
F
G
B4214
H
Richards Castle
Woofferton
Newnham

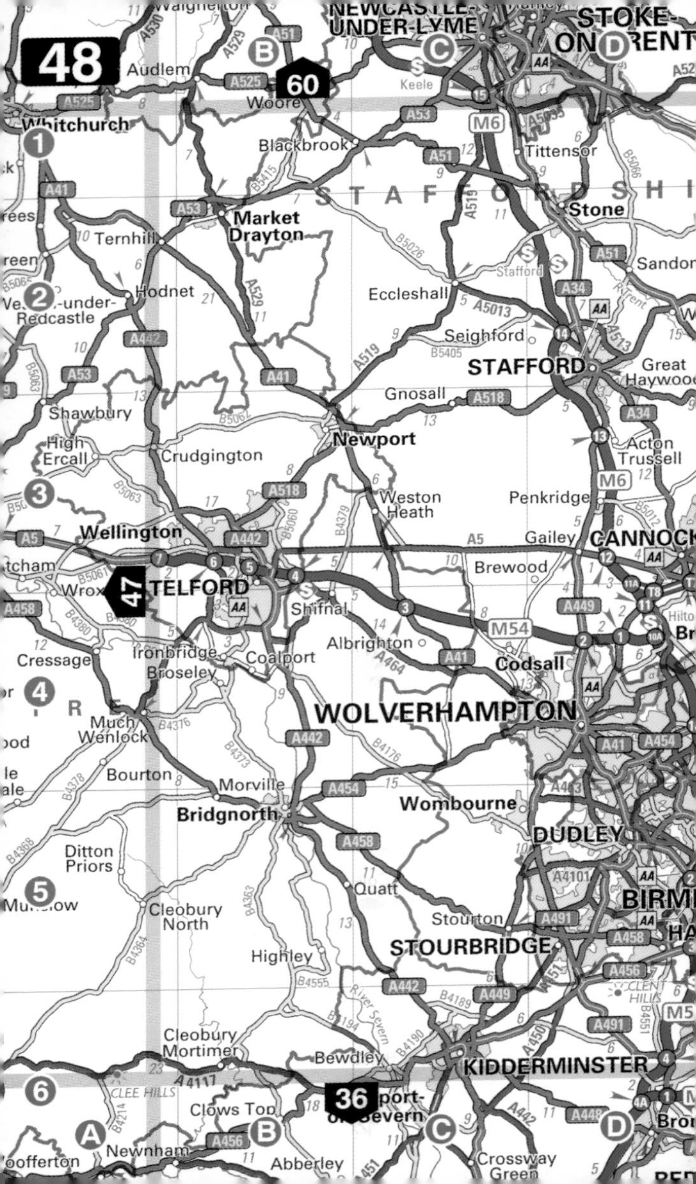
NEWCASTLE-UNDER-LYME
STOKE-ON-TRENT
Audlem
Woore
Keele
Whitchurch
Blackbrook
Tittensor
STAFFORDSHIRE
Market Drayton
Stone
Ternhill
Sandon
Hodnet
Eccleshall
Stafford
Redcastle
Seighford
STAFFORD
Great Haywood
Gnosall
Shawbury
Newport
High Ercall
Crudgington
Acton Trussell
Weston Heath
Penkridge
Wellington
Gailey
CANNOCK
Brewood
TELFORD
Shifnal
Wrox
Albrighton
Codsall
Cressage
Ironbridge
Coalport
Broseley
WOLVERHAMPTON
Much Wenlock
Bourton
Morville
Bridgnorth
Wombourne
DUDLEY
Ditton Priors
Quatt
Munslow
Cleobury North
Stourton
STOURBRIDGE
Highley
River Severn
CLENT HILLS
Cleobury Mortimer
Bewdley
KIDDERMINSTER
CLEE HILLS
Clows Top
Newnham
Abberley
Crossway Green
M6
M54
A5
A41
A442
A449
A458
A454
A53
A51
A519
A518
A525
A529
A34
A5013
A4117
A456
A491
A448

60
47
36

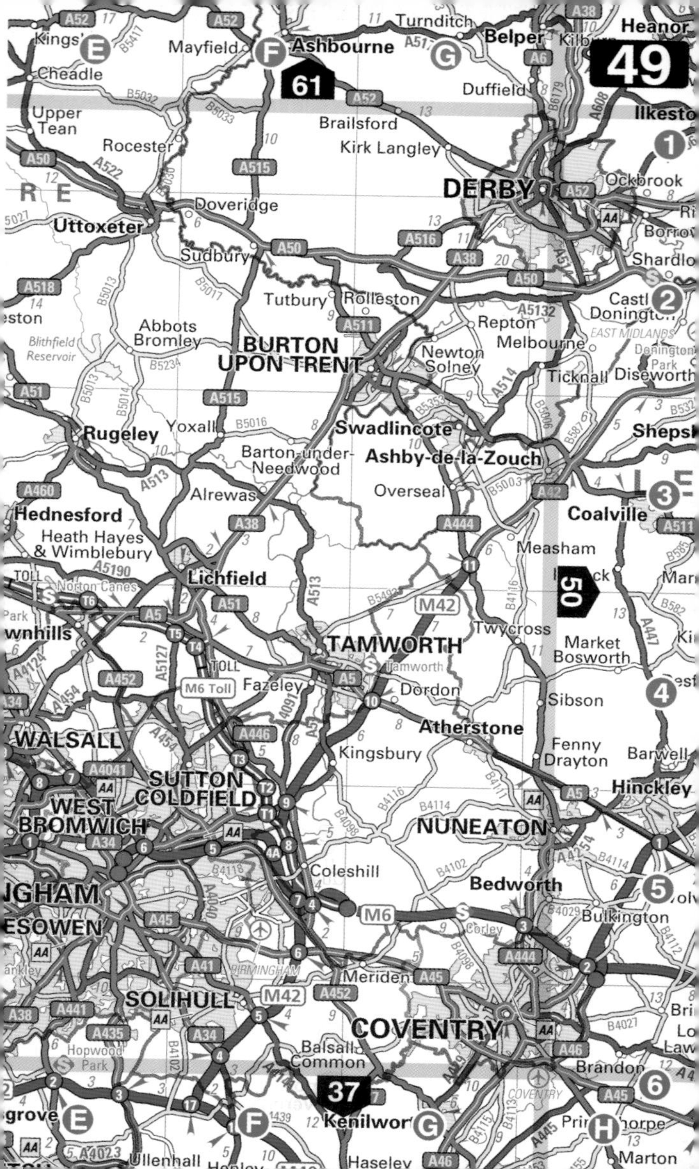

49
61
50
37
Kings'
Cheadle
Upper Tean
Rocester
Mayfield
Ashbourne
Turnditch
Belper
Heanor
Duffield
Ilkeston
Brailsford
Kirk Langley
DERBY
Ockbrook
Borrowash
Shardlow
Castle Donington
EAST MIDLANDS
Donington Park
Diseworth
Doveridge
Uttoxeter
Sudbury
Tutbury
Rolleston
Repton
Melbourne
Ticknall
Blithfield Reservoir
Abbots Bromley
BURTON UPON TRENT
Newton Solney
Swadlincote
Ashby-de-la-Zouch
Shepshed
Rugeley
Yoxall
Barton-under-Needwood
Overseal
Coalville
Alrewas
Hednesford
Heath Hayes & Wimblebury
Measham
Lichfield
Norton Canes
Twycross
Market Bosworth
TAMWORTH
Tamworth
Fazeley
Dordon
Sibson
Atherstone
Fenny Drayton
Barwell
Hinckley
WALSALL
SUTTON COLDFIELD
Kingsbury
WEST BROMWICH
NUNEATON
Coleshill
Bedworth
Bulkington
Corley
BIRMINGHAM
Meriden
SOLIHULL
COVENTRY
Brandon
Hopwood Park
Balsall Common
Kenilworth
Ullenhall
Haseley
Marton
A52
A6
A608
A515
A50
A522
A516
A38
A518
A511
A51
A514
A513
A444
A42
A460
A5190
M42
A5
A447
A452
A5127
M6 Toll
A446
A4041
A34
A45
A4040
M6
A444
A41
A441
A435
A46
A445
B5032
B5033
B5030
B5013
B5017
B5014
B5234
B5016
B5353
B5006
B587
B5003
B5493
B4116
B4114
B4098
B4118
B4102
B4029
B4112
B4027
B4113
B4115
A4023

62
49
38
NOTTINGHAM
DERBY
LEICESTER
NUNEATON
RUGBY
LEICESTERSHIRE
Heanor
Eastwood
Belper
Kilburn
Lowdham
Burton Joyce
Duffield
Ilkeston
Stapleford
Radcliffe on Trent
Ockbrook
West Bridgford
Beeston
Risley
Borrowash
Long Eaton
Plumtree
Shardlow
Ruddington
Bunny
Keyworth
Castle Donington
Kegworth
Widmerpool
Upper Broughton
Repton
Melbourne
Rempstone
Newton Solney
Ticknall
Diseworth
Hathern
Hoton
Shepshed
Loughborough
Barrow upon Soar
Coalville
Mountsorrel
Sileby
East Goscote
Measham
Syston
Ibstock
Markfield
Anstey
Birstall
Groby
Twycross
Market Bosworth
Kirby Muxloe
Desford
Sibson
Oadby
Atherstone
Enderby
Wigston
Fenny Drayton
Barwell
Blaby
Hinckley
Cosby
Countesthorpe
Kibworth Harcourt
Bedworth
Wolvey
Lubenham
Bulkington
Lutterworth
North Kilworth
Husbands Bosworth
Pailton
Swinford
Brinklow
Long Lawford
Cold Ashby
Brandon
West Haddon
Dunchurch
Watford
Marton
Watford Gap
EAST MIDLANDS
Donington Park
BEACON HILL
Leicester Forest East
COVENTRY
M1
M69
M42
A52
A6
A46
A60
A50
A5
A14
A45
A444
A447
A426
A4304
A5199
A453
A606
A6006
A511
A512
A563
A42
A514
A38
A609
A610
A608

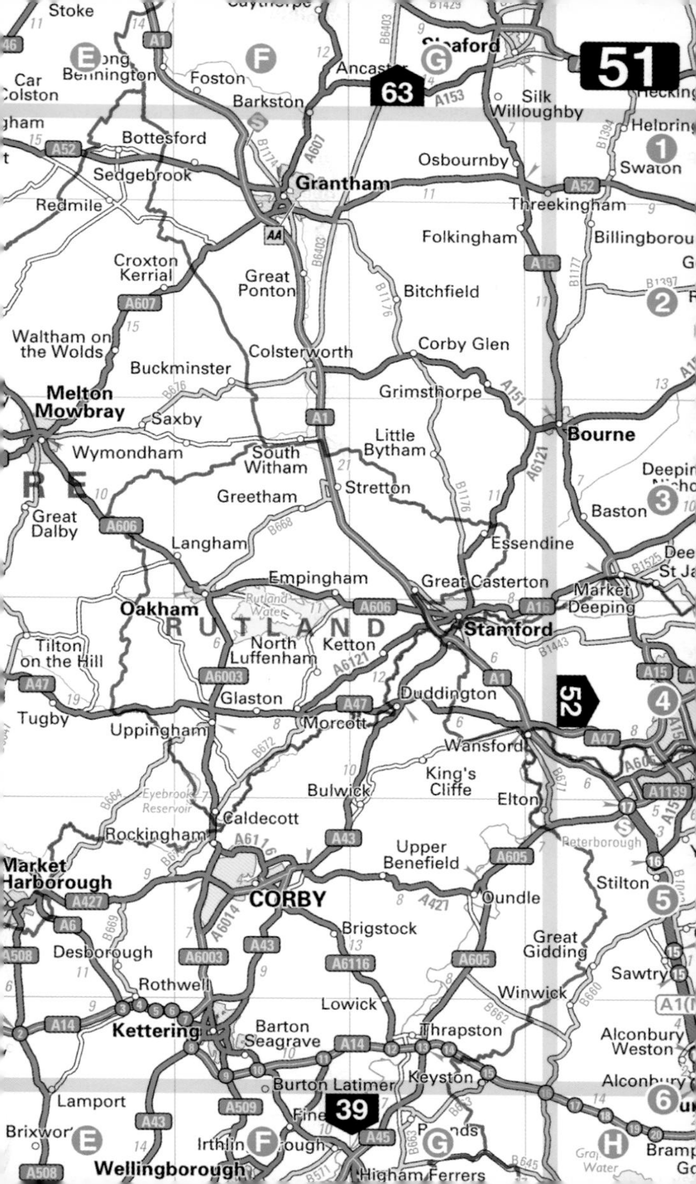
51
63
52
39
Stoke
Long Bennington
Car Colston
Foston
Barkston
Ancaster
Sleaford
Silk Willoughby
Bottesford
Sedgebrook
Redmile
Grantham
Osbournby
Swaton
Helpringham
Threekingham
Folkingham
Billingborough
Croxton Kerrial
Great Ponton
Bitchfield
Waltham on the Wolds
Colsterworth
Corby Glen
Buckminster
Grimsthorpe
Melton Mowbray
Saxby
Bourne
Wymondham
South Witham
Little Bytham
Stretton
Greetham
Baston
Great Dalby
Langham
Essendine
Empingham
Great Casterton
Market Deeping
Oakham
Rutland Water
RUTLAND
Stamford
Tilton on the Hill
North Luffenham
Ketton
Tugby
Glaston
Morcott
Duddington
Uppingham
Wansford
King's Cliffe
Eyebrook Reservoir
Bulwick
Elton
Caldecott
Rockingham
Peterborough
Upper Benefield
Market Harborough
Stilton
CORBY
Oundle
Brigstock
Great Gidding
Desborough
Sawtry
Rothwell
Winwick
Lowick
Kettering
Barton Seagrave
Thrapston
Alconbury Weston
Keyston
Burton Latimer
Alconbury
Lamport
Brixworth
Irthlingborough
Wellingborough
Higham Ferrers
Grafham Water
A1
A52
A607
A606
A15
A151
A6121
A16
A6003
A47
A43
A605
A6116
A427
A6014
A6
A14
A508
A509
A45
A153
A1139
B6403
B1174
B1176
B1394
B1177
B1397
B676
B668
B1525
B1443
B672
B664
B671
B669
B662
B660
B663
B645
B571

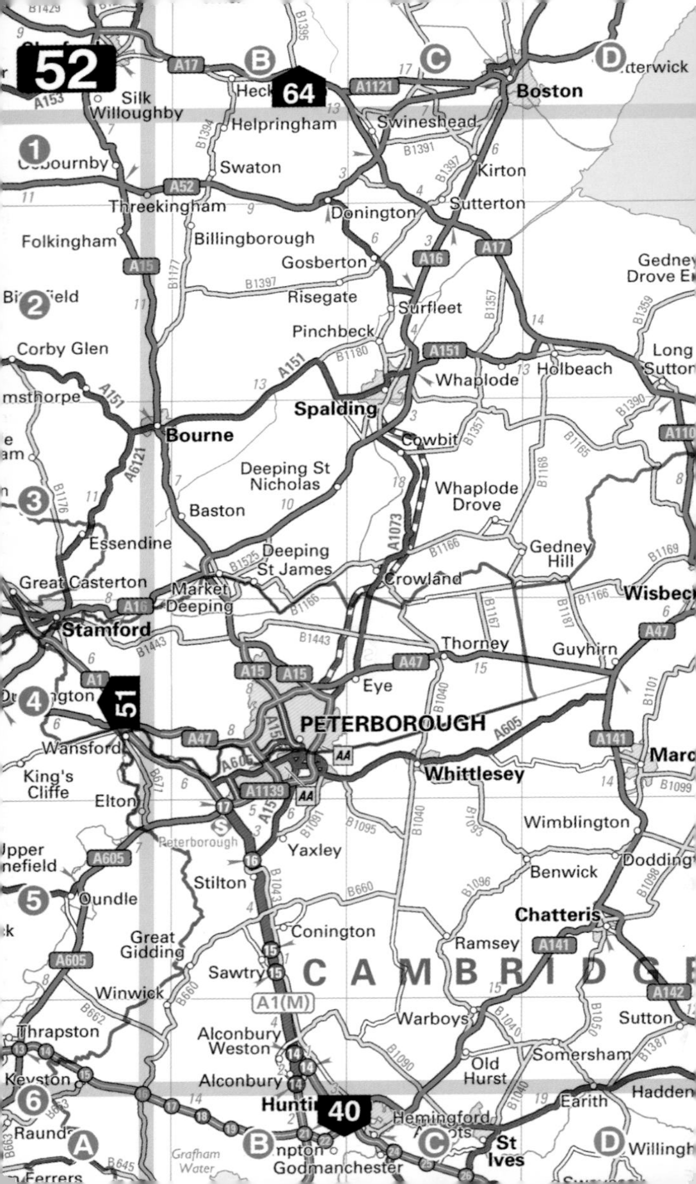

52
64
51
40
A
B
C
D
1
2
3
4
5
6
Boston
Silk Willoughby
Heck
Helpringham
Swineshead
Kirton
Swaton
Threekingham
Donington
Sutterton
Folkingham
Billingborough
Gosberton
Risegate
Surfleet
Pinchbeck
Corby Glen
Whaplode
Holbeach
Long Sutton
Spalding
Bourne
Cowbit
Deeping St Nicholas
Whaplode Drove
Baston
Essendine
Deeping St James
Gedney Hill
Great Casterton
Market Deeping
Crowland
Stamford
Thorney
Guyhirn
Eye
PETERBOROUGH
Wansford
Whittlesey
King's Cliffe
Elton
Wimblington
Yaxley
Benwick
Stilton
Oundle
Conington
Chatteris
Great Gidding
Ramsey
Sawtry
CAMBRIDGE
Winwick
Warboys
Sutton
Thrapston
Alconbury Weston
Somersham
Old Hurst
Keyston
Alconbury
Earith
Hemingford
St Ives
Godmanchester
Grafham Water
A17
A1121
A52
A15
A16
A151
A6121
A1073
A47
A1
A605
A1139
A141
A142
A1(M)
B1395
B1394
B1391
B1397
B1177
B1357
B1359
B1180
B1390
B1165
B1168
B1176
B1166
B1525
B1169
B1167
B1187
B1443
B1040
B1101
B1099
B671
B1091
B1095
B1093
B1043
B660
B1096
B1098
B662
B1090
B1050
B1381
B663
B645
Peterborough

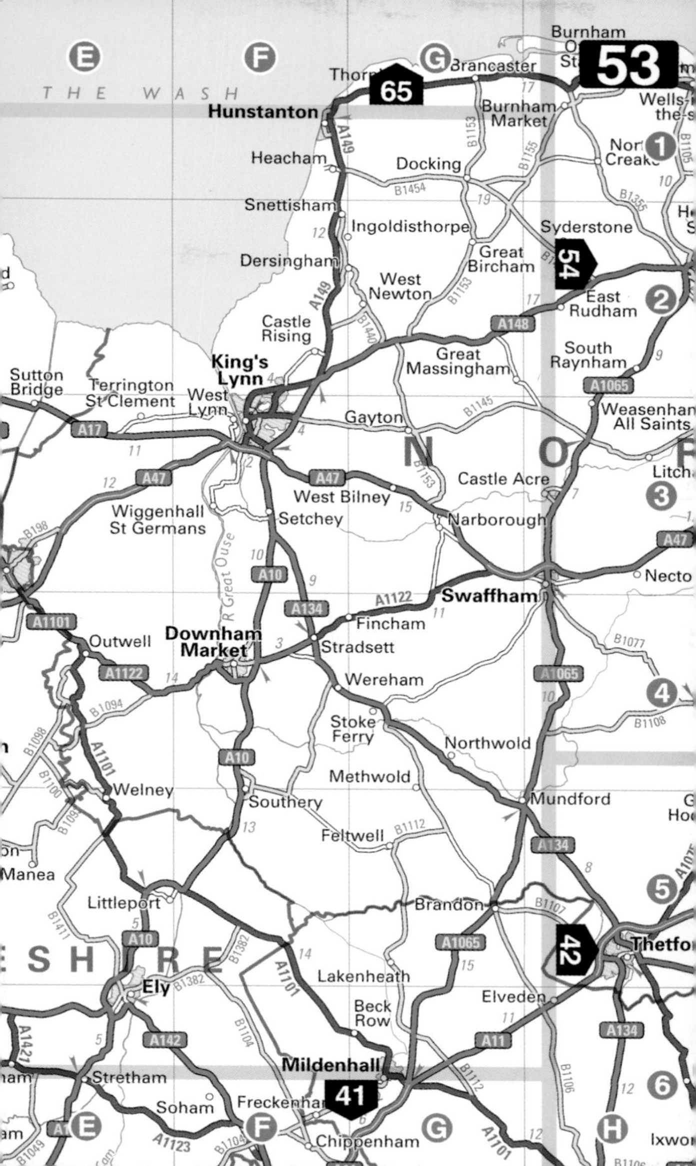
THE WASH
Hunstanton
Heacham
Snettisham
Ingoldisthorpe
Dersingham
West Newton
Castle Rising
King's Lynn
West Lynn
Sutton Bridge
Terrington St Clement
Wiggenhall St Germans
Setchey
West Bilney
Gayton
Brancaster
Burnham Market
Docking
Syderstone
Great Bircham
East Rudham
South Raynham
Great Massingham
Weasenham All Saints
Castle Acre
Narborough
Swaffham
Fincham
Stradsett
Downham Market
Outwell
Wereham
Stoke Ferry
Northwold
Methwold
Southery
Welney
Feltwell
Mundford
Manea
Littleport
Brandon
Lakenheath
Ely
Elveden
Beck Row
Mildenhall
Stretham
Soham
Freckenham
Chippenham
Thetford
Ixworth
Necton
R Great Ouse
53
65
54
42
41

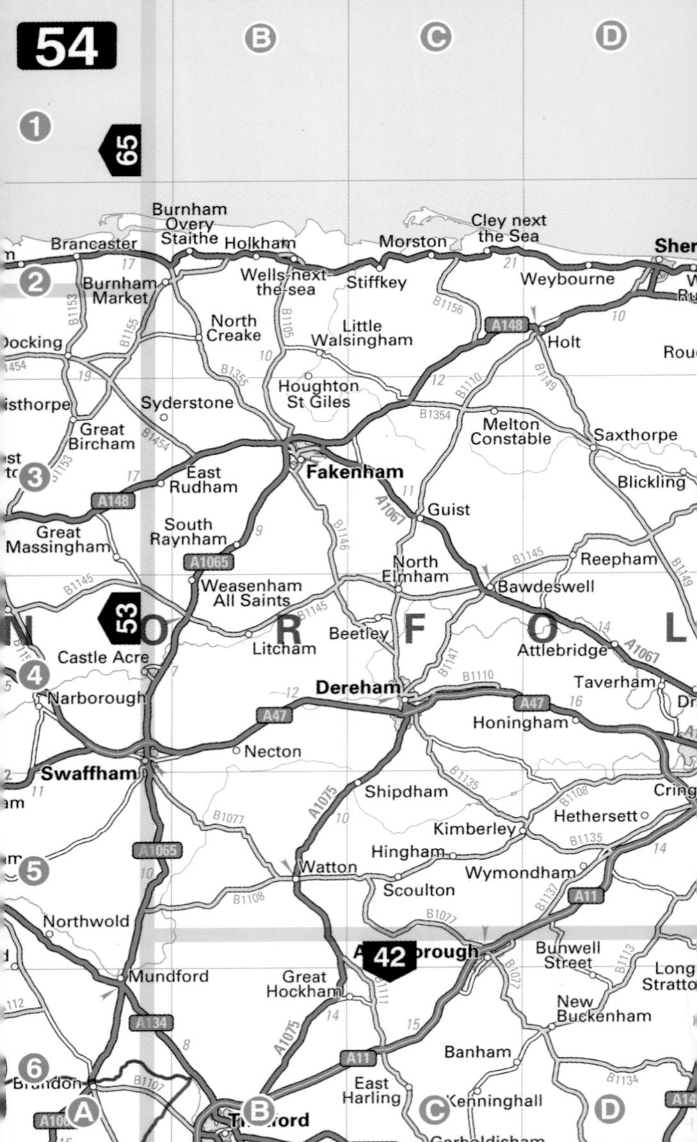

54
65
53
42
NORFOLK
Brancaster
Burnham Overy Staithe
Holkham
Morston
Cley next the Sea
Burnham Market
Wells-next-the-sea
Stiffkey
Weybourne
Docking
North Creake
Little Walsingham
Holt
Houghton St Giles
Syderstone
Great Bircham
Melton Constable
Saxthorpe
Fakenham
East Rudham
Blickling
Guist
Great Massingham
South Raynham
Reepham
North Elmham
Weasenham All Saints
Bawdeswell
Beetley
Litcham
Castle Acre
Attlebridge
Narborough
Dereham
Taverham
Honingham
Necton
Swaffham
Shipdham
Hethersett
Kimberley
Hingham
Watton
Wymondham
Scoulton
Northwold
Bunwell Street
Mundford
Great Hockham
New Buckenham
Banham
East Harling
Kenninghall
Garboldisham
A148
A1065
A47
A1067
A1075
A11
A134
B1153
B1155
B1454
B1355
B1105
B1156
B1110
B1149
B1354
B1145
B1146
B1147
B1135
B1108
B1077
B1137
B1113
B1107
B1111
B1134

E
F
G
1
2
3
4
5
6
H
Cromer
Trimingham
Southrepps
Mundesley
Bacton
Happisburgh
North Walsham
Aylsham
Sea Palling
Stalham
Hickling Broad
Catfield
Horsey
Coltishall
Wroxham
Ludham
Hemsby
Spixworth
Rollesby
Ormesby Broad
Ormesby St Margaret
NORWICH
Rackheath
South Walsham
Thorpe End
Filby
Caister-on-Sea
Acle
GREAT YARMOUTH
NORWICH
Brundall
THE BROADS
Burgh Castle
Caistor St Edmund
Yelverton
Belton
Reedham
Hopton on Sea
Brooke
Loddon
Hales
Fritton
Corton
Haddiscoe
Hempnall
43
Ellingham
Gillingham
LOWESTOFT
Bungay
Beccles
Earsham
Pulham St Mary
Homersfield
Henst
Kessingland
Harleston
A140
A149
A1151
A47
A1064
A146
A143
A12
B1145
B1159
B1150
B1354
B1140
B1332
B1136
B1074
B1527
B1062
B1127
B1436
B1113

56
Dublin
Dun Laoghaire
Cemaes
Amlwch
ISLE OF
ANGLESEY
Llyn Alaw
Llanerchymedd
A5025
B5111
Holyhead
SOUTH STACK
Llanfachraeth
B5112
Benllech
B5109
Trearddur Bay
B4545
Holy
Island
A55
A5
B5110
Llangefni
B5420
Rhosneigr
A4080
ANGLESEY
B4422
B4419
Llanfair
P G
Aberffraw
B4421
Y Felinheli
A487
Newborough
Caernarfon
Bontnewydd
CAERNARFON
Llandwrog
Llanwnda
Caernarfon
Bay
B4418
A499
Penygroes
Clynnog-fawr
Llanaelhaearn
PENINSULA
B4411
Morfa Nefyn
Nefyn
B4354
Llanystumdwy
Trem
Porthm
B4417
A497
Bodfuan
Criccieth
Bor
LLEYN
B4415
Pwllheli
Sarn
B4413
Llanbedrog
Aberdaron
Y Rhiw
Abersoch
Bardsey
Island
44
A
B
C
D
1
2
3
4
5
6

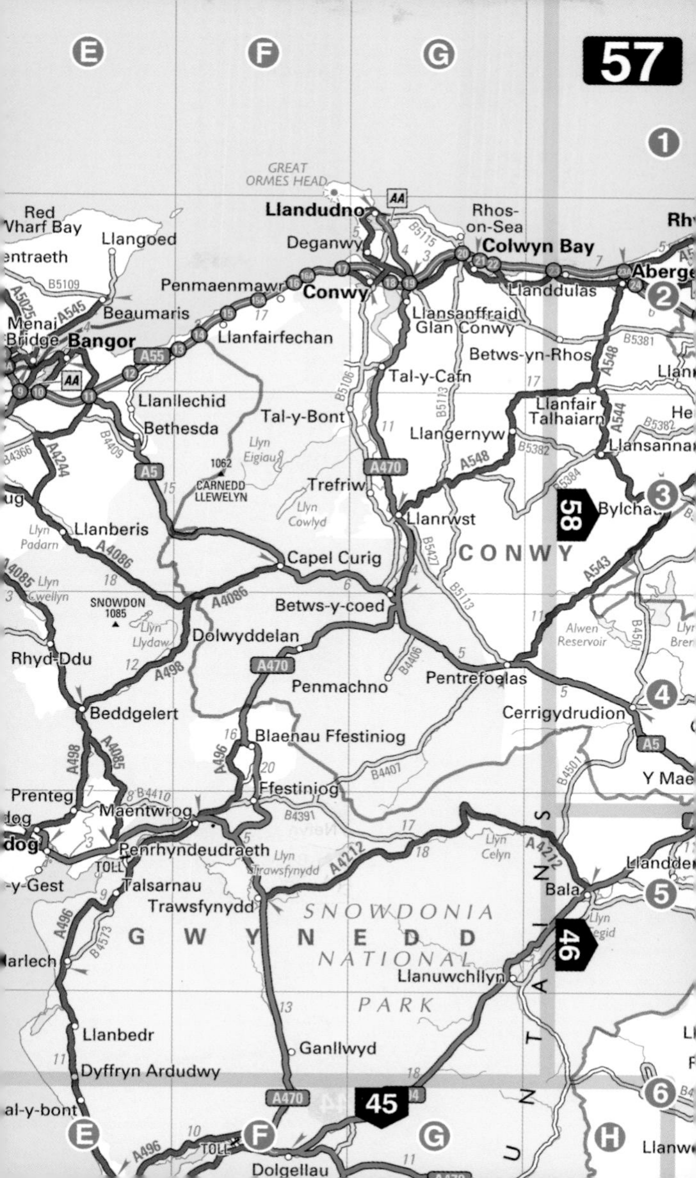
E
F
G
1
2
3
4
5
6
H
GREAT ORMES HEAD
Llandudno
Red Wharf Bay
Llangoed
Deganwy
Rhos-on-Sea
Colwyn Bay
Penmaenmawr
Conwy
Llanddulas
Beaumaris
Menai Bridge
Bangor
Llanfairfechan
Llansanffraid Glan Conwy
Betws-yn-Rhos
Tal-y-Cafn
Llanllechid
Bethesda
Tal-y-Bont
Llyn Eigiau
Llanfair Talhaiarn
Llangernyw
Llansannan
CARNEDD LLEWELYN
1062
Trefriw
Llyn Cowlyd
Llanrwst
Bylchau
Llanberis
Llyn Padarn
Capel Curig
CONWY
Llyn Cwellyn
SNOWDON 1085
Betws-y-coed
Llyn Llydaw
Dolwyddelan
Alwen Reservoir
Rhyd-Ddu
Penmachno
Pentrefoelas
Beddgelert
Cerrigydrudion
Blaenau Ffestiniog
Ffestiniog
Y Maerdy
Prenteg
Maentwrog
Penrhyndeudraeth
Llyn Trawsfynydd
Llyn Celyn
Bala
TOLL
Talsarnau
Trawsfynydd
SNOWDONIA NATIONAL PARK
Llyn Tegid
GWYNEDD
Harlech
Llanuwchllyn
Llanbedr
Ganllwyd
Dyffryn Ardudwy
Tal-y-bont
Dolgellau
MOUNTAINS
58
46
45
A55
A5
A470
A548
A543
A4086
A498
A4085
A496
A4212
A4244
A545
A5025
A544
B5109
B5115
B5106
B5113
B4409
B4366
B5381
B5382
B5384
B5427
B4406
B4407
B4410
B4391
B4501
B4573

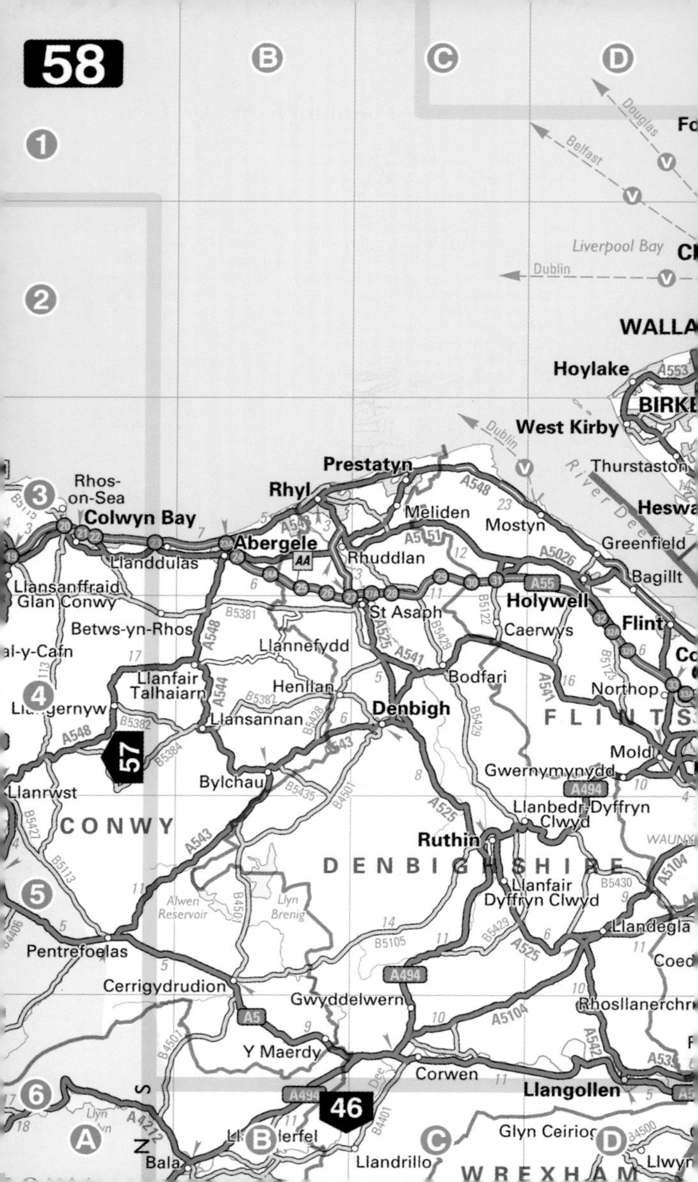
Liverpool Bay
Douglas
Belfast
Dublin
WALLA
Hoylake
BIRKE
West Kirby
Thurstaston
Heswa
River Dee
Prestatyn
Rhyl
Meliden
Mostyn
Greenfield
Bagillt
Rhos-on-Sea
Colwyn Bay
Abergele
Rhuddlan
Llanddulas
Llansanffraid Glan Conwy
Betws-yn-Rhos
St Asaph
Holywell
Flint
Caerwys
Llannefydd
Bodfari
Northop
Llanfair Talhaiarn
Henllan
Denbigh
Llansannan
FLINTS
Mold
Gwernymynydd
Bylchau
Llanrwst
CONWY
Llanbedr-Dyffryn Clwyd
Ruthin
DENBIGHSHIRE
Llanfair Dyffryn Clwyd
Alwen Reservoir
Llyn Brenig
Llandegla
Pentrefoelas
Cerrigydrudion
Gwyddelwern
Rhosllanerchr
Y Maerdy
Corwen
Llangollen
Glyn Ceiriog
Llandrillo
Bala
WREXHAM
57
46

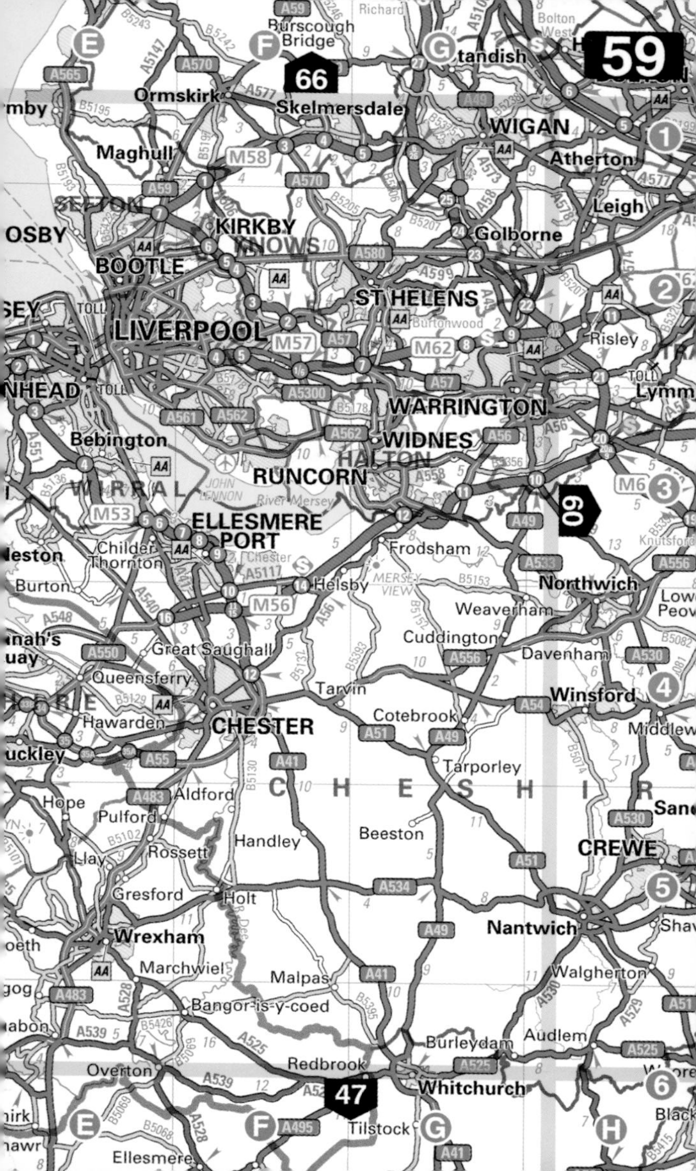
59
66
60
47
Burscough Bridge
Standish
Ormskirk
Skelmersdale
WIGAN
Maghull
Atherton
Leigh
KIRKBY
KNOWSLEY
Golborne
BOOTLE
ST HELENS
Burtonwood
LIVERPOOL
Risley
Lymm
WARRINGTON
WIDNES
HALTON
RUNCORN
Bebington
WIRRAL
JOHN LENNON
River Mersey
ELLESMERE PORT
Frodsham
Childer Thornton
Helsby
MERSEY VIEW
Northwich
Weaverham
Burton
Cuddington
Great Saughall
Davenham
Queensferry
Tarvin
Winsford
Hawarden
CHESTER
Cotebrook
Tarporley
C H E S H I R E
Aldford
Hope
Pulford
Handley
Beeston
Rossett
CREWE
Gresford
Holt
Wrexham
Nantwich
Marchwiel
Malpas
Walgherton
Bangor-is-y-coed
Audlem
Burleydam
Redbrook
Overton
Whitchurch
Tilstock
Ellesmere
Knutsford
M58
M57
M62
M53
M56
M6
A59
A565
A570
A5147
A577
A580
A57
A5300
A561
A562
A56
A5117
A550
A55
A51
A49
A41
A483
A534
A530
A556
A533
A54
A539
A528
A525
A495
A5114
A558
A548
A540
A551
A573
A58
A578
A529

60
67
59
48
Horwich
BOLTON
BURY
ROCHDALE
WIGAN
Prestwich
Chadderton
OLDHAM
Atherton
Failsworth
Leigh
SALFORD
Ashton
Golborne
MANCHESTER
Stretford
Denton
Hyde
Burtonwood
Risley
TRAFFORD
Sale
STOCKPORT
WARRINGTON
Lymm
Cheadle
Hazel Grove
Altrincham
WIDNES
Disley
Bucklow Hill
Poynton
Mobberley
Wilmslow
Alderley Edge
Knutsford
Frodsham
Bollington
Prestbury
Northwich
Lower Peover
Chelford
Macclesfield
Cuddington
Davenham
Goostrey
Holmes Chapel
Winsford
Middlewich
Brereton Green
Tarporley
Congleton
Arclid Green
Sandbach
Biddulph
CREWE
Alsager
Kidsgrove
Nantwich
Shavington
Audley
Walgherton
NEWCASTLE-UNDER-LYME
Hanley
STOKE-ON-TRENT
Burleydam
Audlem
Woore
Keele
Whitchurch
Tittensor
CHESHIRE
STAFFORDSHIRE

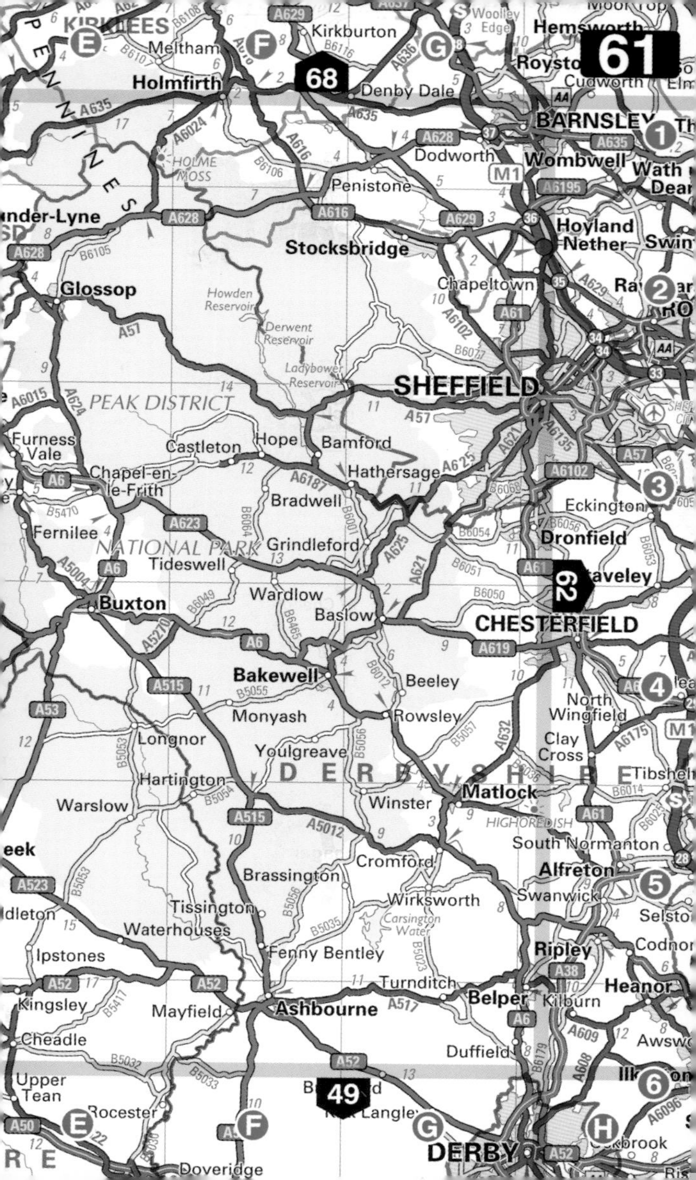
61
68
62
49
KIRKLEES
PENNINES
Meltham
Holmfirth
Kirkburton
Denby Dale
Hemsworth
Royston
Cudworth
BARNSLEY
Wombwell
Dodworth
Penistone
Stocksbridge
HOLME MOSS
Hoyland Nether
Chapeltown
Glossop
Howden Reservoir
Derwent Reservoir
Ladybower Reservoir
SHEFFIELD
PEAK DISTRICT
Furness Vale
Castleton
Hope
Bamford
Hathersage
Chapel-en-le-Frith
Bradwell
Fernilee
NATIONAL PARK
Grindleford
Tideswell
Dronfield
Eckington
Staveley
Wardlow
Buxton
Baslow
CHESTERFIELD
Bakewell
Beeley
Monyash
Rowsley
North Wingfield
Longnor
Youlgreave
Clay Cross
DERBYSHIRE
Hartington
Tibshelf
Warslow
Winster
Matlock
HIGHOREDISH
South Normanton
Cromford
Brassington
Alfreton
Wirksworth
Swanwick
Tissington
Carsington Water
Waterhouses
Ripley
Codnor
Ipstones
Fenny Bentley
Turnditch
Heanor
Belper
Kilburn
Kingsley
Mayfield
Ashbourne
Cheadle
Duffield
Upper Tean
Rocester
Kirk Langley
DERBY
Doveridge
M1
A628
A616
A629
A635
A57
A6
A623
A625
A621
A619
A515
A5012
A52
A517
A38
A61
A6102
A6135
A624
A6015
A5004
A5270
A53
A523
A50
A609
A608
A6096
A6175
A632
A6024
A636
A6195
A6187
B6105
B6106
B6077
B6068
B6054
B6051
B6050
B6049
B6465
B5055
B6012
B5056
B5053
B5054
B5057
B6014
B5035
B5023
B5417
B5032
B5033
B5030
B6179
B6064
B6001
B5470
B6107
B6108
B6116
B6056
B6053
B6025

62
69
61
50
A
B
C
D
1
2
3
4
5
6
Woolley Edge
Moor Top
Hemsworth
Royston
Cudworth
Askern
Thorne
Doncaster North
Hatfield
Adwick Le Street
Dale
BARNSLEY
Thurnscoe
Dodworth
Wombwell
Wath upon Dearne
DONCASTER
Mexborough
Blaxton
Hoyland Nether
Swinton
Conisbrough
Finningley
Chapeltown
Rawmarsh
ROTHERHAM
Tickhill
Bawtry
Maltby
SHEFFIELD
Thurcroft
SHEFFIELD CITY
Dinnington
Barnby Moor
Woodall
Eckington
Worksop
Dronfield
Whitwell
Staveley
Elkesley
Clowne
CHESTERFIELD
Bolsover
NOTTINGHAMSHIRE
Cuckney
Warsop
Edwinstowe
Ollerton
Heath
Glapwell
North Wingfield
Rowsley
Pleasley
Clay Cross
DERBYSHIRE
Tibshelf
MANSFIELD
Bilsthorpe
Matlock
HIGHOREDISH
Kirkby in Ashfield
South Normanton
Blidworth
SHERWOOD FOREST
Alfreton
Pinxton
Southwell
Wirksworth
Swanwick
Selston
Oxton
Ripley
Codnor
Hucknall
Heanor
Eastwood
Lowdham
Belper
Kilburn
Burton Joyce
Gunthorpe
Awsworth
Duffield
Ilkeston
NOTTINGHAM
Stapleford
West Bridgford
DERBY
Ockbrook
Beeston
Risley
M1
A1(M)
M18
A1
A614
A60
A57
A61
A619
A617
A38
A6
A610
A609
A52
A46
A631
A638
A630
A635
A628
A6195
A629
A6102
A616
A632
A6175
A611
A6097
A612
A620
A634
A621
A6135
A6075
A18

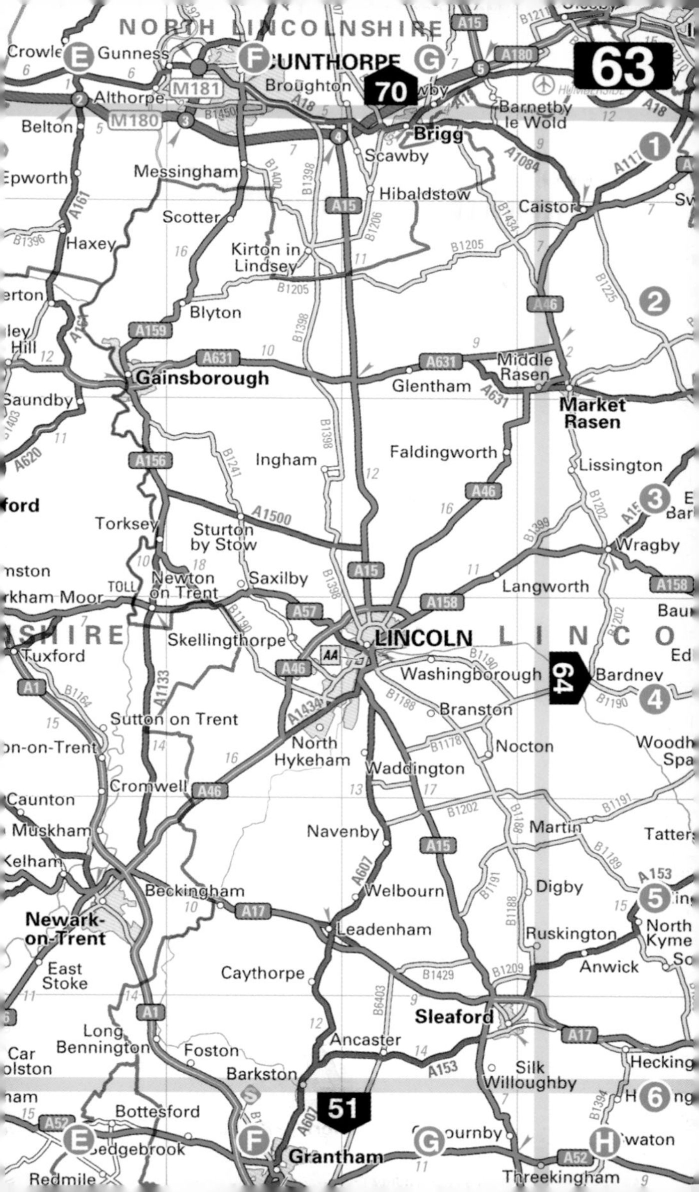
NORTH LINCOLNSHIRE
63
70
SCUNTHORPE
Crowle
Gunness
Broughton
Althorpe
Belton
M181
M180
B1450
A18
A15
A180
B1211
HUMBERSIDE
Barnetby le Wold
Brigg
Scawby
Epworth
Messingham
B1400
B1398
Hibaldstow
A1084
Caistor
A161
Scotter
B1206
B1434
B1396
Haxey
Kirton in Lindsey
B1205
B1225
A46
Blyton
A159
A631
Middle Rasen
Glentham
Gainsborough
Market Rasen
Saundby
A620
B1241
Ingham
Faldingworth
Lissington
A156
A1500
Torksey
Sturton by Stow
B1202
B1399
Wragby
Newton on Trent
Saxilby
A158
Langworth
TOLL
A57
B1190
Skellingthorpe
LINCOLN
LINCO
SHIRE
Tuxford
AA
Washingborough
64
Bardney
A1
B1164
A1133
B1188
Branston
Sutton on Trent
A1434
North Hykeham
B1178
Nocton
Waddington
Cromwell
Caunton
Muskham
Kelham
B1191
Navenby
Martin
A607
Digby
Welbourn
Beckingham
A17
Leadenham
Newark-on-Trent
Ruskington
North Kyme
Anwick
East Stoke
Caythorpe
B1429
B1209
B6403
Sleaford
Long Bennington
Ancaster
Foston
A153
Silk Willoughby
Barkston
51
Bottesford
B1394
A52
Sedgebrook
Grantham
Threekingham
Redmile

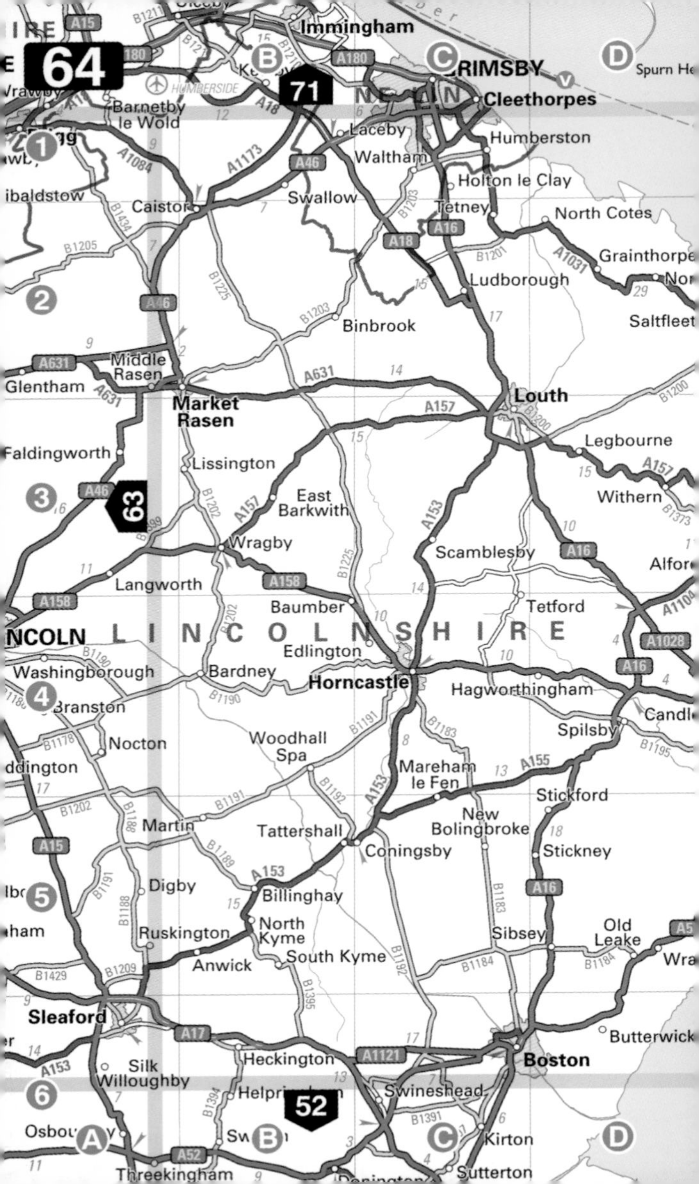

64
71
63
52
Immingham
GRIMSBY
Cleethorpes
Spurn Head
HUMBERSIDE
Barnetby le Wold
Laceby
Humberston
Waltham
Holton le Clay
Caistor
Swallow
Tetney
North Cotes
Grainthorpe
Ludborough
Binbrook
Saltfleet
Middle Rasen
Glentham
Market Rasen
Louth
Legbourne
Faldingworth
Lissington
East Barkwith
Withern
Wragby
Scamblesby
Alford
Langworth
Baumber
Tetford
LINCOLN
LINCOLNSHIRE
Edlington
Washingborough
Bardney
Horncastle
Hagworthingham
Branston
Candlesby
Spilsby
Nocton
Woodhall Spa
Mareham le Fen
Stickford
Martin
Tattershall
New Bolingbroke
Coningsby
Stickney
Digby
Billinghay
North Kyme
Ruskington
Sibsey
Old Leake
Anwick
South Kyme
Sleaford
Butterwick
Heckington
Boston
Silk Willoughby
Swineshead
Kirton
Threekingham
Sutterton
A15
A180
A18
A1173
A1084
A46
A16
A1031
A631
A157
A153
A158
A1028
A155
A17
A1121
A153
A52
B1205
B1434
B1225
B1203
B1201
B1200
B1202
B1373
B1190
B1191
B1183
B1195
B1178
B1188
B1189
B1192
B1184
B1209
B1429
B1395
B1394
B1391

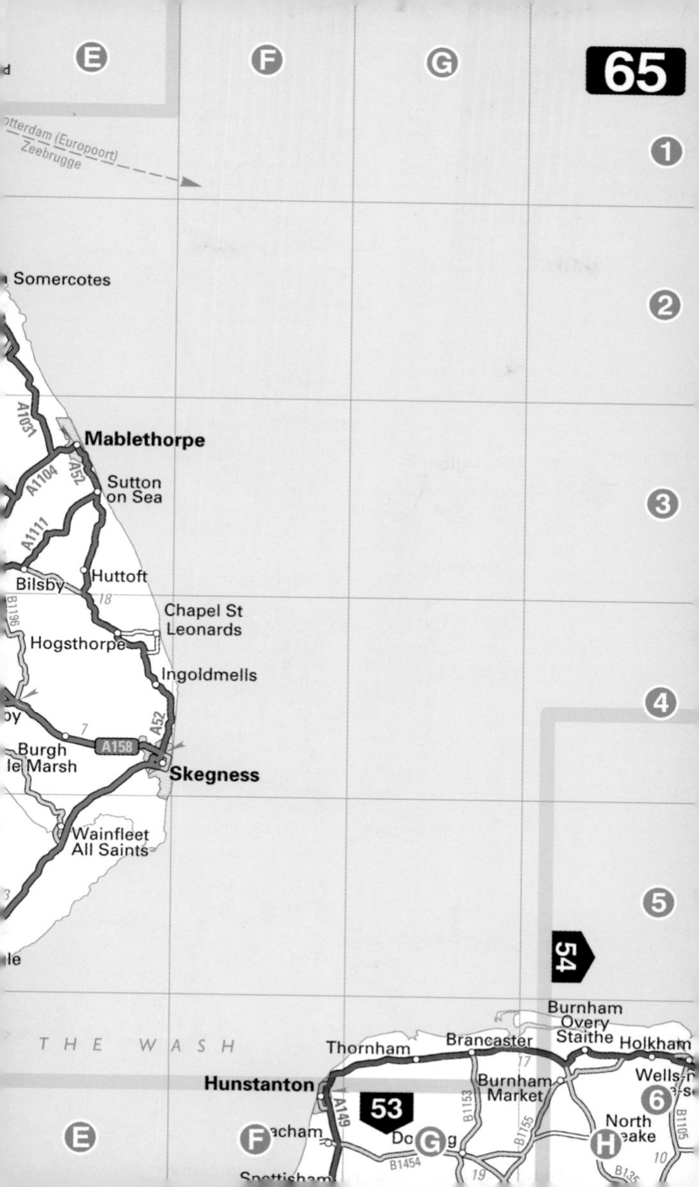
E
F
G
1
2
3
4
5
6
d
otterdam (Europoort)
Zeebrugge
Somercotes
A1031
Mablethorpe
A52
A1104
Sutton
on Sea
A1111
Huttoft
Bilsby
18
B1196
Chapel St
Leonards
Hogsthorpe
Ingoldmells
by
A52
7
A158
Burgh
le Marsh
Skegness
Wainfleet
All Saints
le
54
Burnham
Overy
Staithe
Holkham
Brancaster
Thornham
T H E   W A S H
17
Wells-n
Hunstanton
Burnham
Market
53
A149
B1153
B1155
North
eake
B1105
E
F
acham
Do
G
g
H
B1454
19
10
B135
Snettisham

66
73
59
Ulverston
Cartmel
Lindale
Grange-over-Sands
Cark
Arnside
Silverdale
Burton-in-Kendal (Northbound only)
Arkholme
Carnforth
Hornby
Bolton le Sands
Bardsea
Baycliff
Rampside
Morecambe Bay
Morecambe
Caton
Lancaster
Heysham
Belfast (summer only)
Douglas
Galgate
Lancaster (Forton)
Forton
Larne
Fleetwood
Pilling
Preesall
Garstang
Cleveleys
Hambleton
Poulton-le-Fylde
Barton
BLACKPOOL
Kirkham
PRESTON
Warton
Freckleton
Lytham St Anne's
Longton
Bamber Bridge
Leyland
Tarleton
SOUTHPORT
Rufford
Charnock Richard
Burscough Bridge
Ormskirk
Skelmersdale
Formby
Maghull
M6
M55
A595
A590
A5087
A6
A683
A588
A587
A586
A585
A583
A584
A59
A565
A581
A570
A5209
A5147
A577
B6254
B5272
B5268
B5412
B5269
B5266
B5260
B5259
B5261
B5253
B5250
B5246
B5243
B5242
B5195
B5197

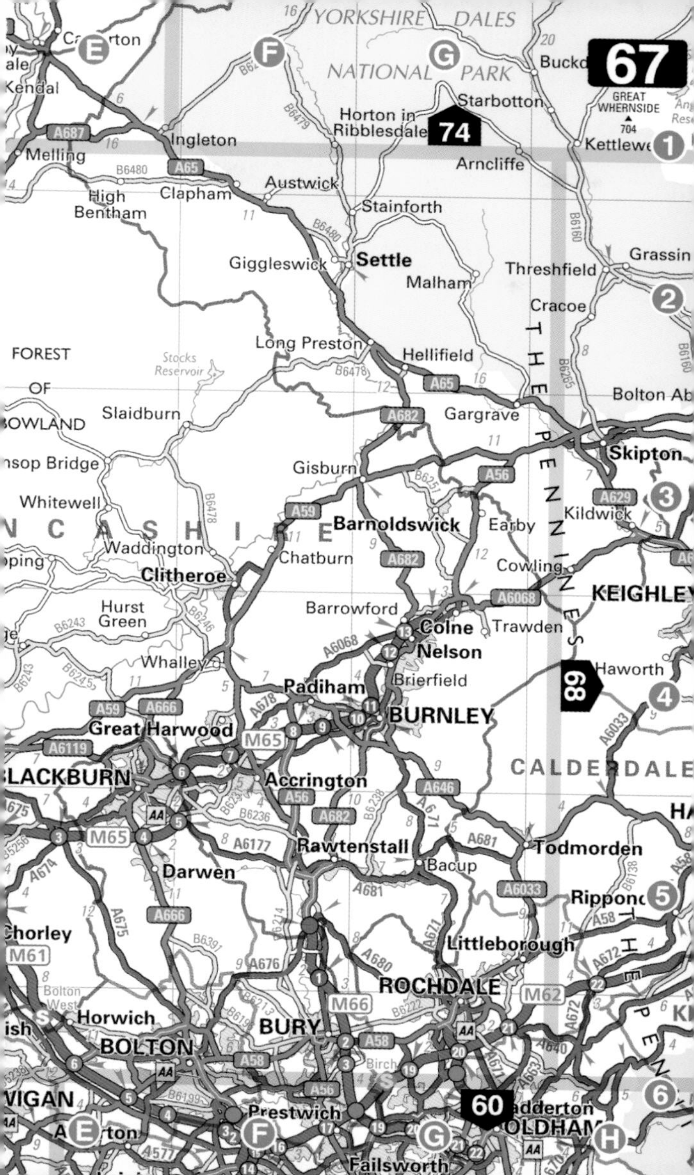

YORKSHIRE DALES
NATIONAL PARK
Horton in Ribblesdale
Starbotton
Kettlewell
Arncliffe
Ingleton
Melling
Kendal
Austwick
Clapham
High Bentham
Stainforth
Giggleswick
Settle
Malham
Threshfield
Cracoe
Long Preston
Hellifield
FOREST OF BOWLAND
Stocks Reservoir
Slaidburn
Gargrave
Skipton
Gisburn
Whitewell
Kildwick
Barnoldswick
Earby
Waddington
Chatburn
Cowling
Clitheroe
KEIGHLEY
Hurst Green
Barrowford
Colne
Trawden
Nelson
Whalley
Haworth
Brierfield
Padiham
BURNLEY
Great Harwood
THE PENNINES
CALDERDALE
BLACKBURN
Accrington
Rawtenstall
Todmorden
Darwen
Bacup
Ripponden
Chorley
Littleborough
ROCHDALE
Horwich
BURY
BOLTON
WIGAN
Prestwich
Chadderton
OLDHAM
Failsworth
GREAT WHERNSIDE
704
74
68
60

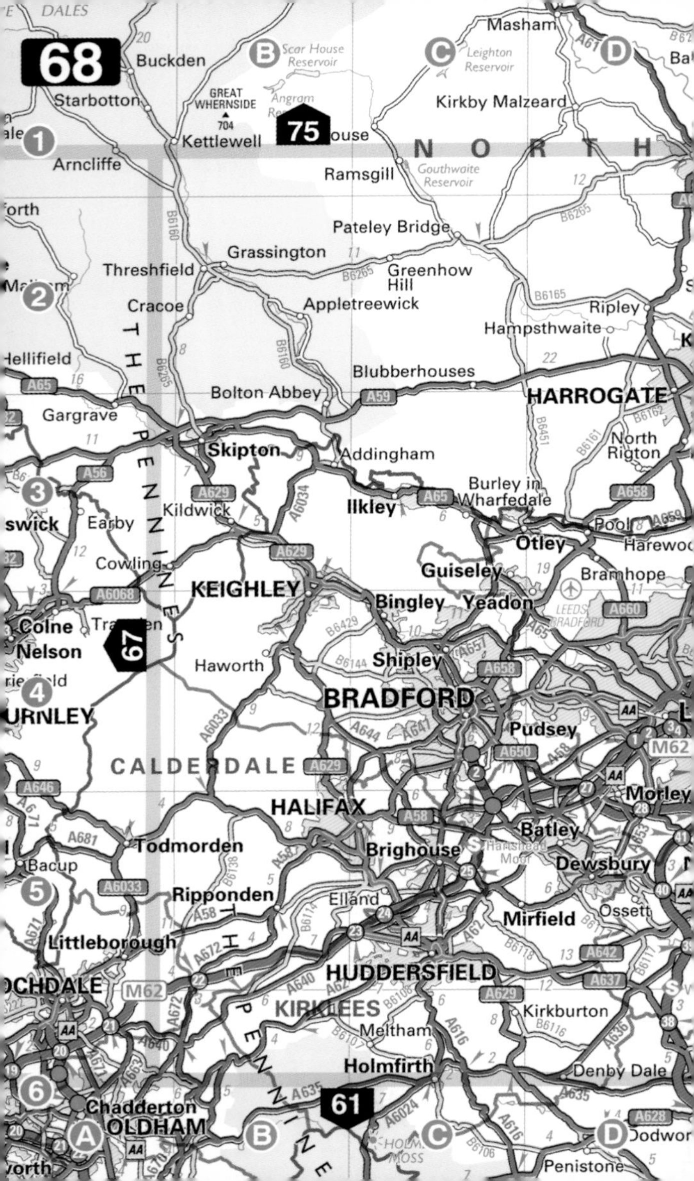
68
75
67
61
Buckden
Starbotton
GREAT WHERNSIDE
Kettlewell
Arncliffe
Scar House Reservoir
Leighton Reservoir
Masham
Kirkby Malzeard
Ramsgill
Gouthwaite Reservoir
NORTH
Pateley Bridge
Grassington
Threshfield
Greenhow Hill
Cracoe
Appletreewick
Ripley
Hampsthwaite
Hellifield
Blubberhouses
Bolton Abbey
HARROGATE
Gargrave
Skipton
Addingham
North Rigton
Burley in Wharfedale
Kildwick
Ilkley
Earby
Otley
Pool
Harewood
Cowling
Guiseley
Bramhope
KEIGHLEY
Bingley
Yeadon
Colne
Nelson
Haworth
Shipley
BRADFORD
Pudsey
CALDERDALE
HALIFAX
Morley
Batley
Todmorden
Brighouse
Hartshead Moor
Dewsbury
Bacup
Ripponden
Elland
Mirfield
Ossett
Littleborough
HUDDERSFIELD
KIRKLEES
Kirkburton
Meltham
Holmfirth
Denby Dale
Chadderton
OLDHAM
Penistone
THE PENNINES
M62
A65
A59
A629
A56
A6068
A658
A660
A650
A58
A646
A6033
A642
A637
A628
A635

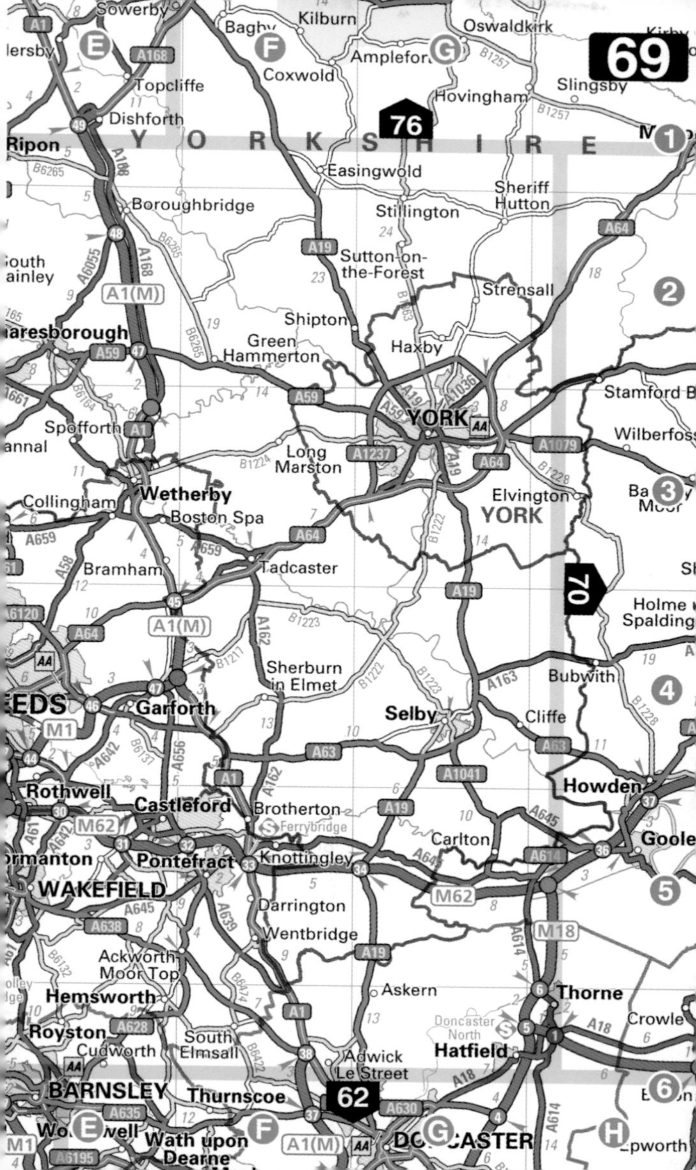

Sowerby
Kilburn
Oswaldkirk
Bagby
Coxwold
Ampleforth
Topcliffe
Dishforth
Hovingham
Slingsby
76
YORKSHIRE
Ripon
Easingwold
Sheriff Hutton
Stillington
Boroughbridge
Sutton-on-the-Forest
Strensall
Shipton
Haxby
Green Hammerton
Stamford Bridge
YORK
Wilberfoss
Long Marston
Elvington
Spofforth
Wetherby
Collingham
Boston Spa
Tadcaster
Bramham
70
Holme upon Spalding Moor
Sherburn in Elmet
Bubwith
Garforth
Selby
Cliffe
Howden
Rothwell
Castleford
Brotherton
Ferrybridge
Goole
Pontefract
Knottingley
Carlton
WAKEFIELD
Darrington
Wentbridge
Ackworth Moor Top
Askern
Hemsworth
Thorne
Crowle
Royston
Doncaster North
Hatfield
Cudworth
South Elmsall
Adwick Le Street
BARNSLEY
Thurnscoe
62
Wath upon Dearne
Epworth
A1
A168
A1(M)
A59
A64
A19
A1079
A1237
A163
A63
A1041
A162
A656
A642
A645
A614
A638
A639
A628
A635
A630
A18
A6195
A6120
A659
A58
A61
A6055
A1036
M1
M62
M18
B6265
B1257
B1363
B1224
B1228
B1222
B1223
B1217
B6164
B6137
B6132
B6474
B6422

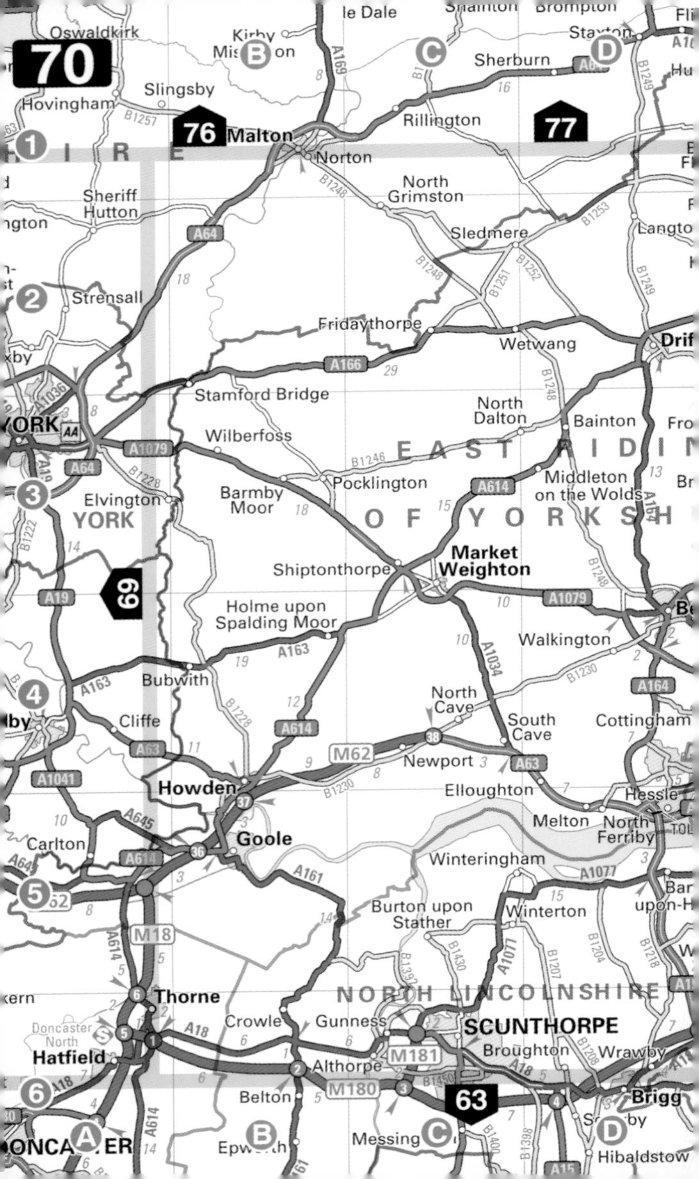
70
Oswaldkirk
Kirby Misperton
Slingsby
Hovingham
76
Malton
Norton
Rillington
Sherburn
Staxton
77
North Grimston
Sheriff Hutton
Sledmere
Strensall
Fridaythorpe
Wetwang
Stamford Bridge
YORK
North Dalton
Bainton
Wilberfoss
Pocklington
Barmby Moor
Elvington
YORK
EAST RIDING OF YORKSHIRE
Middleton on the Wolds
Shiptonthorpe
Market Weighton
69
Holme upon Spalding Moor
Walkington
Bubwith
North Cave
South Cave
Cliffe
Cottingham
Newport
Howden
Elloughton
Hessle
Goole
Carlton
Melton
North Ferriby
Winteringham
Burton upon Stather
Winterton
Thorne
NORTH LINCOLNSHIRE
Crowle
Gunness
SCUNTHORPE
Doncaster North
Hatfield
Broughton
Wrawby
Althorpe
Belton
63
Brigg
Messingham
Epworth
Hibaldstow
DONCASTER
M62
M18
M181
M180
A64
A166
A1079
A614
A163
A1034
A63
A19
A1041
A645
A161
A18
A1077
A15

Filey
Reighton
Bempton
Flamborough Head
Flamborough
Carnaby
Bridlington
Burton Agnes
Barmston
Skipsea
Beeford
Atwick
Hornsea
Goxhill
Leven
Aldbrough
Sproatley
Hedon
KINGSTON UPON HULL
Withernsea
New Holland
Goxhill
Patrington
Easington
River Humber
Immingham Dock
Ulceby
Immingham
Keelby
GRIMSBY
Spurn Head
Cleethorpes
Barnetby le Wold
Laceby
Humberston
Holton le Clay
Swallow
Caistor
HUMBERSIDE
Rotterdam (Europoort)
Zeebrugge
A165
A614
A1035
A1174
A1033
A160
A180
A18
A46
A1173
A1084
B1229
B1255
B1249
B1242
B1244
B1243
B1238
B1240
B1239
B1362
B1445
B1210
B1211
64

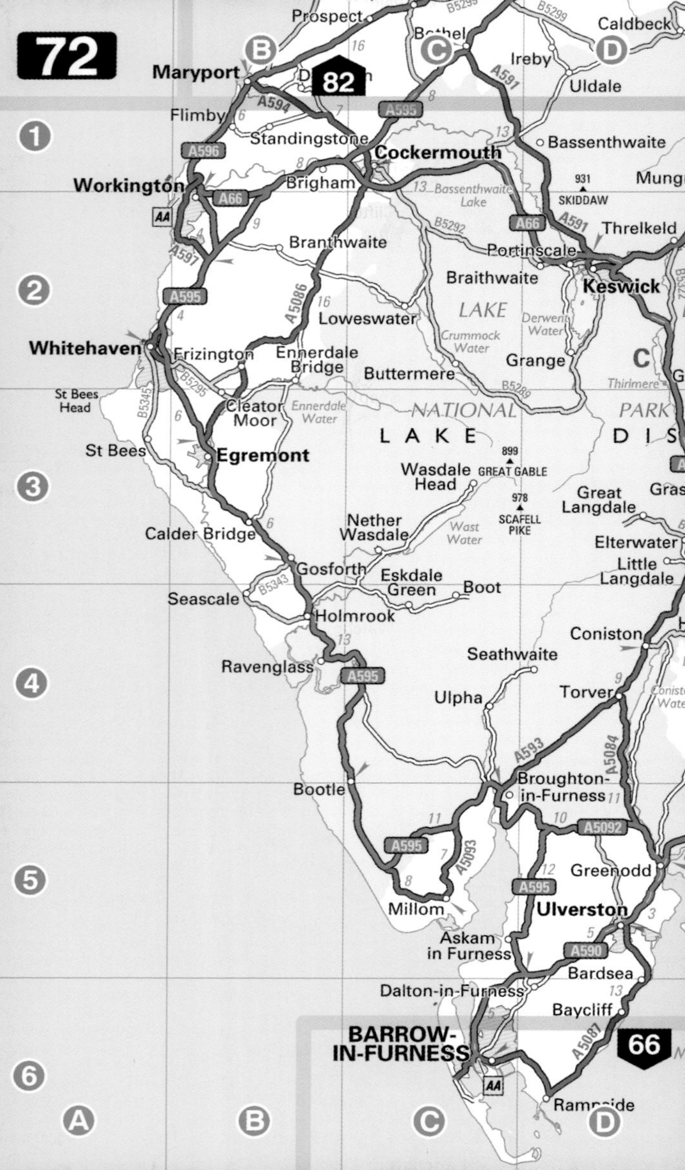

Prospect
Bothel
Caldbeck
Maryport
82
Ireby
Uldale
Flimby
Standingstone
Cockermouth
Bassenthwaite
Workington
Brigham
Bassenthwaite Lake
931
SKIDDAW
Mungr
Threlkeld
Branthwaite
Portinscale
Braithwaite
Keswick
Loweswater
LAKE
Derwent Water
Crummock Water
Whitehaven
Frizington
Ennerdale Bridge
Grange
Buttermere
Thirlmere
St Bees Head
Cleator Moor
Ennerdale Water
NATIONAL
PARK
St Bees
Egremont
LAKE
DIS
899
GREAT GABLE
Wasdale Head
978
SCAFELL PIKE
Great Langdale
Calder Bridge
Nether Wasdale
Wast Water
Elterwater
Gosforth
Eskdale Green
Boot
Little Langdale
Seascale
Holmrook
Coniston
Seathwaite
Ravenglass
Ulpha
Torver
Bootle
Broughton-in-Furness
Greenodd
Millom
Ulverston
Askam in Furness
Bardsea
Dalton-in-Furness
Baycliff
BARROW-IN-FURNESS
66
A594
A595
A591
A596
A66
A597
A5086
B5292
B5289
B5295
B5345
B5343
A593
A5084
A5092
A5093
A590
A5087
B5299
B5322
AA
1
2
3
4
5
6
A
B
C
D

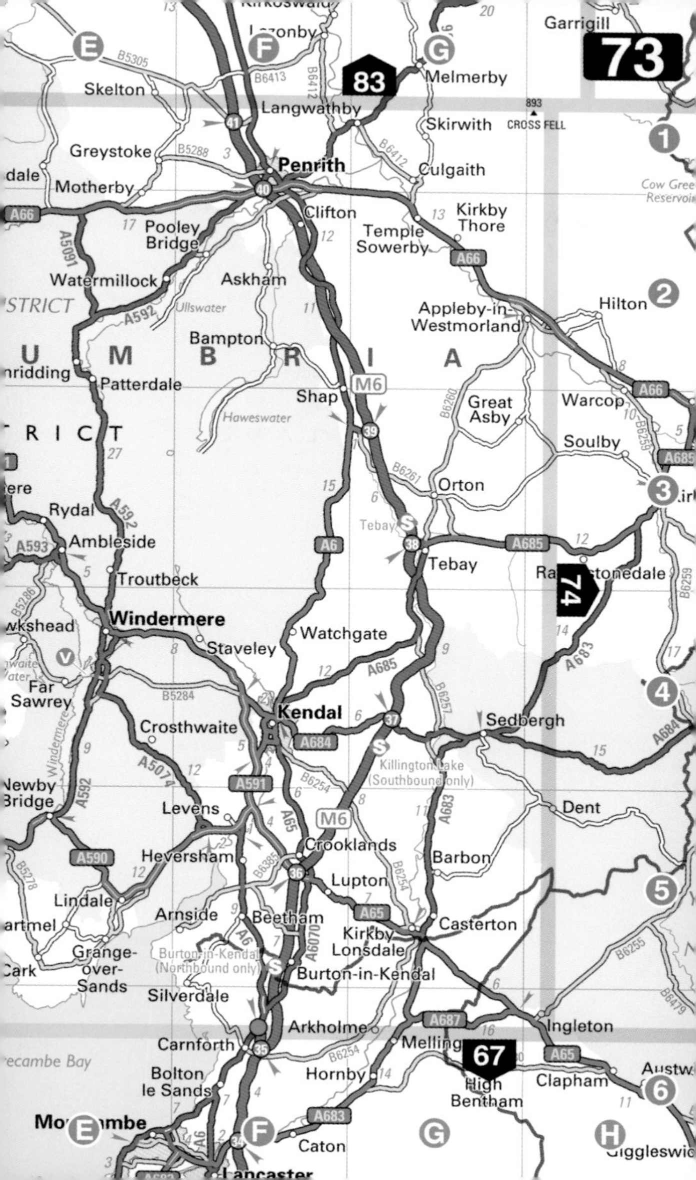

73
83
74
67
Garrigill
Melmerby
Skelton
Langwathby
Skirwith
CROSS FELL
893
Greystoke
Penrith
Culgaith
Motherby
Clifton
Kirkby Thore
Temple Sowerby
Pooley Bridge
Watermillock
Askham
Ullswater
Appleby-in-Westmorland
Hilton
Bampton
Patterdale
Shap
Haweswater
Great Asby
Warcop
Soulby
Orton
Rydal
Ambleside
Tebay
Troutbeck
Windermere
Staveley
Watchgate
Far Sawrey
Kendal
Crosthwaite
Sedbergh
Killington Lake (Southbound only)
Levens
Dent
Newby Bridge
Heversham
Crooklands
Barbon
Lupton
Lindale
Arnside
Beetham
Casterton
Kirkby Lonsdale
Grange-over-Sands
Burton-in-Kendal (Northbound only)
Burton-in-Kendal
Silverdale
Arkholme
Ingleton
Carnforth
Melling
Bolton le Sands
Hornby
High Bentham
Clapham
Caton
Cow Green Reservoir
M6
A66
A6
A685
A684
A683
A591
A592
A593
A590
A65
A687
A6070
A5074
A5091
B5305
B6413
B6412
B5288
B6260
B6261
B6259
B6257
B6254
B6255
B6479
B6385
B5284
B5286
B5278

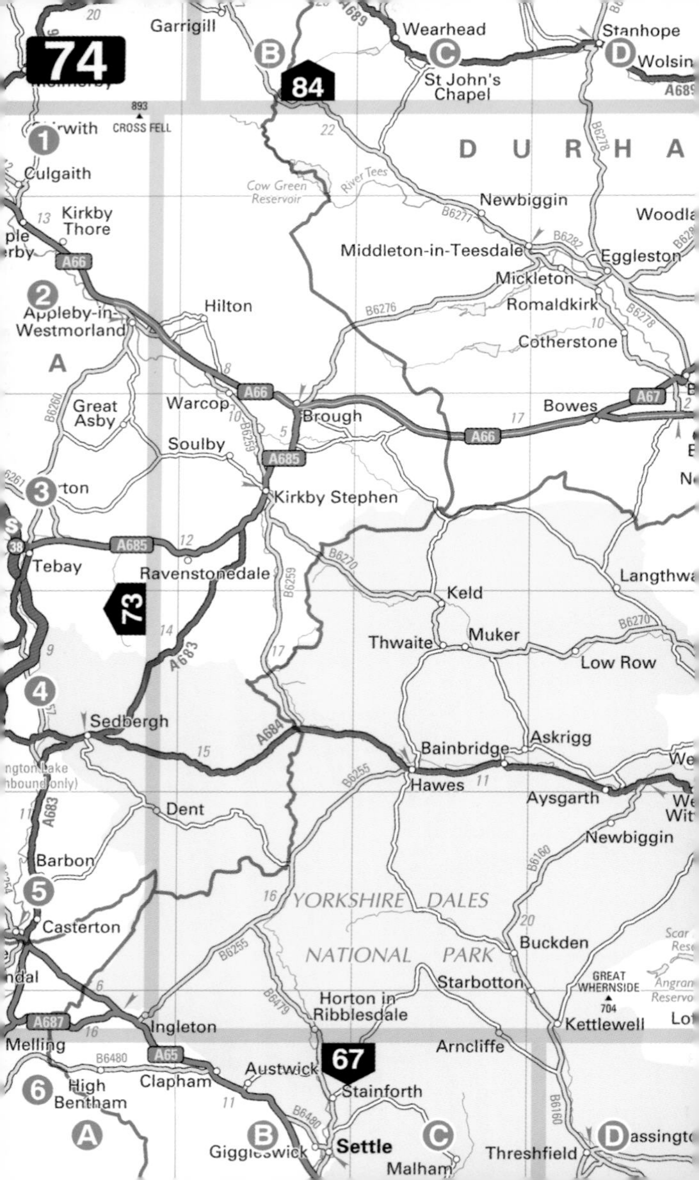

74
84
73
67
Garrigill
Wearhead
Stanhope
St John's Chapel
CROSS FELL
893
Culgaith
Kirkby Thore
DURHAM
Cow Green Reservoir
River Tees
Newbiggin
Middleton-in-Teesdale
Eggleston
Mickleton
Romaldkirk
Cotherstone
Hilton
Appleby-in-Westmorland
Great Asby
Warcop
Brough
Bowes
Soulby
Kirkby Stephen
Tebay
Ravenstonedale
Langthwaite
Keld
Thwaite
Muker
Low Row
Sedbergh
Askrigg
Bainbridge
Hawes
Aysgarth
Dent
Newbiggin
Barbon
YORKSHIRE DALES
NATIONAL PARK
Casterton
Buckden
Starbotton
GREAT WHERNSIDE
704
Horton in Ribblesdale
Kettlewell
Ingleton
Melling
Arncliffe
Austwick
High Bentham
Clapham
Stainforth
Giggleswick
Settle
Malham
Threshfield

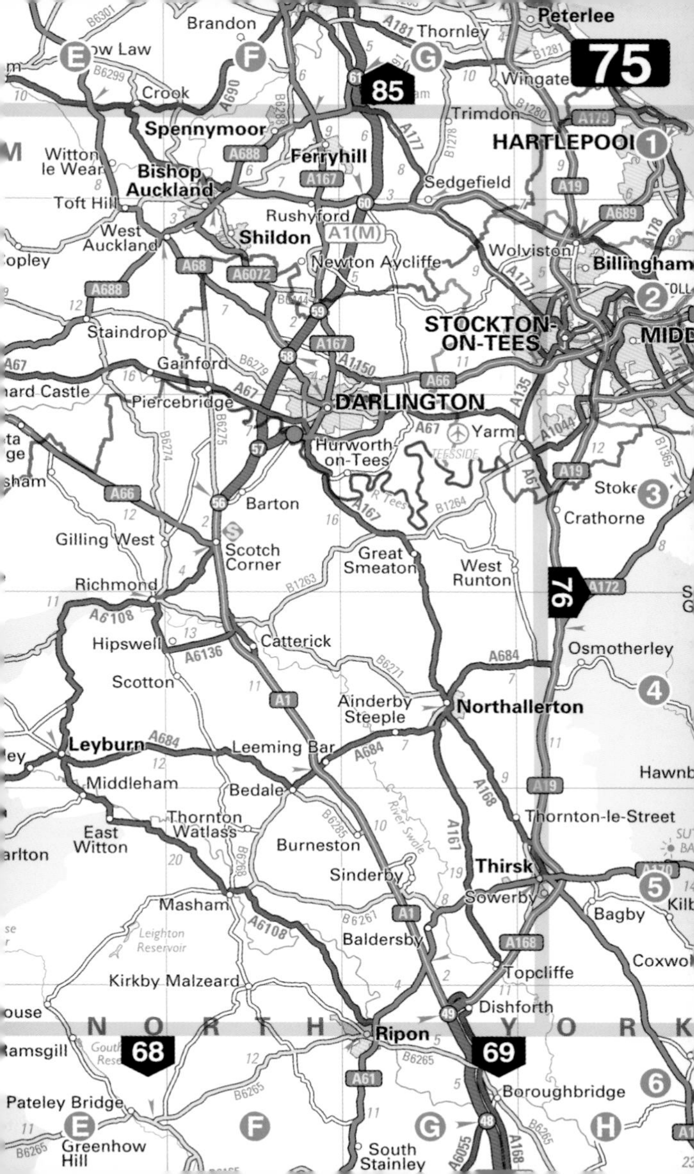

Peterlee
Brandon
Thornley
75
Wingate
Crook
85
Trimdon
Spennymoor
HARTLEPOOL
Witton le Wear
Bishop Auckland
Ferryhill
Sedgefield
Toft Hill
Rushyford
West Auckland
Shildon
Wolviston
Billingham
Newton Aycliffe
Staindrop
STOCKTON-ON-TEES
Gainford
Piercebridge
DARLINGTON
Yarm
Hurworth-on-Tees
Teesside
R Tees
Barton
Crathorne
Scotch Corner
Gilling West
Great Smeaton
West Runton
Richmond
76
Hipswell
Catterick
Osmotherley
Scotton
Ainderby Steeple
Northallerton
Leyburn
Leeming Bar
Middleham
Bedale
Thornton-le-Street
Thornton Watlass
East Witton
Burneston
Sinderby
River Swale
Thirsk
Masham
Sowerby
Bagby
Leighton Reservoir
Baldersby
Topcliffe
Kirkby Malzeard
Dishforth
NORTH YORK
Ripon
Ramsgill
68
69
Pateley Bridge
Boroughbridge
Greenhow Hill
South Stainley

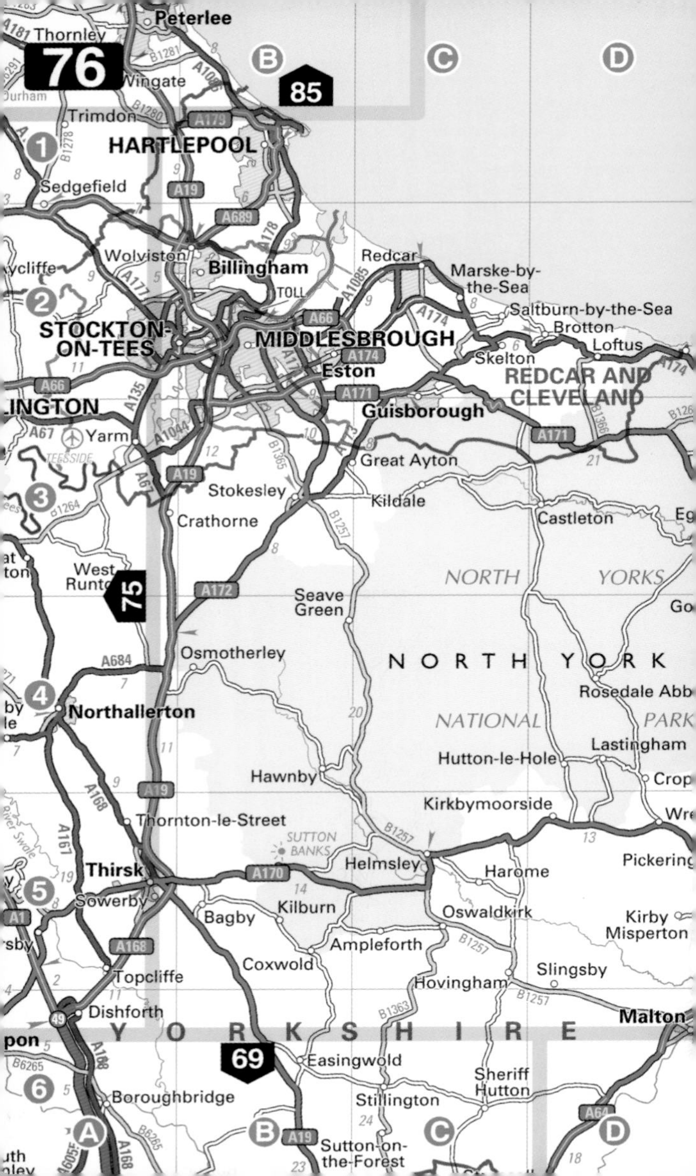

76
85
75
69
Peterlee
Thornley
Wingate
Trimdon
HARTLEPOOL
Sedgefield
Wolviston
Billingham
Redcar
Marske-by-the-Sea
Saltburn-by-the-Sea
Brotton
Loftus
Skelton
REDCAR AND CLEVELAND
STOCKTON-ON-TEES
MIDDLESBROUGH
Eston
Guisborough
Yarm
TEESSIDE
Great Ayton
Stokesley
Kildale
Castleton
Crathorne
West Runton
NORTH YORKS
Seave Green
Osmotherley
NORTH YORK
Rosedale Abb
Northallerton
NATIONAL PARK
Lastingham
Hutton-le-Hole
Hawnby
Kirkbymoorside
Thornton-le-Street
SUTTON BANKS
Helmsley
Harome
Pickering
Thirsk
Sowerby
Kilburn
Bagby
Oswaldkirk
Kirby Misperton
Ampleforth
Coxwold
Slingsby
Topcliffe
Hovingham
Dishforth
Malton
YORKSHIRE
Easingwold
Sheriff Hutton
Boroughbridge
Stillington
Sutton-on-the-Forest
TOLL

E
F
G
1
2
3
4
5
6
H
thes
inderwell
Runswick
Lythe
Sandsend
Whitby
Ruswarp
B1447
Sleights
B1416
Grosmont
Robin Hood's Bay
tton
idge
A171
Ravenscar
and
A169
O O R S
20
Cloughton
A165
Hackness
Scalby
Lockton
Scarborough
n
East Ayton
AA
A165
B1261
A170
17
Seamer
Cayton
Thornton le Dale
Shainton
Brompton
Flixton
Filey
Staxton
A1039
A169
B1258
Sherburn
A64
B1249
Hunmanby
16
Reighton
Rillington
11
B1229
Bempton
A165
orton
Burton Fleming
70
71
B1255
Flambo
North Grimston
B1248
Rudston
B1253
Carnaby
Bridlington
Sledmere
Langtoft
B1248
B1252
A614
Kilham
Burton

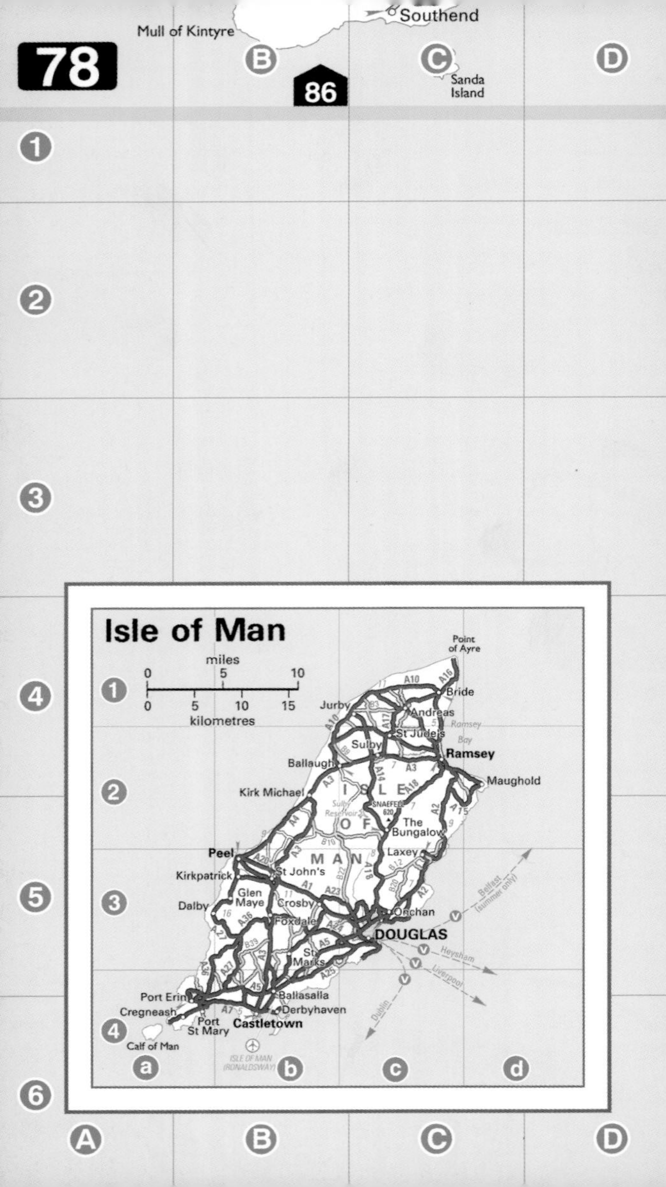

Southend
Mull of Kintyre
Sanda Island
86
Isle of Man
miles
kilometres
Point of Ayre
Bride
Jurby
Andreas
St Judes
Ramsey
Ramsey Bay
Sulby
Ballaugh
Maughold
Kirk Michael
ISLE OF MAN
Snaefell 620
Sulby Reservoir
The Bungalow
Laxey
Peel
St John's
Kirkpatrick
Glen Maye
Crosby
Dalby
Foxdale
Onchan
DOUGLAS
St Marks
Belfast (summer only)
Heysham
Liverpool
Dublin
Port Erin
Ballasalla
Derbyhaven
Cregneash
Port St Mary
Castletown
Calf of Man
Isle of Man (Ronaldsway)

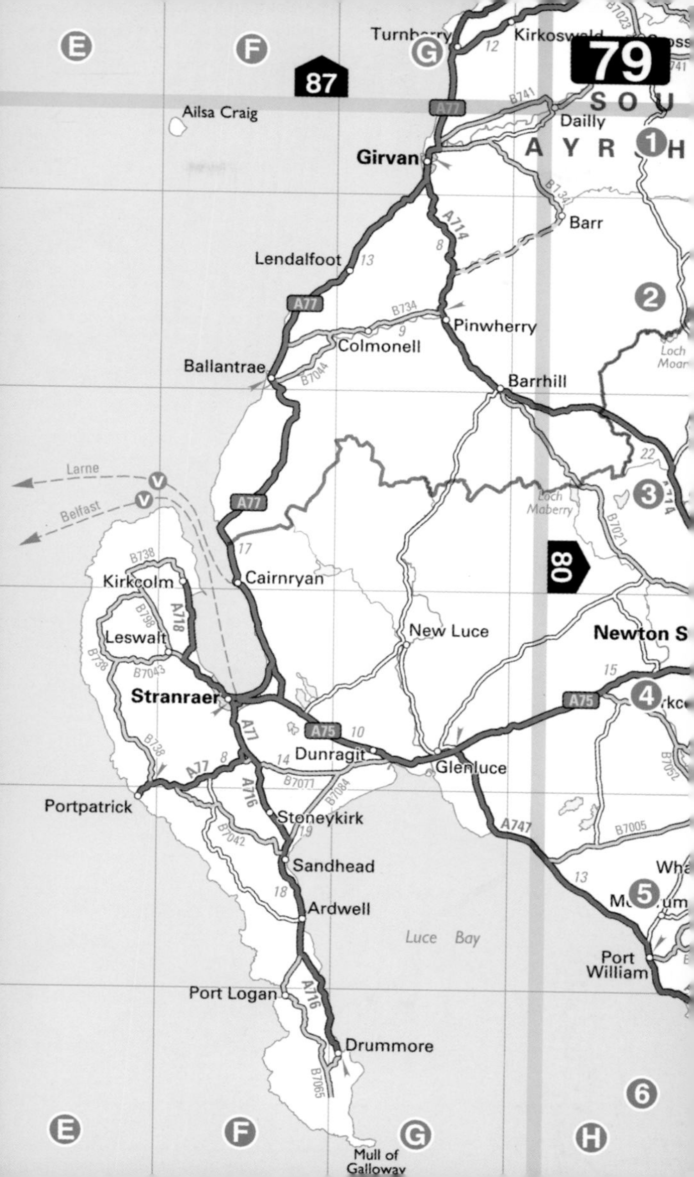

79
87
80
E
F
G
H
Turnberry
Kirkoswald
Girvan
Dailly
Ailsa Craig
Barr
Lendalfoot
Pinwherry
Colmonell
Ballantrae
Barrhill
Loch Moan
Loch Maberry
Larne
Belfast
Kirkcolm
Cairnryan
Leswalt
New Luce
Newton S
Stranraer
Dunragit
Glenluce
Portpatrick
Stoneykirk
Sandhead
Ardwell
Luce Bay
Port William
Port Logan
Drummore
Mull of Galloway
A77
A714
A75
A716
A718
A747
B734
B7044
B738
B798
B7043
B7077
B7084
B7042
B7065
B7021
B7005
B741

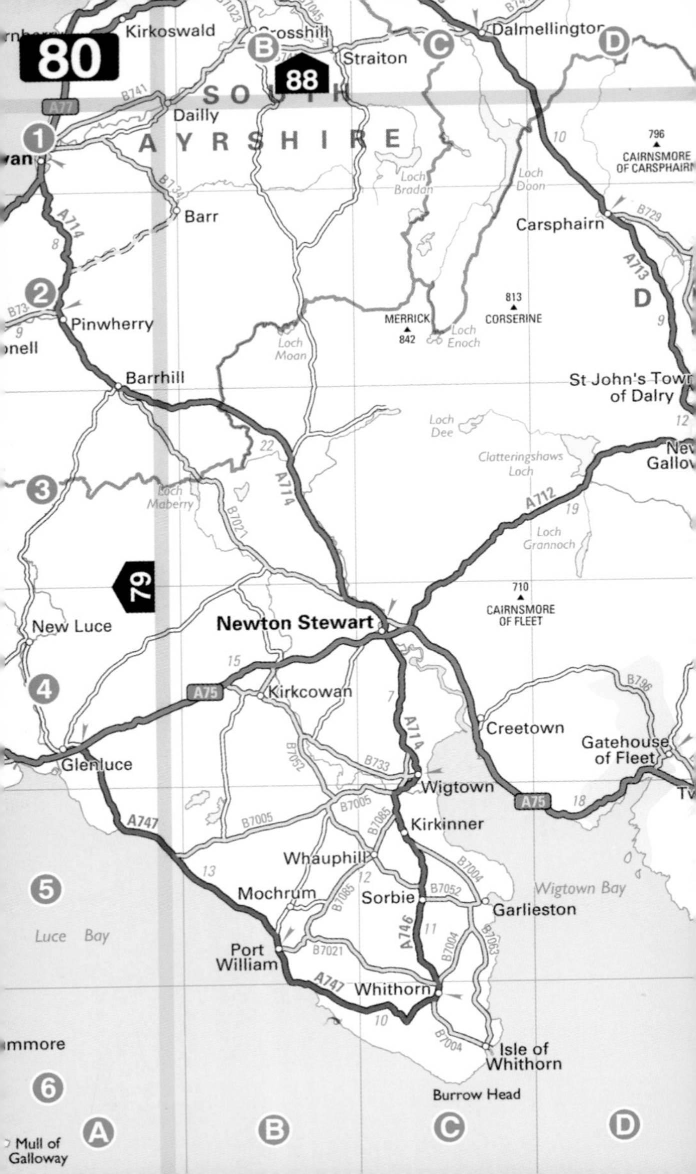

80
88
79
Kirkoswald
Crosshill
Straiton
Dalmellington
Dailly
SOUTH AYRSHIRE
Barr
Pinwherry
Barrhill
Carsphairn
796
CAIRNSMORE OF CARSPHAIRN
Loch Bradan
Loch Doon
813
CORSERINE
MERRICK
842
Loch Enoch
Loch Moan
St John's Town of Dalry
Loch Dee
Clatteringshaws Loch
Loch Maberry
Loch Grannoch
710
CAIRNSMORE OF FLEET
New Luce
Newton Stewart
Kirkcowan
Creetown
Gatehouse of Fleet
Glenluce
Wigtown
Kirkinner
Whauphill
Mochrum
Sorbie
Garlieston
Wigtown Bay
Luce Bay
Port William
Whithorn
Isle of Whithorn
Burrow Head
Mull of Galloway
A77
A714
A713
A712
A75
A747
A746
B741
B734
B729
B7021
B7052
B733
B7005
B7085
B7004
B7063
B796
A
B
C
D
1
2
3
4
5
6

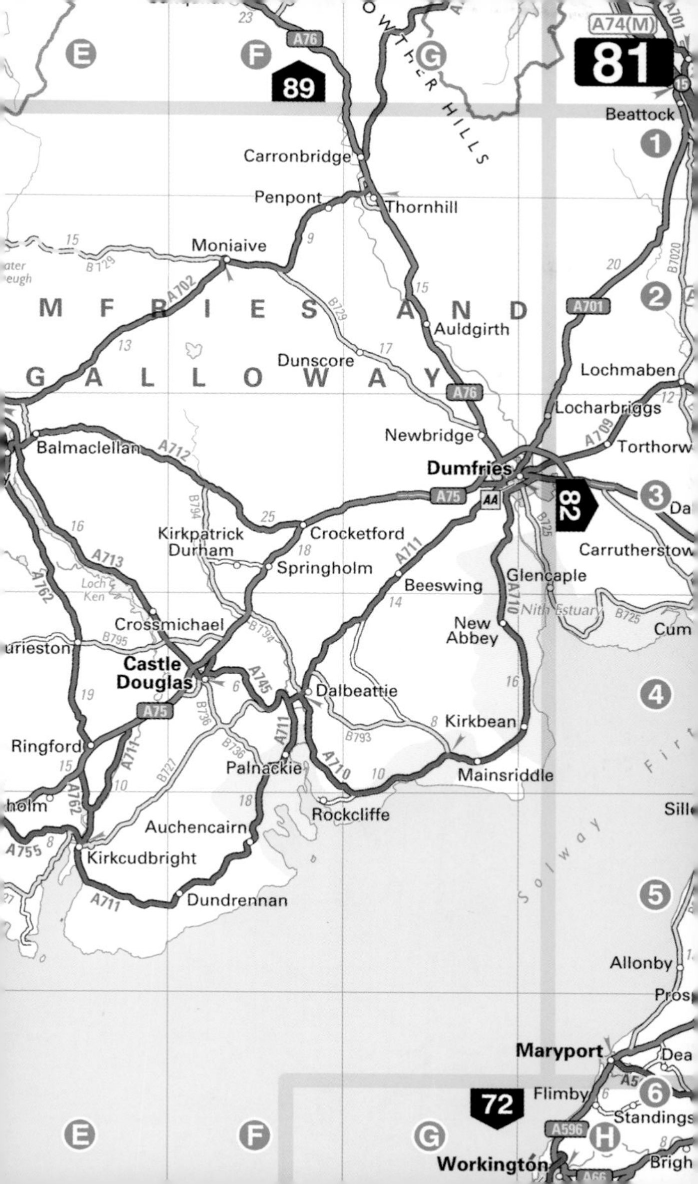

81
89
82
72
DUMFRIES AND GALLOWAY
Beattock
Carronbridge
Penpont
Thornhill
Moniaive
Auldgirth
Dunscore
Lochmaben
Locharbriggs
Newbridge
Torthorw
Dumfries
Balmaclellan
Kirkpatrick Durham
Crocketford
Springholm
Carrutherstow
Glencaple
Beeswing
Crossmichael
New Abbey
Castle Douglas
Dalbeattie
Kirkbean
Ringford
Palnackie
Mainsriddle
Rockcliffe
Auchencairn
Kirkcudbright
Dundrennan
Allonby
Maryport
Flimby
Standings
Workington
Nith Estuary
Solway Firth
Loch Ken

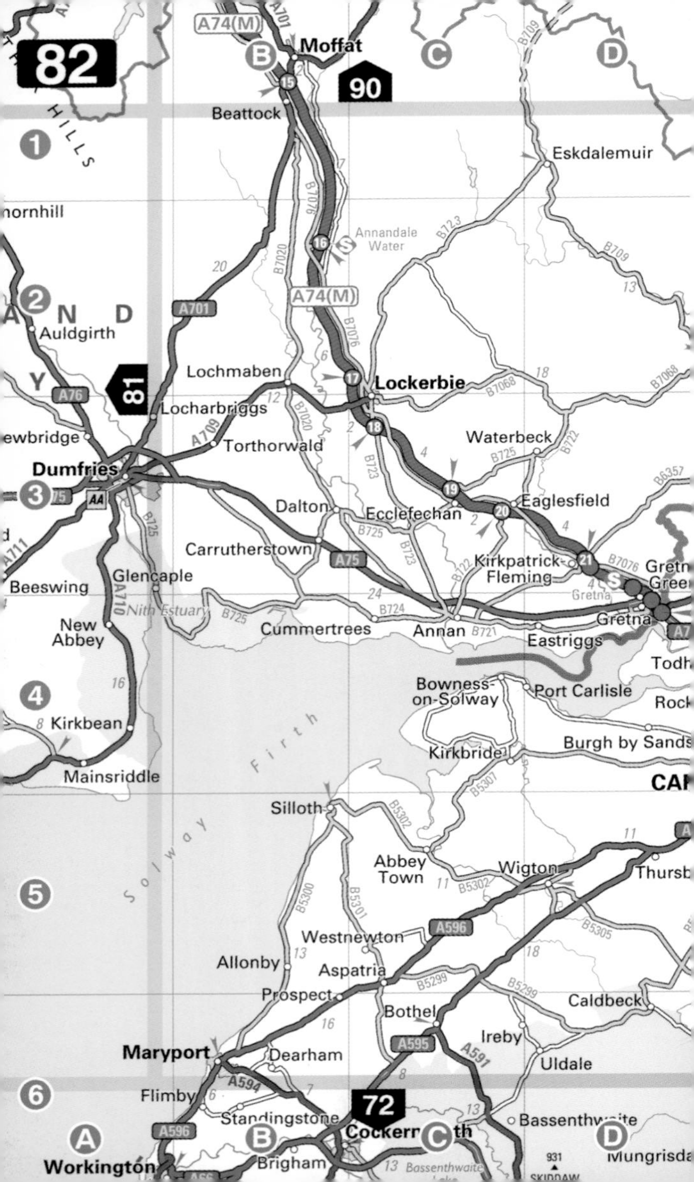
82
90
81
72
Moffat
Beattock
Eskdalemuir
Annandale Water
Auldgirth
Lochmaben
Lockerbie
Locharbriggs
Torthorwald
Dumfries
Waterbeck
Eaglesfield
Dalton
Ecclefechan
Carrutherstown
Kirkpatrick-Fleming
Glencaple
Beeswing
New Abbey
Nith Estuary
Cummertrees
Annan
Eastriggs
Gretna
Bowness-on-Solway
Port Carlisle
Burgh by Sands
Kirkbean
Mainsriddle
Kirkbride
Solway Firth
Silloth
Abbey Town
Wigton
Westnewton
Allonby
Aspatria
Prospect
Bothel
Caldbeck
Ireby
Uldale
Maryport
Dearham
Flimby
Standingstone
Bassenthwaite
Workington
Brigham
Cockermouth
Bassenthwaite Lake

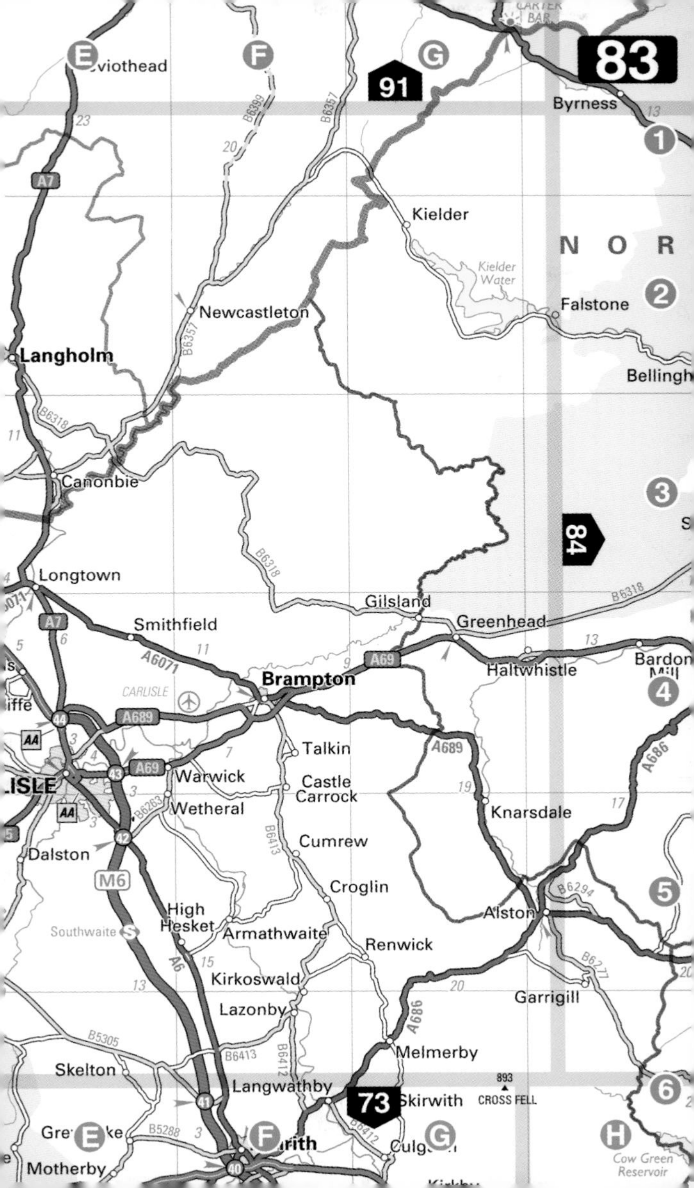
83
91
84
73
CARTER BAR
Byrness
Kielder
Kielder Water
N O R
Falstone
Bellingh
Newcastleton
Langholm
Canonbie
Longtown
Smithfield
Gilsland
Greenhead
Haltwhistle
Bardon Mill
Brampton
CARLISLE
Talkin
Warwick
Castle Carrock
Wetheral
Cumrew
Dalston
Croglin
Knarsdale
Alston
High Hesket
Southwaite
Armathwaite
Renwick
Kirkoswald
Garrigill
Lazonby
Melmerby
Skelton
Langwathby
Skirwith
CROSS FELL
893
Motherby
Cow Green Reservoir
A7
A6071
A69
A689
A686
A6
M6
B6399
B6357
B6318
B6263
B6413
B6412
B5305
B5288
B6294
B6277

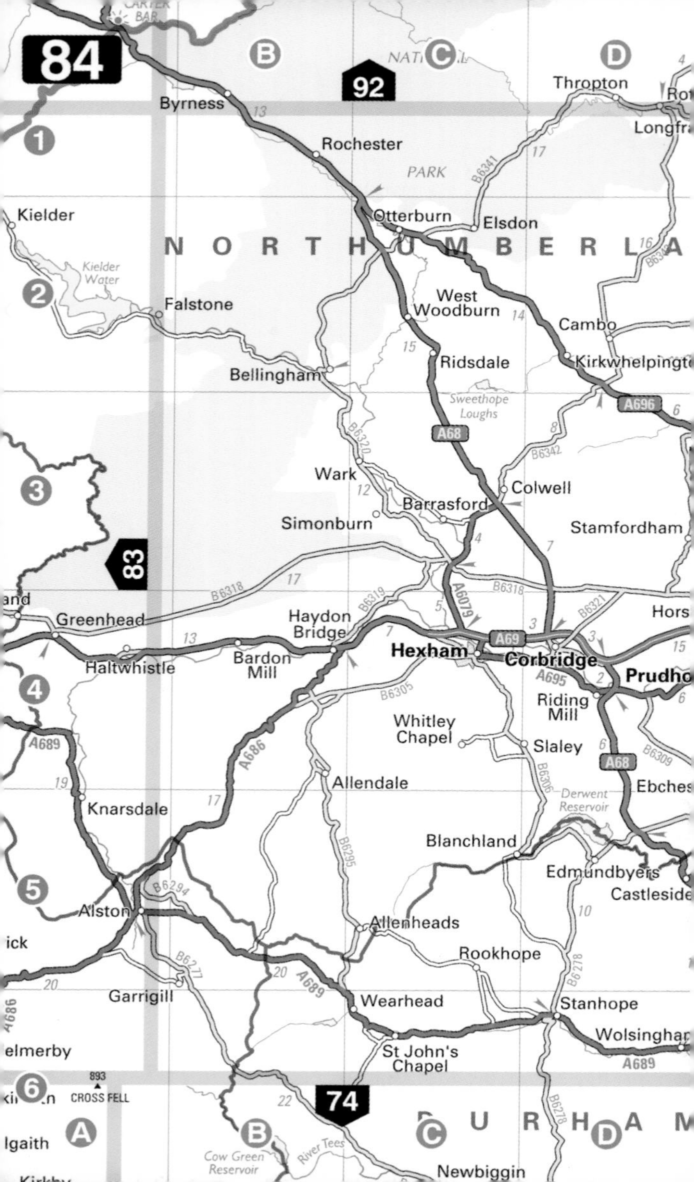

84
92
83
74
B
C
D
1
2
3
4
5
6
A
NORTHUMBERLAND
DURHAM
Byrness
Rochester
PARK
Thropton
Longfra
Kielder
Kielder Water
Otterburn
Elsdon
Falstone
West Woodburn
Cambo
Ridsdale
Kirkwhelpington
Bellingham
Sweethope Loughs
A696
A68
B6320
B6342
B6341
Wark
Colwell
Barrasford
Simonburn
Stamfordham
B6318
B6319
B6321
A6079
Greenhead
Haydon Bridge
Hexham
Corbridge
A69
Haltwhistle
Bardon Mill
A695
Prudho
Riding Mill
B6305
Whitley Chapel
Slaley
A689
A686
Allendale
B6306
B6309
Ebches
Knarsdale
Derwent Reservoir
Blanchland
B6295
Edmundbyers
Castleside
B6294
Alston
Allenheads
Rookhope
B6277
B6278
Garrigill
Wearhead
Stanhope
Wolsinghar
St John's Chapel
893
CROSS FELL
Cow Green Reservoir
River Tees
Newbiggin

93
Newton-on-the-Moor
Warkworth
Amble
Broomhill
Felton
Red Row
Widdrington
Ashington
Newbiggin-by-the-Sea
Morpeth
Blyth
Bedlington
Stannington
Cramlington
Seaton Delaval
Ponteland
Whitley Bay
Darras Hall
Gosforth
North Shields
Tynemouth
Stavanger
Bergen
Haugesund
Kristiansand
Göteborg
Amsterdam
NEWCASTLE UPON TYNE
Jarrow
SOUTH SHIELDS
GATESHEAD
Blaydon
Whickham
Birtley
SUNDERLAND
Burnopfield
WASHINGTON
Stanley
Annfield Plain
Chester-le-Street
Seaham
Consett
Houghton le Spring
Lanchester
Easington
Durham
Peterlee
Brandon
Thornley
Tow Law
Wingate
Crook
Trimdon
Spennymoor
75
76
Bishop Auckland
Sedgefield
Toft Hill

86
95
BEINN AN OIR
Craighouse
Kilberry
Tarbe
Kennacraig
Whitehous
Claonaig
Clachan
Loch Garasdale
Gigha
Ardminish
Tayinloan
KINTYRE
Carradale
Dippen
Glenbarr
Saddell
Bellochantuy
Torbe
Kilkenzie
CAMPBELTOWN
Machrihanish
Campbeltown
Southend
Mull of Kintyre
Sanda Island
rdbeg
A83
B8024
B842
B843
A841

Colintraive
Kames
Portavadie
Bute
Port Bannatyne
Innellan
Inverkip
Rothesay
Ascog
Kilchattan
Sound of Bute
Great Cumbrae Island
Millport
Firth of Clyde
Skelmorlie
Largs
Lochwinnoch
NORTH AYRSHIRE
Fairlie
Kilbirnie
Dalry
West Kilbride
Kilwinning
Ardrossan
Saltcoats
Irvine
Lochranza
North Arran
Corrie
874
GOATFELL
ARRAN
Brodick
Lamlash
Blackwaterfoot
Whiting Bay
Troon
Prestwick
Ayr
Belfast
Alloway
Dunure
Maybole
Kirkoswald
Turnberry
Dailly
Ailsa Craig
Girva
96
88
79
A78
A815
A886
A844
B878
B881
B896
A760
B784
B780
B781
B707
A737
B778
B785
A738
A841
B880
A719
B7024
B7023
A77
B741
A79
B734
E
F
G
H
1
2
3
4
5
6

Dumbarton
Milngavie
Inverkip
Port Glasgow
INVERCLYDE
Kilmacolm
97
Renfrew
CLYDEBANK
Skelmorlie
Bridge of Weir
Johnstone
PAISLEY
GLA
RENFREWSHIRE
Rutherglen
Cambu
Largs
Lochwinnoch
Barrhead
M77
NORTH
Newton Mearns
EAST
RENFREWSHIRE
Fairlie
Kilbirnie
Beith
Lugton
KILB
Eaglesham
AYRSHIRE
Dalry
Dunlop
West Kilbride
Stewarton
Kilwinning
Fenwick
Ardrossan
Stevenston
Kilmaurs
Saltcoats
Irvine
KILMARNOCK
Darvel
Galston
87
Dundonald
Troon
Symington
Belfast
Monkton
Tarbolton
Mauchline
Prestwick
PRESTWICK
Catrine
Ayr
Ochiltree
Auchinleck
Cumnock
Coylton
Alloway
Dunure
EAST
Dalrymple
AYRSHIRE
Patna
Maybole
Kirkmichael
Kirkoswald
Crosshill
Dalmellington
Straiton
SOUTH
Dailly
80
AYRSHIRE
Loch Bradan
Loch Doon
796
CAIRNSMORE OF CARSPHAIRN

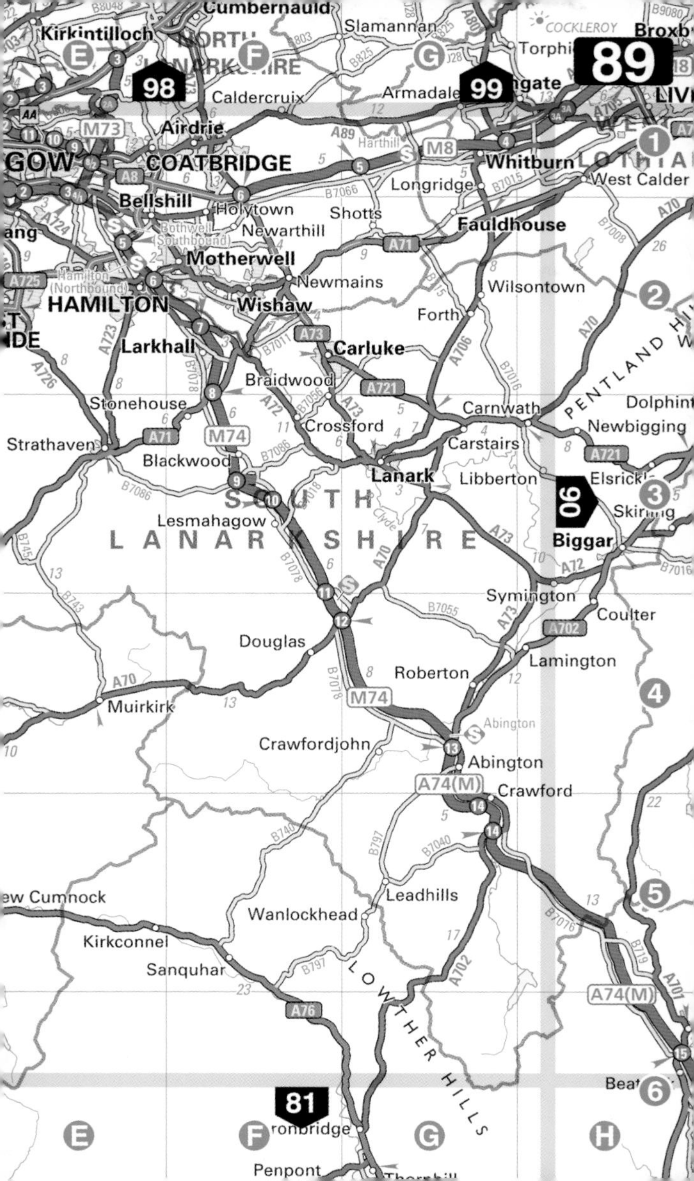
89
98
99
90
81
Cumbernauld
Kirkintilloch
NORTH LANARKSHIRE
Slamannan
Torphichen
COCKLEROY
Broxburn
Caldercruix
Armadale
Bathgate
Airdrie
COATBRIDGE
Harthill
Whitburn
WEST LOTHIAN
West Calder
Longridge
Bellshill
Holytown
Shotts
Bothwell (Southbound)
Newarthill
Fauldhouse
Motherwell
Hamilton (Northbound)
HAMILTON
Newmains
Wilsontown
Wishaw
Forth
Larkhall
Carluke
PENTLAND HILLS
Braidwood
Dolphinton
Stonehouse
Carnwath
Newbigging
Crossford
Carstairs
Strathaven
Blackwood
Lanark
Libberton
Elsrickle
SOUTH LANARKSHIRE
Skirling
Lesmahagow
Biggar
Clyde
Symington
Coulter
Douglas
Lamington
Roberton
Muirkirk
Abington
Crawfordjohn
Crawford
Leadhills
New Cumnock
Wanlockhead
Kirkconnel
Sanquhar
LOWTHER HILLS
Beattock
Thornhill
Penpont
Moniaive
Thornhill
M73
M8
A8
A71
A73
A721
A70
A72
A702
A706
A725
A723
A726
A724
A76
M74
A74(M)
A701
E
F
G
H
1
2
3
4
5
6

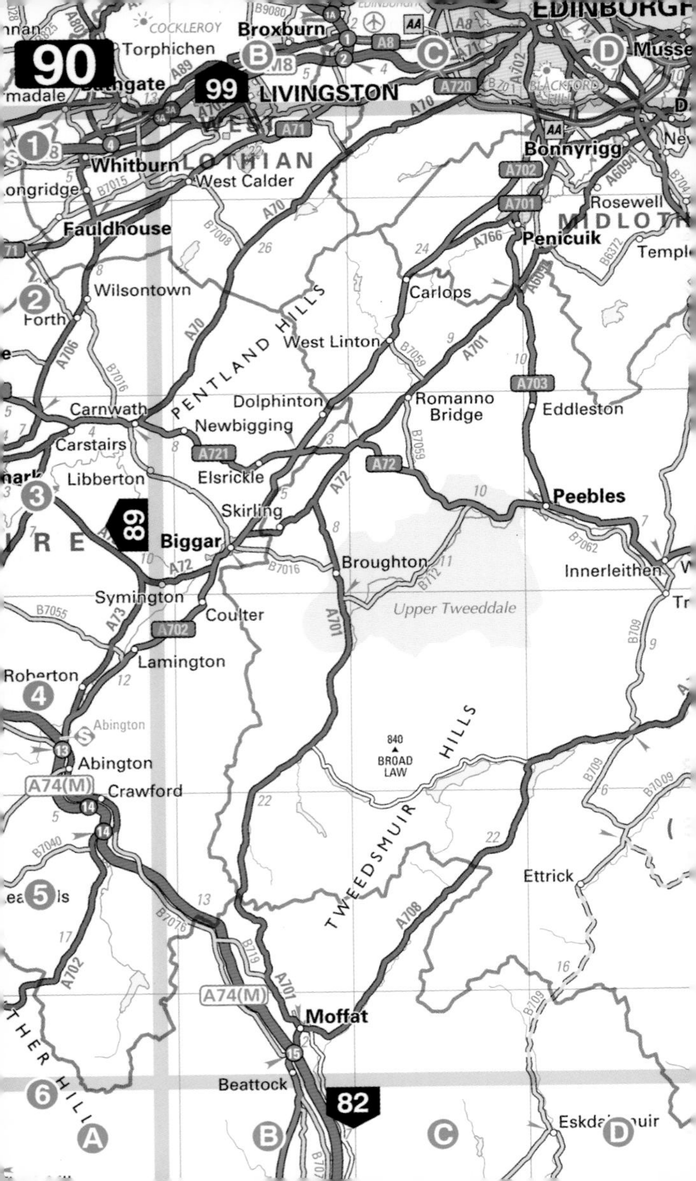

EDINBURGH
90
99
89
82
COCKLEROY
Torphichen
Broxburn
LIVINGSTON
WEST LOTHIAN
Whitburn
West Calder
Fauldhouse
Wilsontown
Forth
Carnwath
Carstairs
Libberton
Biggar
Symington
Coulter
Lamington
Roberton
Abington
Crawford
Moffat
Beattock
PENTLAND HILLS
Carlops
West Linton
Dolphinton
Newbigging
Elsrickle
Skirling
Broughton
Upper Tweeddale
Romanno Bridge
Bonnyrigg
Rosewell
MIDLOTHIAN
Penicuik
Eddleston
Peebles
Innerleithen
840
BROAD LAW
TWEEDSMUIR HILLS
Ettrick
BLACKFORD HILL
A70
A71
A72
A73
A701
A702
A703
A706
A708
A720
A721
A766
A6094
A74(M)
B7008
B7015
B7016
B7040
B7055
B7059
B7062
B7076
B709
B712
B719
M8
A8

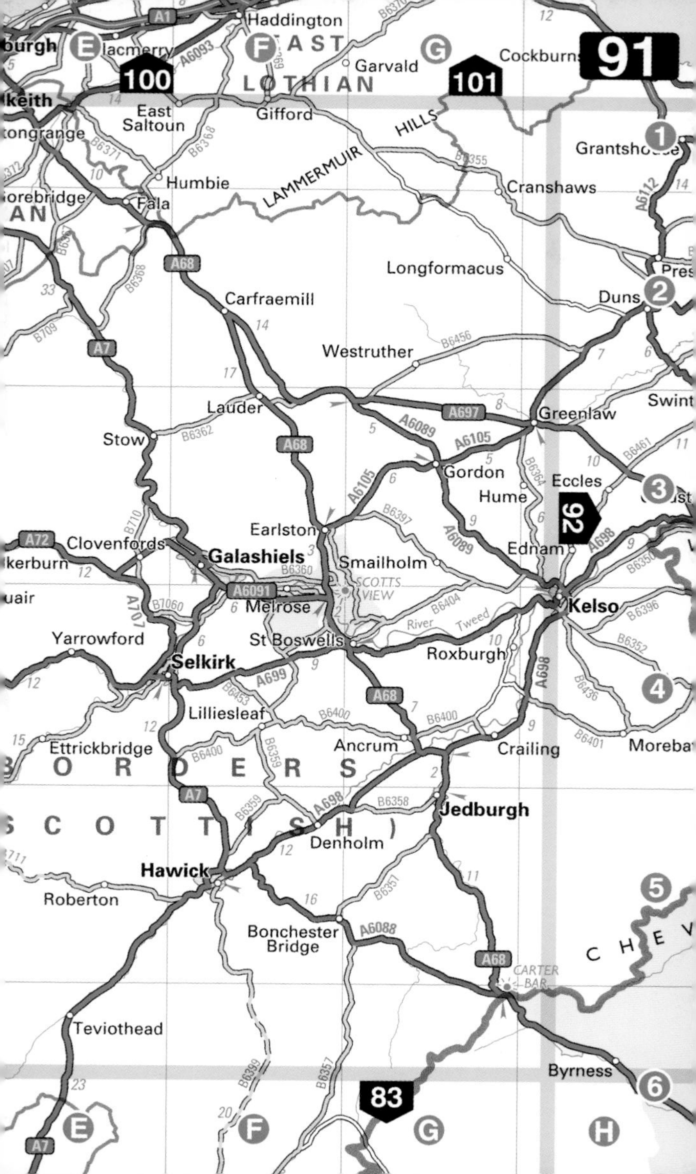

91
100
101
92
83
Haddington
EAST
LOTHIAN
Garvald
Cockburnspath
Gifford
East
Saltoun
Humbie
Fala
LAMMERMUIR
HILLS
Cranshaws
Grantshouse
Longformacus
Duns
Carfraemill
Westruther
Lauder
Stow
Greenlaw
Gordon
Eccles
Hume
Earlston
Clovenfords
Galashiels
Smailholm
Ednam
SCOTTS VIEW
Melrose
Kelso
St Boswells
River Tweed
Yarrowford
Selkirk
Roxburgh
Lilliesleaf
Ettrickbridge
Ancrum
Crailing
BORDERS
SCOTTISH
Jedburgh
Denholm
Hawick
Roberton
Bonchester
Bridge
CARTER BAR
CHEVIOT
Teviothead
Byrness

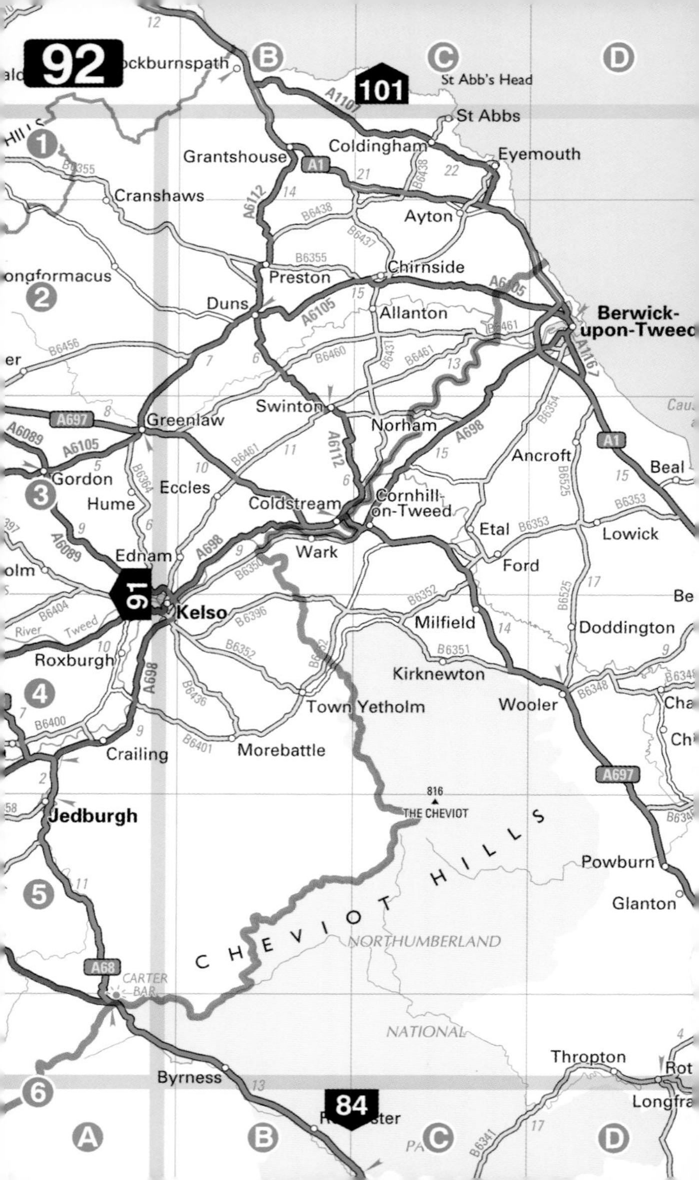
92
ockburnspath
B
C
D
101
St Abb's Head
A1107
St Abbs
Grantshouse
Coldingham
Eyemouth
A1
21
22
B6438
B6355
Cranshaws
A6112
14
B6438
Ayton
B6437
B6355
Chirnside
Preston
ongformacus
Duns
15
A6105
A6105
Allanton
Berwick-
upon-Tweed
B6461
A1167
B6456
B6460
B6437
B6461
13
7
6
Swinton
A697
8
Greenlaw
Norham
B6354
A6089
A6105
A698
B6461
11
A6112
15
A1
Ancroft
Beal
5
Gordon
10
Eccles
B6364
6
Cornhill-
on-Tweed
B6525
15
B6353
Hume
Coldstream
Etal
B6353
Lowick
A6089
9
Ednam
A698
9
Wark
Ford
B6350
17
91
B6352
B6525
Kelso
B6396
B6404
River
Tweed
Milfield
14
Doddington
10
B6352
B6351
9
Roxburgh
A698
Kirknewton
B6348
B6436
Town Yetholm
Wooler
B6400
9
B6401
Crailing
Morebattle
A697
816
THE CHEVIOT
Jedburgh
CHEVIOT HILLS
Powburn
11
Glanton
NORTHUMBERLAND
A68
CARTER
BAR
NATIONAL
Thropton
Byrness
13
84
ster
17
B6341
A
B
C
D

E
F
G
1
2
3
4
5
6
way flooded
high tide
Holy Island
Holy Island
Farne Islands
Bamburgh
Seahouses
Beadnell
Warenford
B1342
B1341
B1340
A1
14
Embleton
B6347
Craster
Eglingham
B1339
B6341
B6346
Longhoughton
Boulmer
Alnwick
B6341
7
8
Alnmouth
A1
A1068
Newton-on-the-Moor
Warkworth
Amble
19
6
Broomhill
B6345
B1330
Felton
B6345
Red Row
Widdrington
A697
85
G
H

102
A
B
C
D
1
2
3
4
5
6
Colonsay
B8087
B8086
Scalasaig
B8085
Oronsay
784
Jur
Sanaigmore
Port Askaig
B8018
B8017
Ballygrant
8
Loch Gorm
A846
A847
Bridgend
3
Port Charlotte
A847
Bowmore
I S L A Y
15
11
B8016
Portnahaven
ISLAY
A846
3
Ardbeg
Port Ellen

95
103
96
86
Scarba, Lunga and Garvallachs
Scarba
Gulf of Corryvreckan
ARGYLL AND BUTE
Loch Avich
Ford
Kilmartin
Crinan
Lochgair
Lochgilphead
Ardrishaig
Tayvallich
Knapdale
Ardlussa
JURA
Sound of Jura
Otter Ferry
Kilfinan
Loch Fyne
Portavadie
Tarbert
Kennacraig
Whitehouse
Skipness
Claonaig
Kilberry
Craighouse
Clachan
Loch Garasdale
Gigha
Ardminish
Tayinloan
KINTYRE
Lochranza
North Arran
Carradale
Dippen
Saddell
ARRAN
A816
A83
A846
A841
B8002
B8025
B841
B8000
B8024
B8001
B842
B880

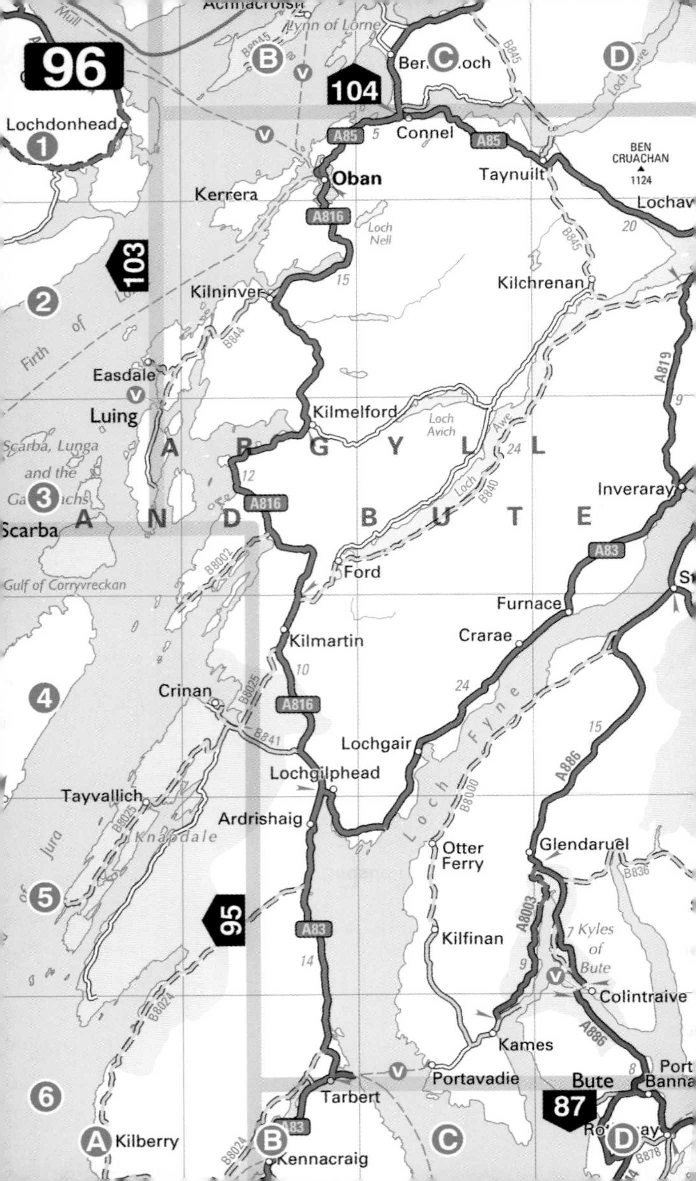

96
104
103
95
87
Oban
Connel
Taynuilt
BEN CRUACHAN
1124
Lochdonhead
Kerrera
Loch Nell
Kilninver
Kilchrenan
Firth of
Easdale
Luing
Scarba, Lunga and the
Kilmelford
Loch Avich
A R G Y L L
A N D B U T E
Inveraray
Scarba
Ford
Gulf of Corryvreckan
Furnace
Kilmartin
Crarae
Crinan
Lochgair
Lochgilphead
Tayvallich
Ardrishaig
Knapdale
Jura
Loch Fyne
Otter Ferry
Glendaruel
Kilfinan
Kyles of Bute
Colintraive
Kames
Portavadie
Bute
Tarbert
Kilberry
Kennacraig
A85
A816
A819
A83
A886
A8003
B845
B844
B840
B8002
B8025
B841
B8000
B836
B8024
B878

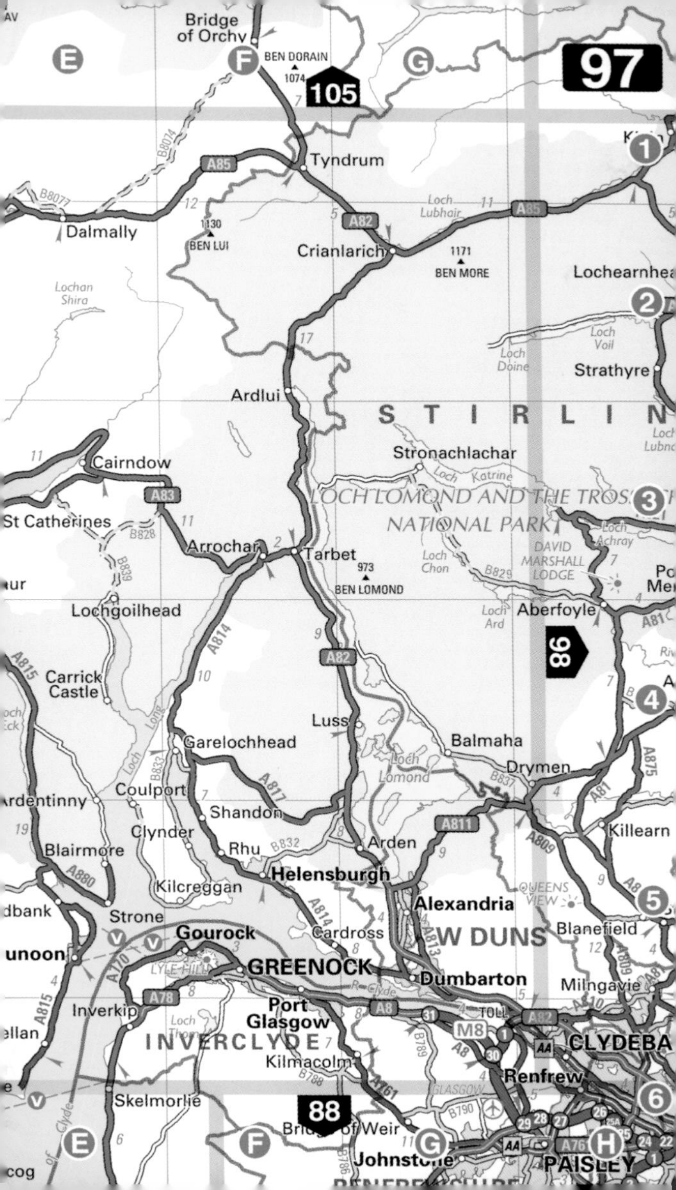
97
105
86
88
Bridge of Orchy
BEN DORAIN 1074
Tyndrum
Dalmally
BEN LUI 1130
Crianlarich
Loch Lubhair
BEN MORE 1171
Lochan Shira
Loch Voil
Loch Doine
Strathyre
Ardlui
STIRLING
Stronachlachar
Loch Katrine
Cairndow
St Catherines
LOCH LOMOND AND THE TROSSACHS NATIONAL PARK
Loch Achray
DAVID MARSHALL LODGE
Arrochar
Tarbet
BEN LOMOND 973
Loch Chon
Lochgoilhead
Aberfoyle
Loch Ard
Carrick Castle
Loch Long
Luss
Garelochhead
Balmaha
Loch Lomond
Drymen
Coulport
Shandon
Killearn
Clynder
Rhu
Arden
Blairmore
Helensburgh
Kilcreggan
QUEENS VIEW
Alexandria
Strone
Gourock
Cardross
Blanefield
LYLE HILL
GREENOCK
Dumbarton
Milngavie
Port Glasgow
Inverkip
INVERCLYDE
CLYDEBANK
Kilmacolm
Renfrew
Skelmorlie
GLASGOW
Bridge of Weir
Johnstone
PAISLEY
A85
A82
A83
A814
A815
A817
A811
A809
A81
A875
A880
A770
A78
A8
M8
A761
A76
B8074
B8077
B828
B839
B829
B837
B833
B832
B789
B788
B790
B786
TOLL
AA

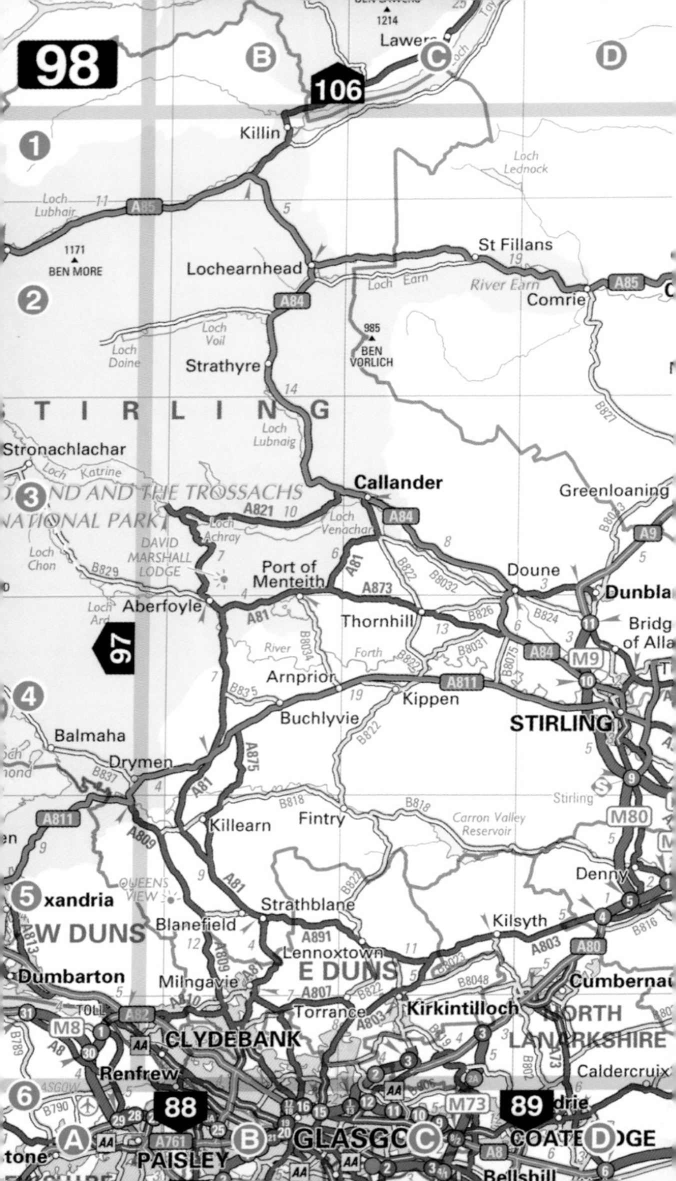
98
106
97
88
89
Killin
Lawers
1214
Loch Lubhair
A85
1171
BEN MORE
Lochearnhead
St Fillans
Loch Earn
River Earn
Comrie
Loch Lednock
A84
Loch Voil
Loch Doine
Strathyre
985
BEN VORLICH
B827
STIRLING
Loch Lubnaig
Stronachlachar
Loch Katrine
Callander
Greenloaning
LOCH LOMOND AND THE TROSSACHS NATIONAL PARK
A821
Loch Achray
Loch Venachar
Loch Chon
DAVID MARSHALL LODGE
B829
Port of Menteith
A81
A873
B822
B8032
Doune
Dunblane
Aberfoyle
Loch Ard
Thornhill
B826
B824
Bridge of Allan
River Forth
B8034
B8031
B8075
M9
Arnprior
A811
Kippen
B835
Buchlyvie
STIRLING
Balmaha
A875
Drymen
B837
B818
Stirling
Killearn
Fintry
Carron Valley Reservoir
M80
A809
Denny
QUEENS VIEW
Alexandria
Strathblane
Blanefield
Kilsyth
A891
A803
A80
WEST DUNS
A813
Lennoxtown
E DUNS
B8023
B8048
Cumbernauld
Dumbarton
Milngavie
A807
Torrance
Kirkintilloch
NORTH LANARKSHIRE
TOLL
A82
M8
CLYDEBANK
B789
A8
Renfrew
B8048
A73
Caldercruix
B790
M73
Airdrie
A761
GLASGOW
COATBRIDGE
PAISLEY
Bellshill
A
B
C
D
1
2
3
4
5
6

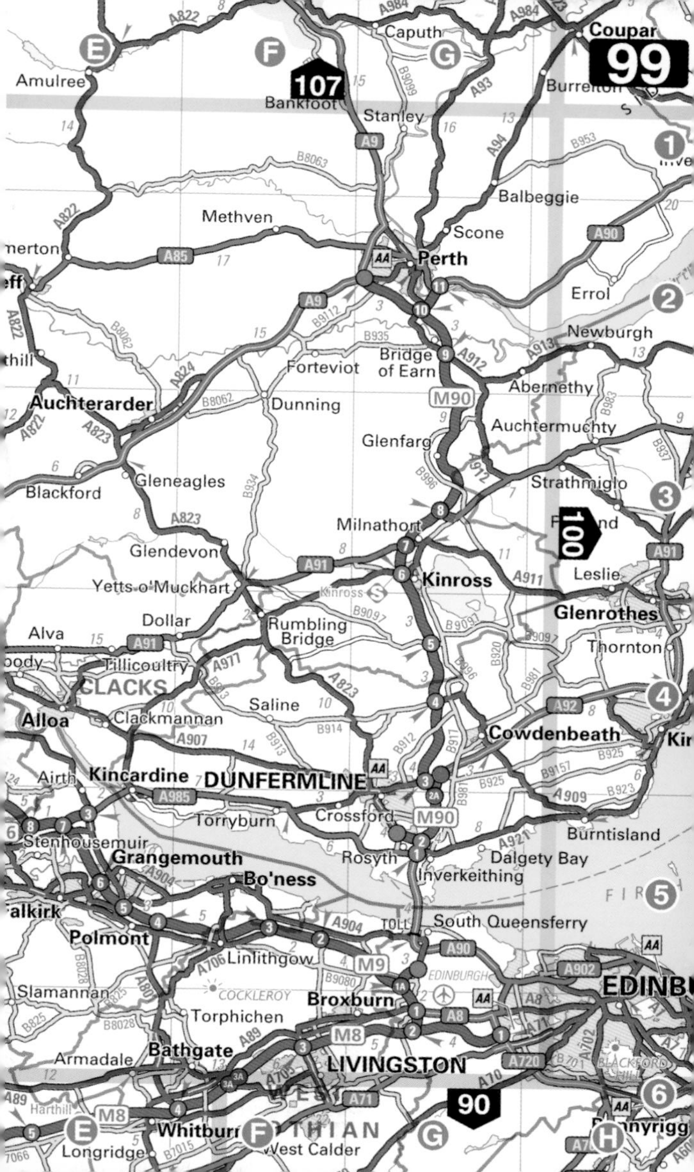

107
99
100
90
Amulree
Caputh
Coupar
Bankfoot
Stanley
Burrelton
Methven
Balbeggie
Scone
Perth
Errol
Newburgh
Forteviot
Bridge of Earn
Abernethy
Auchterarder
Dunning
Auchtermuchty
Glenfarg
Strathmiglo
Gleneagles
Blackford
Milnathort
Glendevon
Kinross
Leslie
Yetts o'Muckhart
Glenrothes
Dollar
Rumbling Bridge
Thornton
Alva
Tillicoultry
CLACKS
Saline
Alloa
Clackmannan
Cowdenbeath
Airth
Kincardine
DUNFERMLINE
Torryburn
Crossford
Burntisland
Stenhousemuir
Grangemouth
Rosyth
Dalgety Bay
Inverkeithing
Bo'ness
Polmont
South Queensferry
Linlithgow
EDINBURGH
Slamannan
COCKLEROY
Broxburn
Torphichen
Bathgate
Armadale
LIVINGSTON
BLACKFORD HILL
Harthill
Whitburn
Longridge
West Calder
A822
A984
A93
A94
A9
B9099
B953
B8063
A90
A85
B9112
B935
A912
A913
A824
B8062
M90
B983
B996
B937
A823
B934
A91
A911
B9097
B920
A977
B981
A92
B914
B913
B912
B917
A907
B925
B9157
A985
B981
A909
B923
A921
A904
A706
M9
B9080
A902
B8028
A801
B8025
A8
A71
A702
A720
B701
M8
A89
A705
A70
A71
B7015
AA
TOLL

Coupar Angus
Newtyle
SIDLAW HILLS
Burrelton
Muirhead
108
DUNDEE
Monifieth
Invergowrie
Balbeggie
Scone
Perth
Tayport
Newport-on-Tay
Wormit
Firth of Tay
Kilmany
Errol
Leuchars
St Andrews Bay
Guardbridge
Newburgh
Dairsie
St Andrews
Abernethy
Cupar
Auchtermuchty
Ceres
Craigrothie
Ladybank
Strathmiglo
FIFE
Largoward
Falkland
99
Upper Largo
Kinross
Leslie
Glenrothes
Leven
Methil
Elie
Thornton
Buckhaven
Cowdenbeath
Kirkcaldy
Zeebrugge
Burntisland
Dalgety Bay
Inverkeithing
FIRTH OF FORTH
Gullane
Aberlady
South Queensferry
Longniddry
EDINBURGH
Prestonpans
Haddington
Musselburgh
Macmerry
EAST LOTHIAN
Dalkeith
East Saltoun
Gifford
90
Newtongrange
Bonnyrigg
Humbie

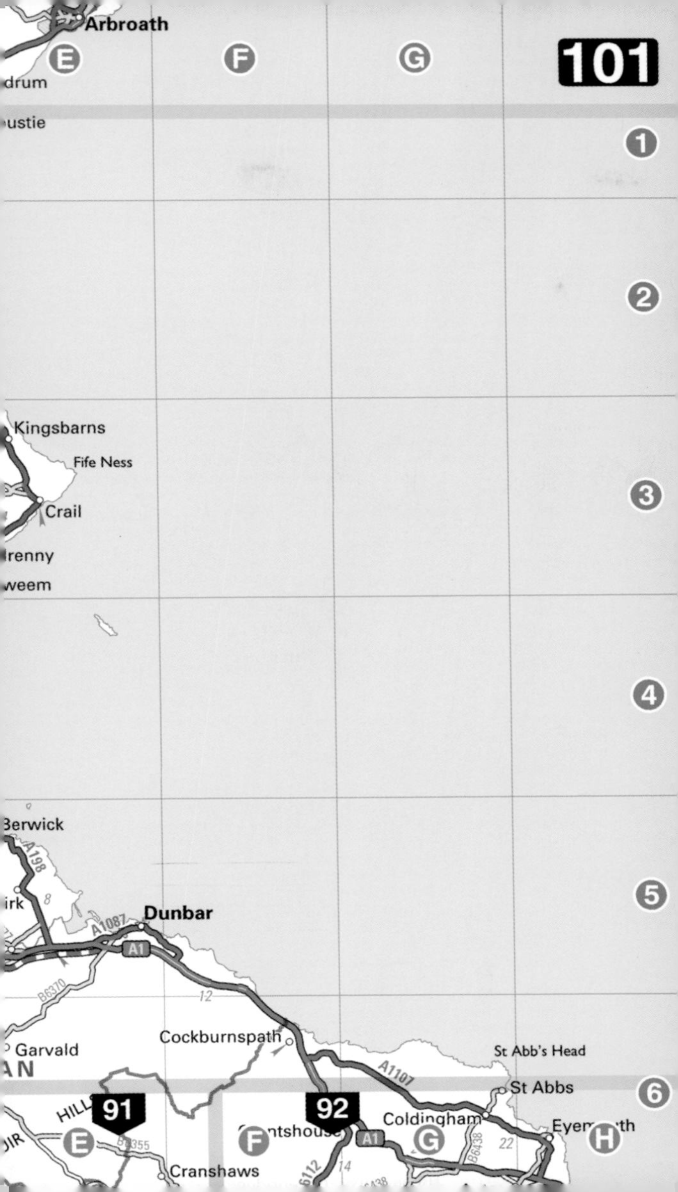
101
E
F
G
H
1
2
3
4
5
6
Arbroath
Kingsbarns
Fife Ness
Crail
Berwick
Dunbar
A198
A1087
A1
B6370
12
8
Cockburnspath
Garvald
St Abb's Head
A1107
St Abbs
Coldingham
B6438
22
14
B6355
Cranshaws
91
92

102
Oban
110
Coll
B8072
B8071
Arinagour
B8070
Calgar
Tiree
Caoles
B8069
TIREE
B8068
Scarinish
B8065
B8066
Hynish
Iona
Fionnphort
94

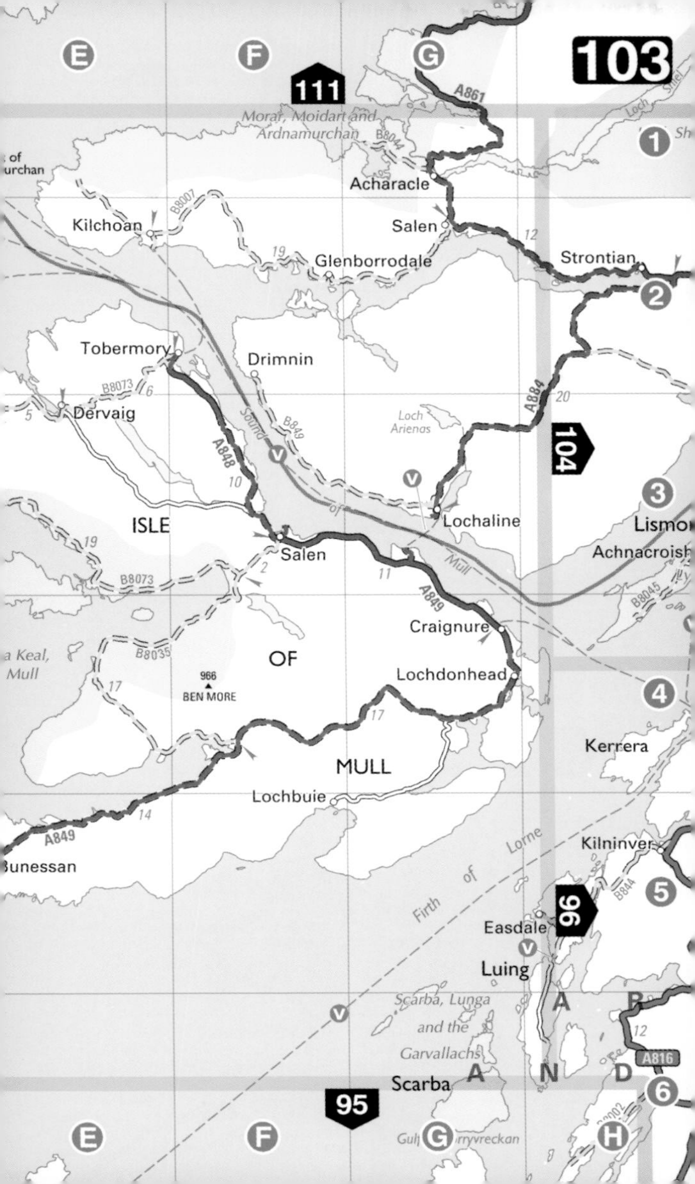
E
F
G
111
A861
Loch Shiel
Morar, Moidart and Ardnamurchan
B8044
1
Acharacle
Kilchoan
B8007
Salen
12
19
Glenborrodale
Strontian
2
Tobermory
Drimnin
B8073
6
5
Dervaig
A884
20
Sound of Mull
B849
Loch Arienas
104
A848
10
3
Lochaline
ISLE
Lismore
Salen
Achnacroish
2
11
19
B8073
A849
B8045
Craignure
a Keal, Mull
B8035
OF
Lochdonhead
966
BEN MORE
17
17
4
Kerrera
MULL
Lochbuie
14
A849
Bunessan
Firth of Lorne
Kilninver
B844
5
96
Easdale
Luing
Scarba, Lunga and the Garvallachs
A
B
12
A816
Scarba
A
N
D
6
95
E
F
G
H
Gulf of Corryvreckan

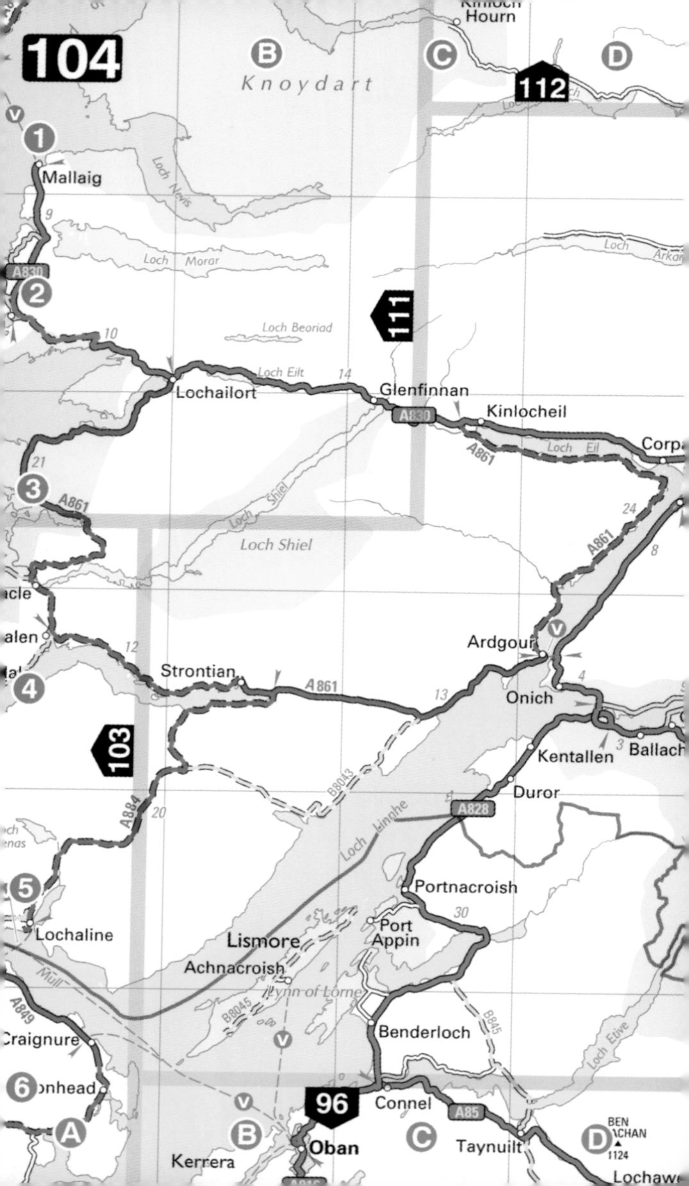
104
Knoydart
Hourn
112
Mallaig
Loch Nevis
Loch Morar
A830
Loch Beoriad
111
Loch Eilt
Lochailort
Glenfinnan
A830
Kinlocheil
Loch Eil
A861
Corpa
Loch Shiel
A861
Loch Shiel
A861
Ardgour
Strontian
A861
Onich
Kentallen
Ballach
Duror
B8043
A828
103
A884
Loch Linnhe
Portnacroish
Port Appin
Lochaline
Lismore
Achnacroish
Lynn of Lorne
Mull
A849
B8045
Benderloch
B845
Loch Etive
Craignure
96
Connel
A85
Oban
Taynuilt
Kerrera
BEN
1124
Lochawe

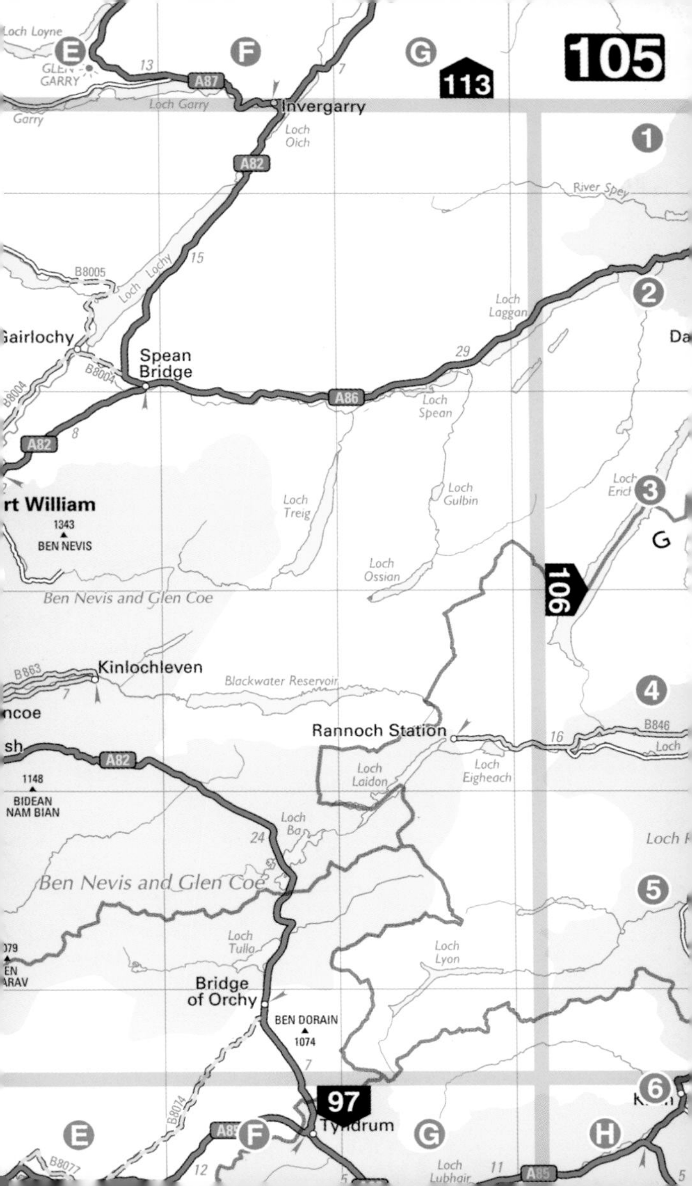

Loch Loyne
E
F
G
113
GLEN GARRY
13
A87
7
Loch Garry
Invergarry
Garry
Loch Oich
1
A82
River Spey
15
Loch Lochy
B8005
Loch
2
Loch Laggan
Gairlochy
Da
Spean Bridge
29
B8004
B8004
A86
Loch Spean
A82
8
Loch Gulbin
Loch Ericht
3
rt William
Loch Treig
G
1343
BEN NEVIS
Loch Ossian
106
Ben Nevis and Glen Coe
Kinlochleven
B863
Blackwater Reservoir
7
4
ncoe
Rannoch Station
B846
16
sh
A82
Loch
Loch Laidon
Loch Eigheach
1148
BIDEAN NAM BIAN
Loch Ba
24
Ben Nevis and Glen Coe
5
Loch Tulla
Loch Lyon
Bridge of Orchy
BEN DORAIN
1074
7
97
6
B8074
Tyndrum
E
F
G
H
B8077
12
Loch Lubhair
11
A85
5

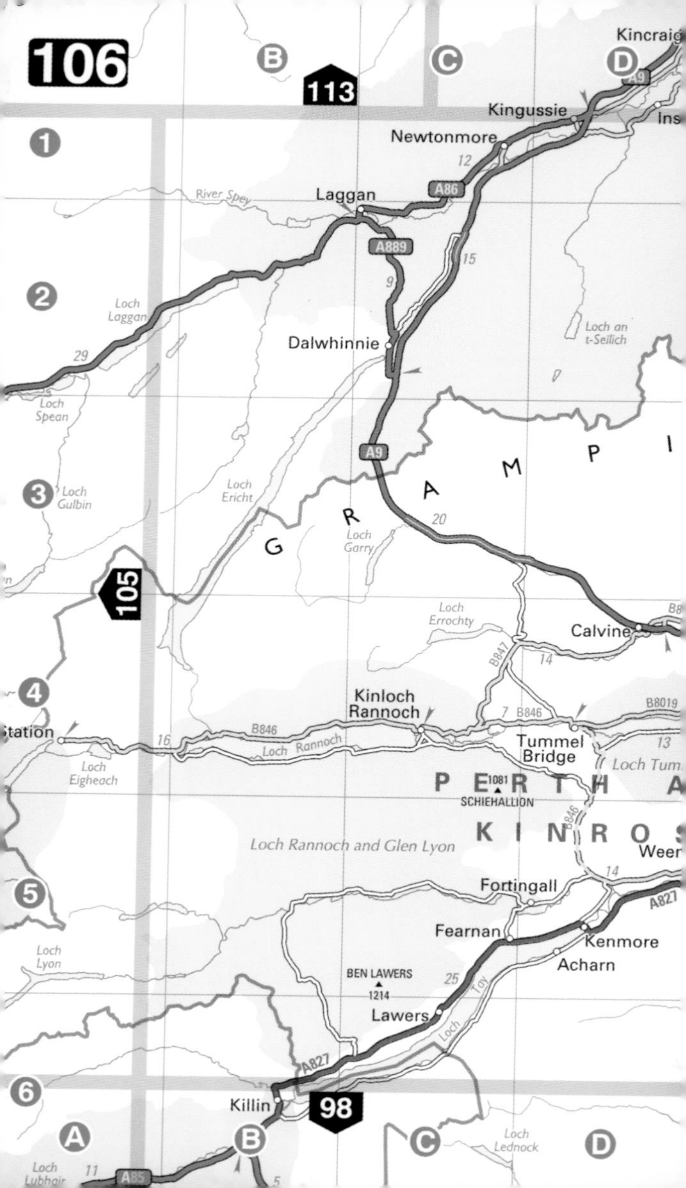
106
113
B
C
D
Kincraig
A9
Kingussie
Newtonmore
1
12
A86
River Spey
Laggan
A889
15
9
2
Loch Laggan
29
Dalwhinnie
Loch an t-Seilich
Loch Spean
A9
G R A M P I
3
Loch Gulbin
Loch Ericht
20
Loch Garry
105
Loch Errochty
Calvine
B847
14
4
Kinloch Rannoch
7
B846
B8019
Station
16
B846
Loch Rannoch
Tummel Bridge
13
Loch Eigheach
Loch Tum
P E R T H A
1081
SCHIEHALLION
B846
K I N R O S
Loch Rannoch and Glen Lyon
Weem
14
5
Fortingall
A827
Fearnan
Kenmore
Loch Lyon
Acharn
BEN LAWERS
1214
25
Tay
Lawers
Loch
A827
6
Killin
98
A
B
C
D
Loch Lednock
Loch Lubhair
11
A85
5

107
114
108
99
CAIRNGORMS NATIONAL PARK
CAIRNGORM MOUNTAINS
CAIRN GORM
BRAERIACH
BEN MACDHUI
CAIRN TOUL
Corgarff
Crathie
Braemar
LOCHNAGAR
Loch Muick
GLAS MAOL
Spittal of Glenshee
Blair Atholl
Killiecrankie
QUEENS VIEW
Pitlochry
Kirkmichael
Ballintuim
Ballinluig
R Tay
Aberfeldy
Dowally
Bridge of Cally
Alyth
River Tay
Blairgowrie
Dunkeld
Caputh
Coupar Angus
Amulree
Burrelton
Bankfoot
Stanley
Balbeggie
SIDLAW
A93
A924
A827
A826
A822
A923
A984
A94
A9
B951
B950
B947
B954
B898
B867
B9099
B8063
B953
B976
B970

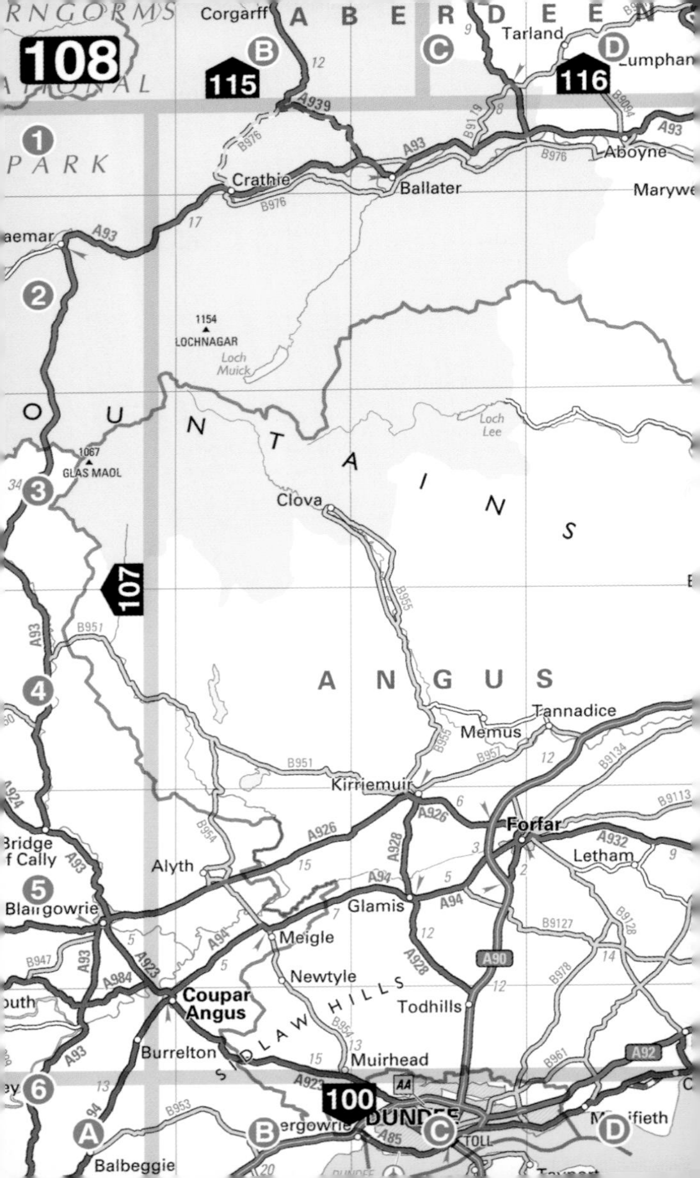
RNGORMS
NATIONAL
PARK
Corgarff
A B E R D E E N
Tarland
Lumphan
115
116
A939
B976
A93
B9094
Aboyne
Crathie
Ballater
Marywe
B976
aemar
1154
LOCHNAGAR
Loch Muick
M O U N T A I N S
Loch Lee
1067
GLAS MAOL
Clova
107
B955
B951
A N G U S
Tannadice
Memus
B957
B9134
Kirriemuir
B9113
A926
Forfar
A932
Letham
A928
B954
Bridge of Cally
Alyth
A94
Blairgowrie
Glamis
B9127
B9128
Meigle
A90
B947
A984
A923
B978
Newtyle
Coupar Angus
Todhills
SIDLAW HILLS
Burrelton
Muirhead
B961
A92
100
DUNDEE
B953
ergowrie
A85
Monifieth
TOLL
Balbeggie

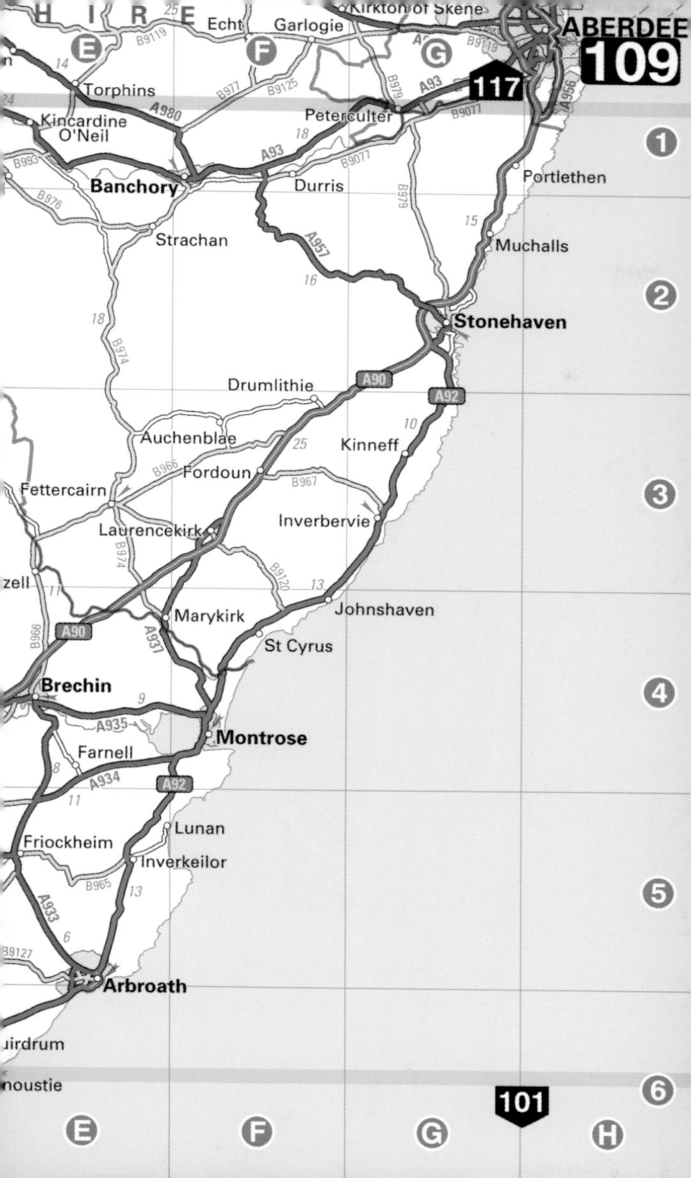

Kirkton of Skene
Echt
Garlogie
ABERDEE
109
117
101
Torphins
Kincardine O'Neil
Banchory
Peterculter
Durris
Portlethen
Strachan
Muchalls
Stonehaven
Drumlithie
Auchenblae
Kinneff
Fordoun
Fettercairn
Laurencekirk
Inverbervie
Johnshaven
Marykirk
St Cyrus
Brechin
Montrose
Farnell
Lunan
Friockheim
Inverkeilor
Arbroath
A90
A92
A93
A980
A957
A937
A935
A934
A933
A956
B9119
B977
B9125
B979
B9077
B993
B976
B974
B966
B967
B9120
B965
B9127
E
F
G
H
1
2
3
4
5
6

118
102
Harlosh
ISLE OF SKYE
A863
B885
Bracadale
A87
B883
Sconser
Drynoch
B8009
Carbost
A863
965
CUILLIN HILLS
The Cuillin Hills
927
BLAVEN
1009
B8083
Elgol
Soay
Tarska
Canna
Sound of Canna
Rùm
Point
The Small Isles
Sound of Rum
Eigg
Sound of Eigg
Muck
Oban

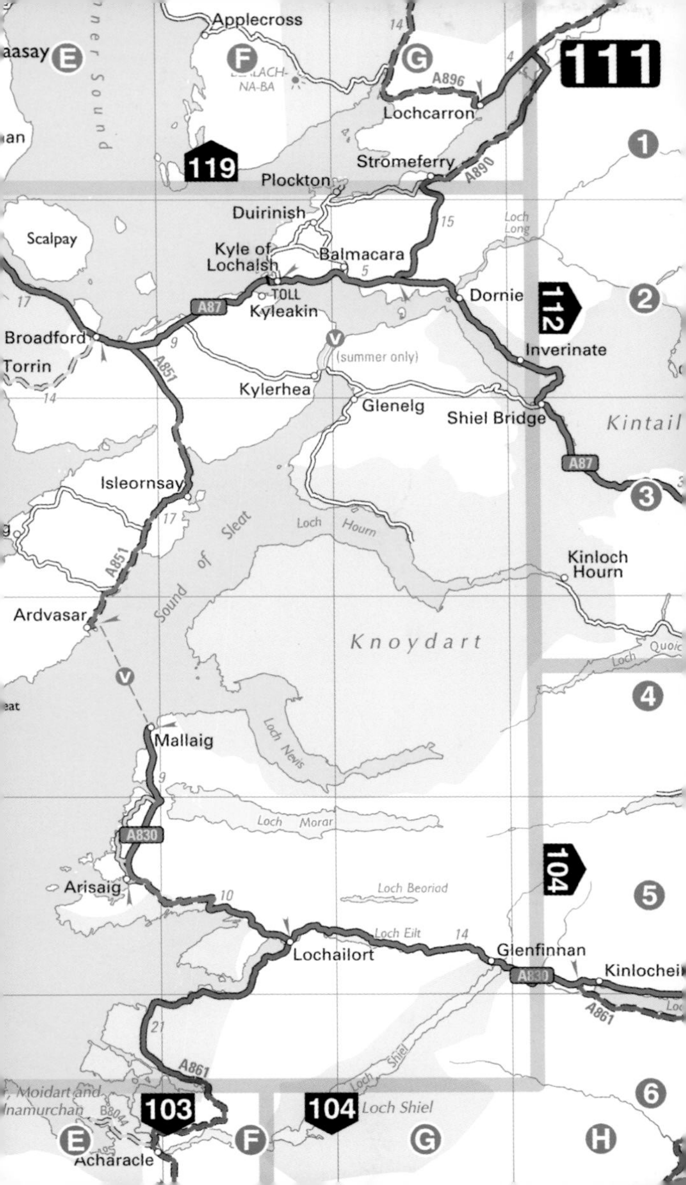

Applecross
Raasay
Inner Sound
BEALACH-NA-BA
Lochcarron
A896
111
119
Plockton
Stromeferry
A890
Duirinish
Scalpay
Kyle of Lochalsh
Balmacara
Loch Long
TOLL
Kyleakin
A87
Dornie
112
Broadford
Torrin
A851
(summer only)
Inverinate
Kylerhea
Glenelg
Shiel Bridge
Kintail
A87
Isleornsay
Sound of Sleat
Loch Hourn
Kinloch Hourn
A851
Ardvasar
Knoydart
Loch Quoich
Mallaig
Loch Nevis
Loch Morar
A830
104
Arisaig
Loch Beoriad
Loch Eilt
Lochailort
Glenfinnan
A830
Kinlocheil
A861
A861
Loch Shiel
Moidart and Ardnamurchan
B8044
103
104
Loch Shiel
Acharacle

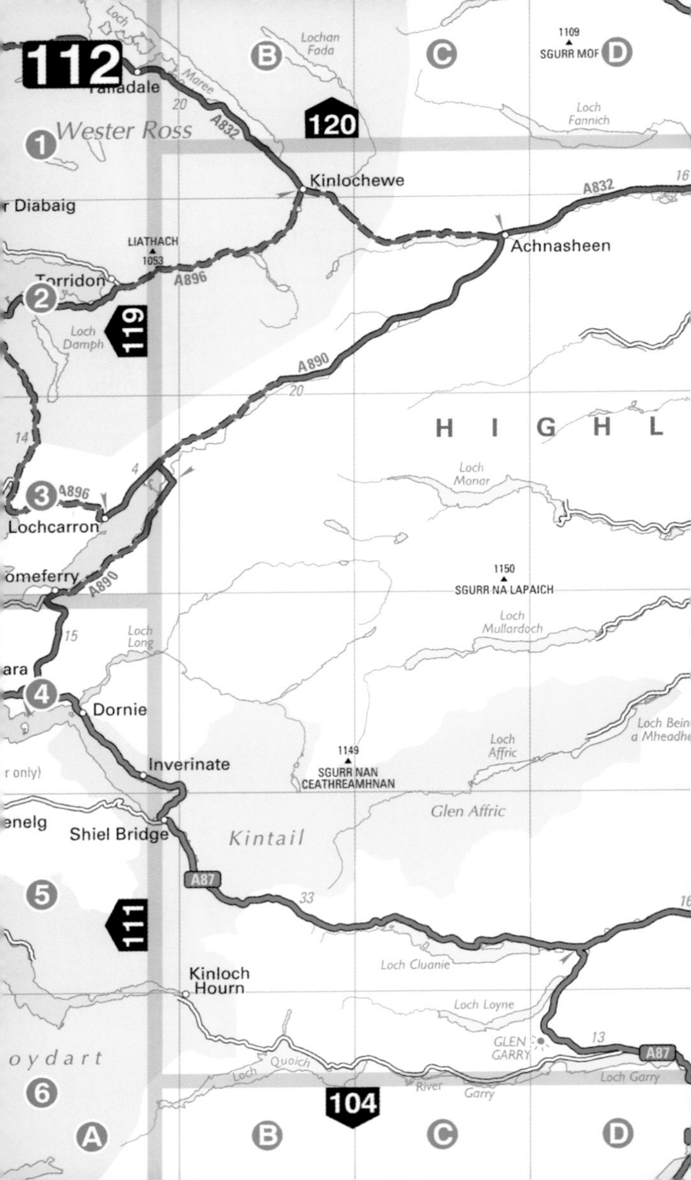
112
Talladale
Loch Maree
Wester Ross
Lochan Fada
120
1109
SGURR MOR
Loch Fannich
Kinlochewe
A832
Diabaig
Achnasheen
LIATHACH
1053
Torridon
A896
119
Loch Damph
A890
HIGHL
Loch Monar
A896
Lochcarron
omeferry
A890
1150
SGURR NA LAPAICH
Loch Mullardoch
Loch Long
ara
Dornie
Loch Beinn a Mheadhe
Loch Affric
1149
SGURR NAN CEATHREAMHNAN
Inverinate
r only)
Glen Affric
enelg
Shiel Bridge
Kintail
A87
111
Loch Cluanie
Kinloch Hourn
Loch Loyne
GLEN GARRY
A87
oydart
Loch Quoich
River Garry
Loch Garry
104

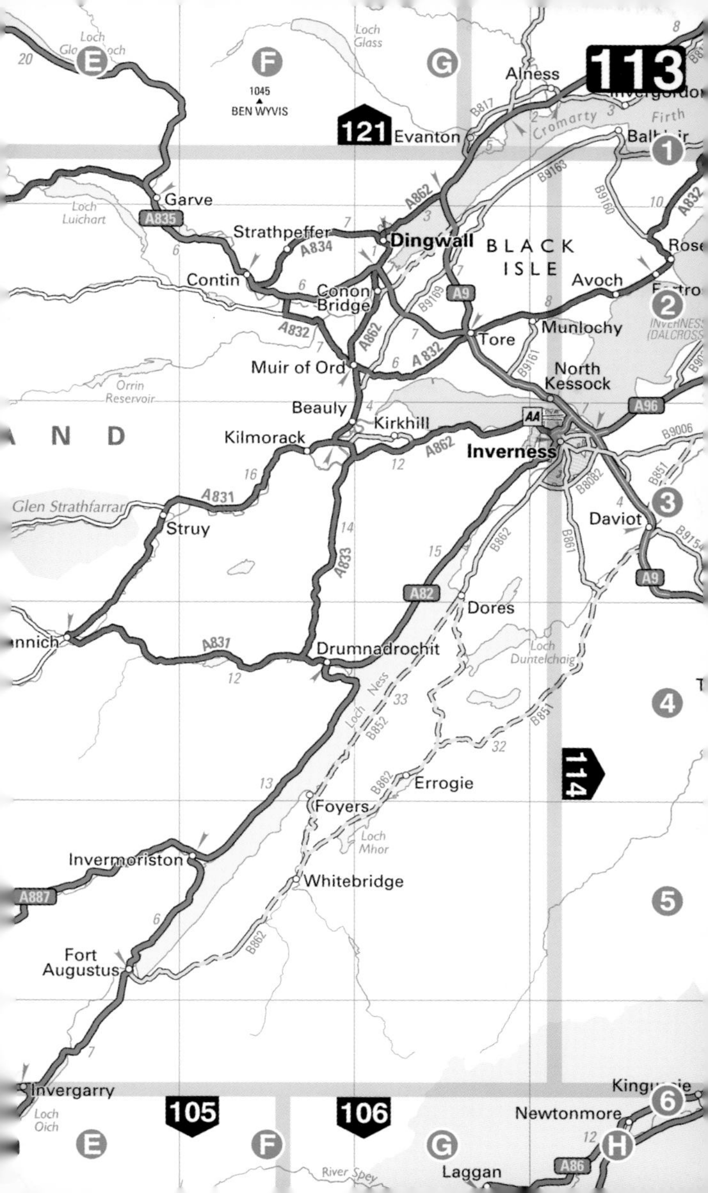

113
121
114
105
106
E
F
G
1
2
3
4
5
6
H
1045
BEN WYVIS
Loch Glass
Alness
Cromarty
Firth
Evanton
B817
Garve
Loch Luichart
A835
Strathpeffer
A834
Dingwall
BLACK ISLE
A862
B9163
B9160
A832
Rose
Avoch
Contin
Conon Bridge
B9169
A9
Tore
Munlochy
A832
Muir of Ord
Orrin Reservoir
B9161
North Kessock
Beauly
Kirkhill
A96
B9006
Kilmorack
A862
Inverness
B8082
B851
Glen Strathfarrar
A831
Struy
A833
B862
B861
Daviot
B9154
A82
A9
Dores
Drumnadrochit
A831
Loch Duntelchaig
Loch Ness
B852
B851
Errogie
B862
Foyers
Loch Mhor
Invermoriston
Whitebridge
A887
B862
Fort Augustus
Invergarry
Loch Oich
Newtonmore
A86
River Spey
Laggan

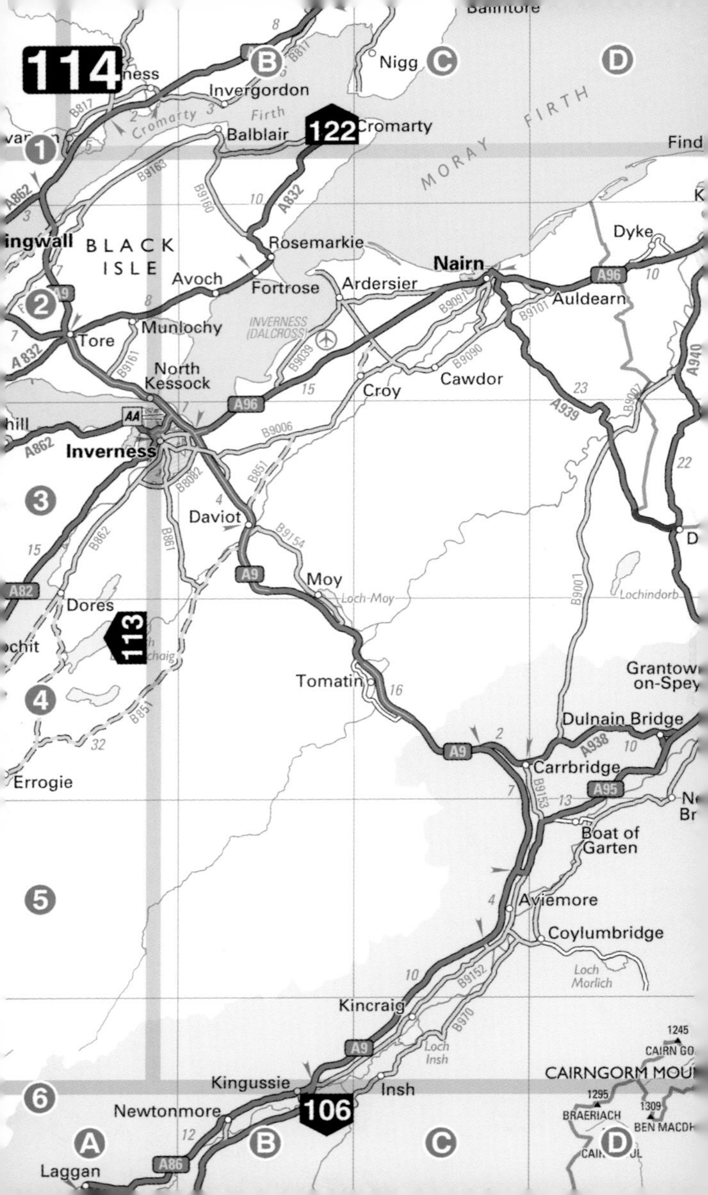

114
Invergordon
Nigg
Cromarty Firth
Balblair
122
Cromarty
MORAY FIRTH
Find
Dingwall
BLACK ISLE
Rosemarkie
Avoch
Fortrose
Nairn
Dyke
Ardersier
Auldearn
Tore
Munlochy
INVERNESS (DALCROSS)
North Kessock
Croy
Cawdor
Inverness
Daviot
Moy
Loch Moy
Lochindorb
Dores
113
Tomatin
Grantown-on-Spey
Dulnain Bridge
Errogie
Carrbridge
Boat of Garten
Aviemore
Coylumbridge
Loch Morlich
Kincraig
Loch Insh
CAIRNGORM MOU
CAIRN GO
BRAERIACH
BEN MACDH
Kingussie
Insh
106
Newtonmore
Laggan

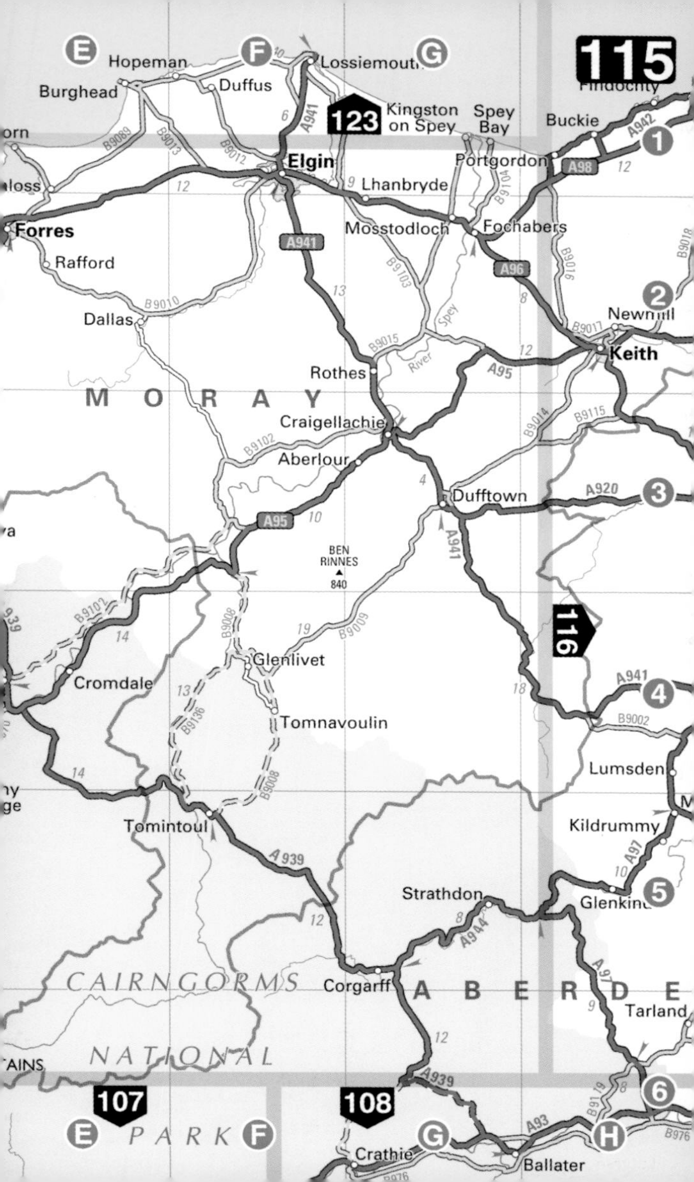
Hopeman
Burghead
Duffus
Lossiemouth
Kingston on Spey
Spey Bay
Buckie
Elgin
Portgordon
Lhanbryde
Forres
Mosstodloch
Fochabers
Rafford
Dallas
Newmill
Keith
Rothes
MORAY
Craigellachie
Aberlour
Dufftown
BEN RINNES
840
Glenlivet
Cromdale
Tomnavoulin
Lumsden
Kildrummy
Tomintoul
Strathdon
Glenkindie
Corgarff
CAIRNGORMS NATIONAL PARK
ABERDE
Tarland
Crathie
Ballater
A941
A98
A96
A95
A920
A939
A944
A97
A93
A942
B9089
B9013
B9012
B9010
B9104
B9103
B9016
B9015
B9017
B9014
B9115
B9102
B9008
B9009
B9136
B9002
B9119
B976
River Spey
123
116
107
108

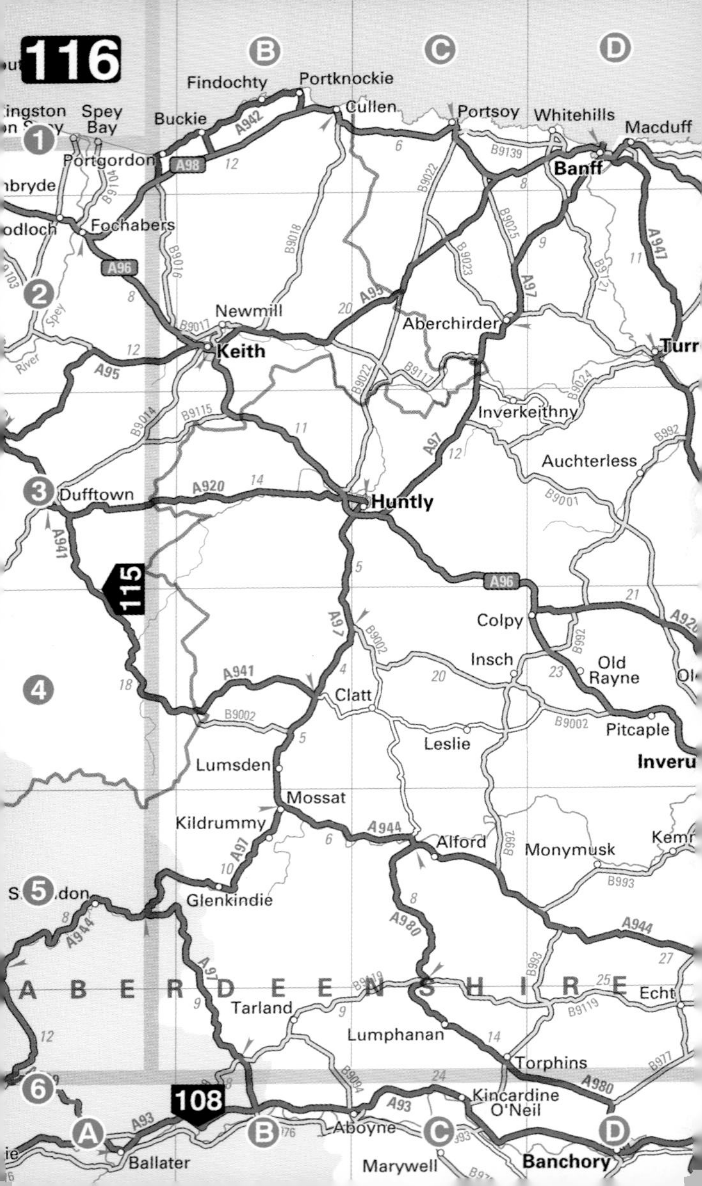
116
B
C
D
Findochty
Portknockie
Cullen
Portsoy
Whitehills
Macduff
Spey Bay
Buckie
Portgordon
Banff
Fochabers
Newmill
Aberchirder
Keith
Inverkeithny
Auchterless
Dufftown
Huntly
115
Colpy
Insch
Old Rayne
Clatt
Pitcaple
Leslie
Lumsden
Mossat
Kildrummy
Alford
Monymusk
Glenkindie
ABERDEENSHIRE
Tarland
Lumphanan
Echt
Torphins
Kincardine O'Neil
108
A
Aboyne
Ballater
Marywell
Banchory
A942
A98
A96
A95
A97
A920
A941
A944
A980
A93
A947
B9139
B9022
B9025
B9023
B9018
B9016
B9104
B9017
B9117
B9024
B9121
B9014
B9115
B9001
B992
B9002
B993
B9119
B977
B9094

E
F
G
Rosehearty
Sandhaven
Fraserburgh
Gardenstown
Pennan
Inverallochy
St Combs
New Aberdour
Memsie
Rathen
Crimond
Strichen
New Pitsligo
St Fergus
Cuminestown
Maud
Mintlaw
New Deer
Old Deer
Longside
Peterhead
Stuartfield
Clola
Boddam
Fyvie
Methlick
Hatton
Cruden Bay
Tarves
Ellon
Collieston
Pitmedden
Newburgh
Balmedie
Kintore
ABERDEEN
Dyce
Stromness
Lerwick
Kirkton of Skene
Garlogie
ABERDEEN
Peterculter
109
Durris
Portlethen
H
A98
A90
A981
A952
A950
A948
A947
A920
A975
A96
A944
A93
A956
B9031
B9032
B9033
B9030
B9093
B9027
B9170
B9106
B9005
B9000
B999
B993
B979
B977
B994
B9126
B9119
B9125
B9077
1
2
3
4
5
6

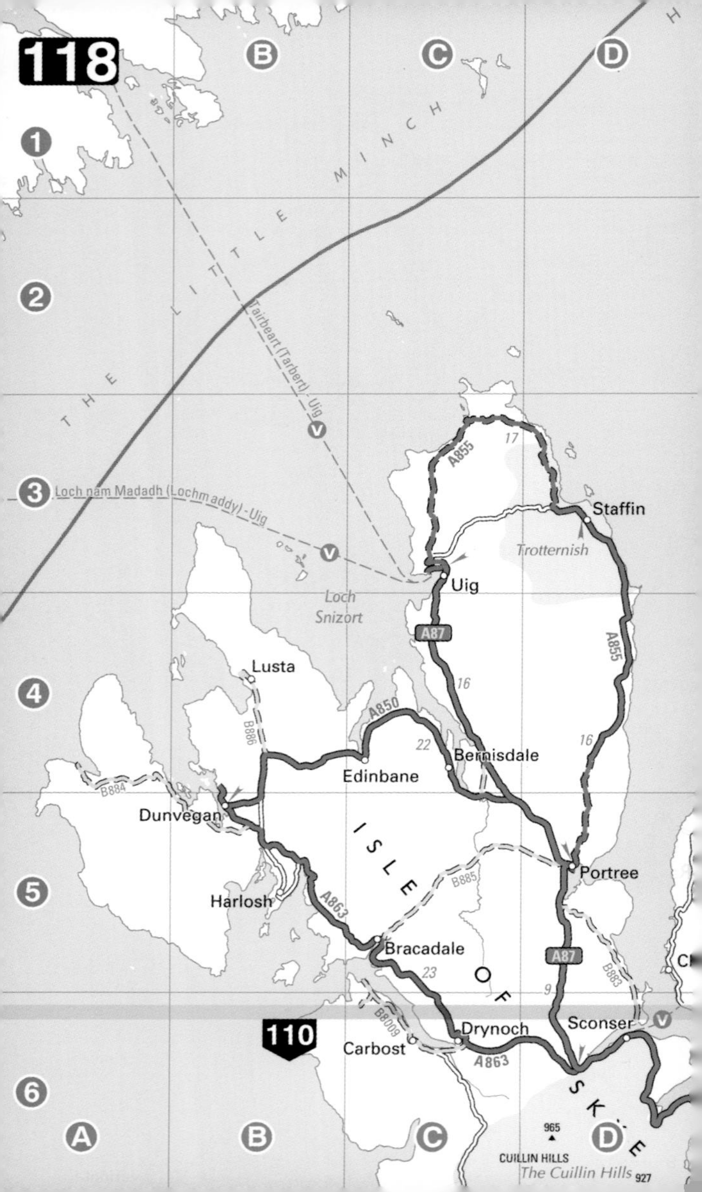

THE LITTLE MINCH
Tairbeart (Tarbert) - Uig
Loch nam Madadh (Lochmaddy) - Uig
Staffin
Trotternish
Uig
Loch Snizort
A855
A87
Lusta
A850
B886
Edinbane
Bernisdale
B884
Dunvegan
ISLE OF SKYE
Portree
B885
Harlosh
A863
Bracadale
B883
Sconser
Drynoch
Carbost
B8009
110
965
CUILLIN HILLS
The Cuillin Hills
927

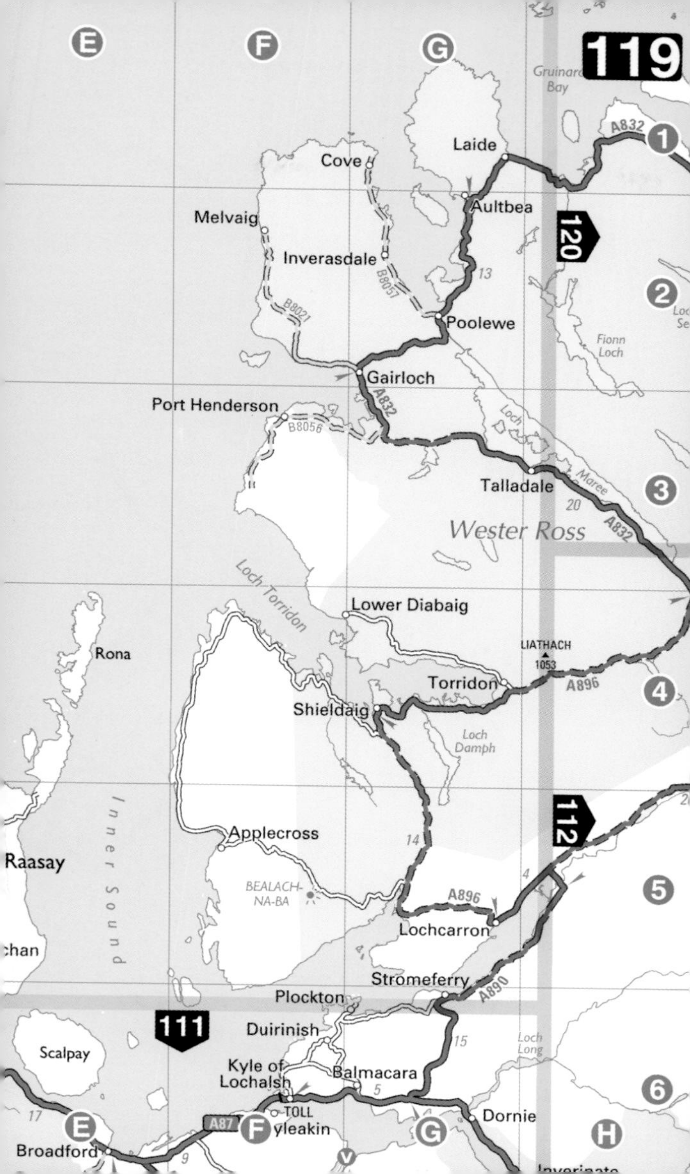

E
F
G
Gruinard Bay
A832
1
Laide
Cove
Aultbea
Melvaig
120
Inverasdale
B8057
13
2
B8021
Poolewe
Fionn Loch
Gairloch
A832
Port Henderson
B8056
Loch
Talladale
Maree
3
20
Wester Ross
A832
Loch Torridon
Lower Diabaig
LIATHACH
1053
Rona
Torridon
A896
4
Shieldaig
Loch Damph
Inner Sound
112
Applecross
14
Raasay
4
BEALACH-NA-BA
A896
5
Lochcarron
Stromeferry
A890
Plockton
111
Duirinish
15
Loch Long
Scalpay
Kyle of Lochalsh
Balmacara
5
6
17
TOLL
A87
Dornie
Broadford
9
H

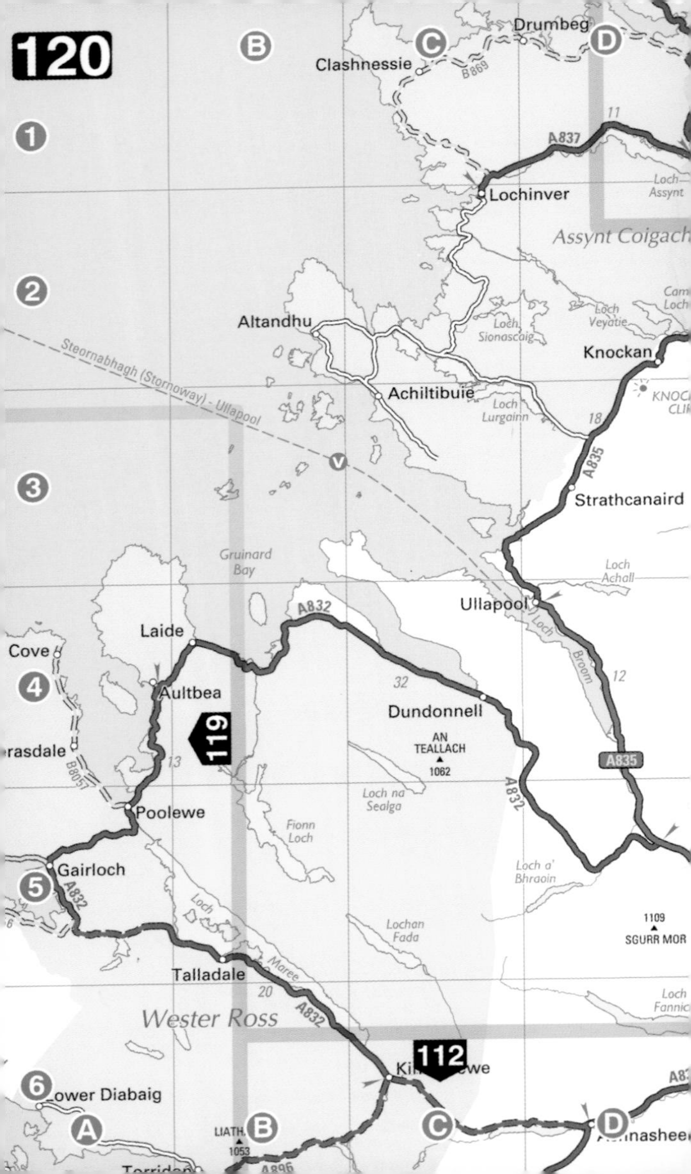

B
C
D
1
2
3
4
5
6
A
Drumbeg
Clashnessie
B869
11
A837
Lochinver
Loch Assynt
Assynt Coigach
Loch Sionascaig
Loch Veyatie
Altandhu
Knockan
Achiltibuie
Loch Lurgainn
18
A835
Steornabhagh (Stornoway) - Ullapool
V
Strathcanaird
Gruinard Bay
Loch Achall
Ullapool
A832
Laide
Cove
Aultbea
119
Loch Broom
12
32
Dundonnell
AN TEALLACH
1062
A835
erasdale
B8057
13
A832
Loch na Sealga
Poolewe
Fionn Loch
Gairloch
A832
Loch a' Bhraoin
Loch
Lochan Fada
1109
SGURR MOR
Talladale
Maree
20
A832
Wester Ross
Loch Fannich
112
Lower Diabaig
LIATH.
1053
A896

121
Altnaharra
Loch Naver
Loch Merkland
Loch a' Bhealaich
Loch Choire
21
37
A838
A836
Inchnadamph
124
998
BEN MORE ASSYNT
A837
Loch Shin
Shinness
Loch Ailsh
Loch Urigill
Lairg
A839
14
Rosehall
27
A837
B864
11
31
A837
Inveran
A836
122
Bonar Bridge
Ardgay
Spinningda
10
A386
15
STRUIE HILL
B9176
1081
EINN DEARG
Loch Morie
19
Loch Glass
Loch Glascarnoch
20
Alness
1045
BEN WYVIS
B817
Cromarty
Evanton
5
2
113
B9163
B916
16
Garve
A862
3
Loch Luichart
A835
Strathpeffer
7
A834
Dingwall
1
BLACK ISLE
Contin
6
Conon
A9
Avoc

Altnaharra
122
Naver
B
C
D
16
Kinbrace
Loch a' Bhealaich
Loch Choire
21
1
125
17
A897
A836
2
Shin
nness
Lairg
Loch Brora
21
A839
14
Brora
3
A839
B864
Golspie
A9
A837
11
Inveran
A836
7
Embo
Bonar Bridge
Spinningdale
Ardgay
A949
10
3
Dornoch
4
121
A386
Dornoch Firth
15
Edderton
6
Dornoch Firth
STRUIE HILL
Tain
Portm
B9176
Hill of Fearn
6
B9165
Loch Morie
B9175
19
5
Balintore
Loch Glass
8
A9
B817
Nigg
Alness
6
Invergordon
B817
2
Cromarty
3
Firth
FIRTH
Cromarty
Evanton
Balblair
MORAY
113
B9163
114
6
A862
B9160
A832
3
7
A
B
C
D
BLACK ISLE
Rosema
Nairn
Avoch
Fortrose
Ardersier

Latheron
Lybster
E
F
G
Dunbeath
20
1
Berriedale
126
A9
2
Helmsdale
3
4
mack
5
B9040
Hopeman
Lossiemouth
Fin
Burghead
Duffus
B9103
Kingston on Spey
Spey Bay
Buckie
6
A941
Findhorn
B9089
B9013
B9012
Elgin
115
Portgordon
A98
Kinloss
12
B9104
6
yke
E
Forres
F
G
H
A941
A96
10
Rafford
B9016

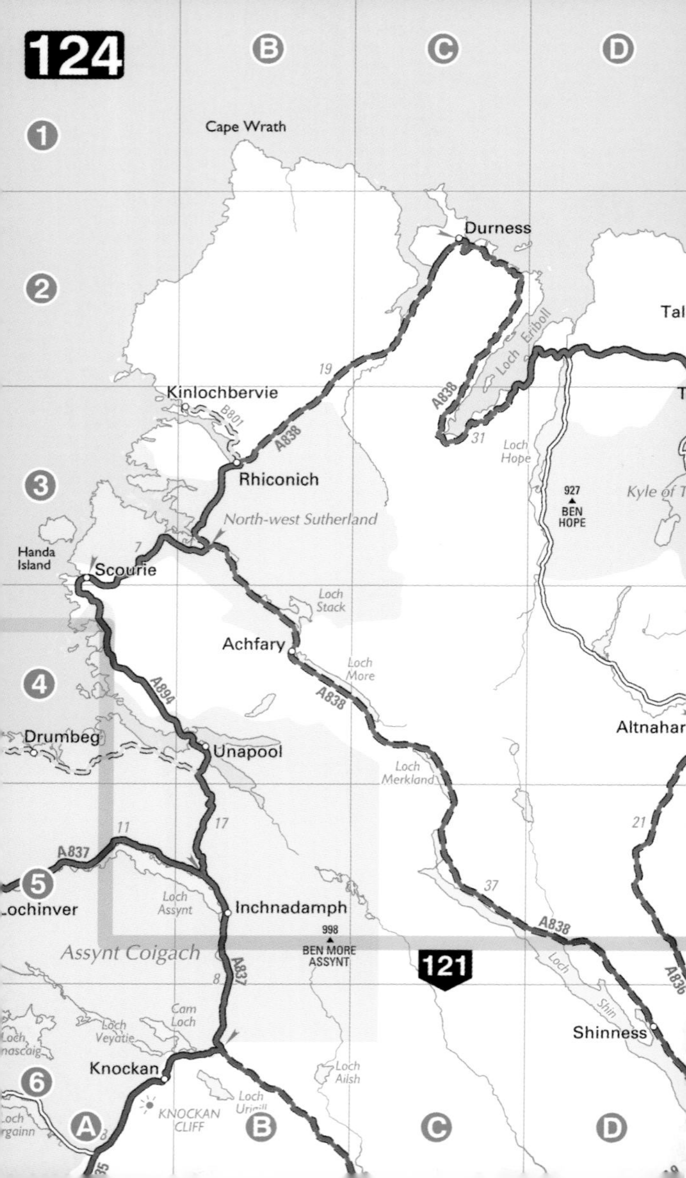

B
C
D
1
2
3
4
5
6
Cape Wrath
Durness
Tal
Loch Eriboll
A838
31
19
Kinlochbervie
B801
A838
Rhiconich
Loch Hope
927
BEN HOPE
Kyle of T
North-west Sutherland
Handa Island
7
Scourie
Loch Stack
Achfary
Loch More
A838
A894
Drumbeg
Unapool
Altnahar
Loch Merkland
11
17
21
A837
Lochinver
Loch Assynt
Inchnadamph
37
A838
998
BEN MORE ASSYNT
Assynt Coigach
121
A837
8
Loch Shin
A836
Cam Loch
Loch Veyatie
Shinness
Knockan
Loch Ailsh
KNOCKAN CLIFF
A
B
C
D

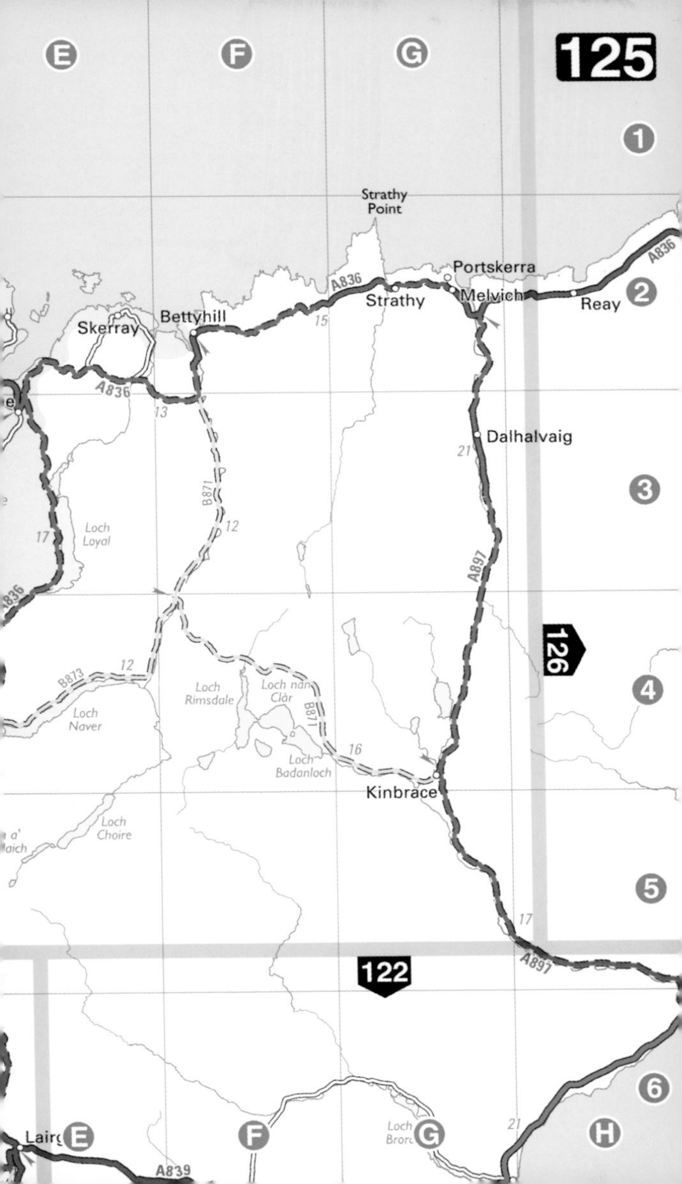
E
F
G
1
2
3
4
5
6
H
Strathy Point
Portskerra
Melvich
Strathy
Reay
A836
Bettyhill
Skerray
A836
13
15
Dalhalvaig
21
B871
12
Loch Loyal
17
A836
A897
126
B873
12
Loch Naver
Loch Rimsdale
Loch nan Clàr
B871
16
Loch Badanloch
Kinbrace
Loch Choire
17
A897
122
21
A839

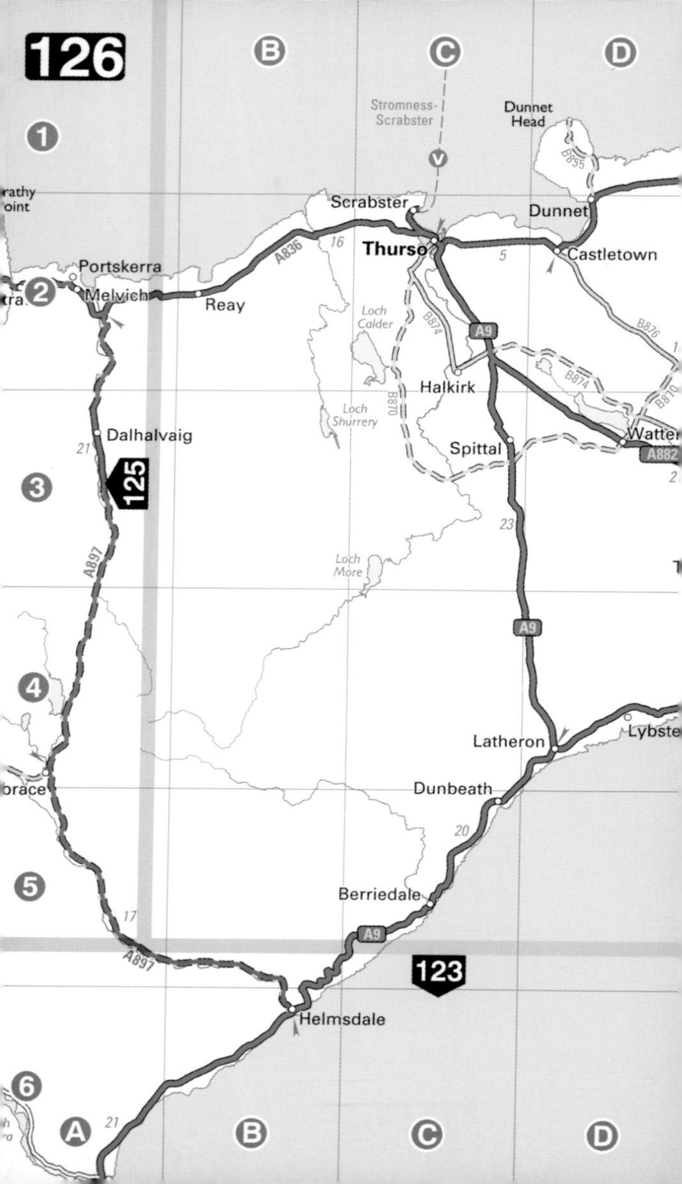

126
B
C
D
1
Stromness-
Scrabster
Dunnet
Head
B855
rathy
oint
Scrabster
Dunnet
Thurso
16
A836
5
Castletown
Portskerra
2
Melvich
Reay
Loch
Calder
B874
A9
B876
Halkirk
B874
B870
Loch
Shurrery
B870
Dalhalvaig
Watten
21
Spittal
A882
3
125
23
A897
Loch
More
A9
4
Latheron
Lybster
Dunbeath
20
5
Berriedale
17
A9
A897
123
Helmsdale
6
21
A
B
C
D

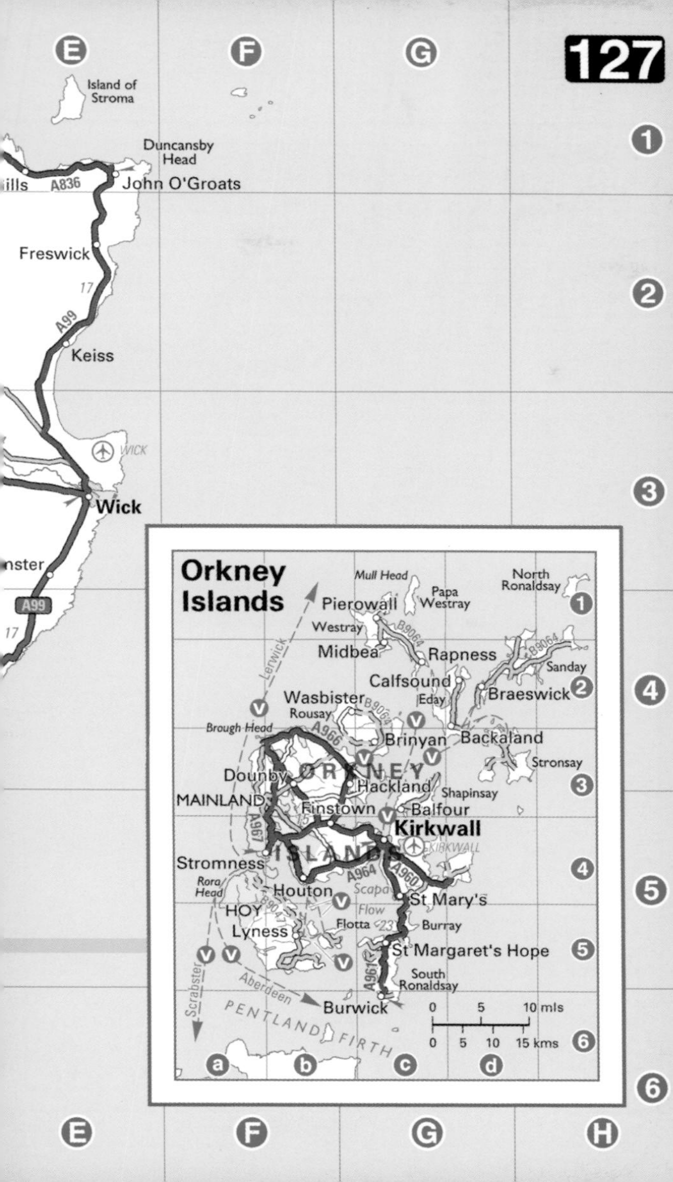
E
F
G
H
1
2
3
4
5
6
Island of Stroma
Duncansby Head
John O'Groats
A836
Freswick
17
A99
Keiss
WICK
Wick
A99
17
Orkney Islands
Mull Head
Papa Westray
North Ronaldsay
Pierowall
Westray
B9064
Midbea
Rapness
Sanday
Calfsound
Braeswick
Lerwick
Wasbister
Rousay
B9064
Eday
Brough Head
A966
Brinyan
Backaland
Stronsay
Dounby
ORKNEY
Hackland
Shapinsay
MAINLAND
Finstown
Balfour
A967
Kirkwall
KIRKWALL
ISLANDS
Stromness
A964
A960
Rora Head
Houton
Scapa Flow
St Mary's
HOY
Lyness
Flotta
Burray
St Margaret's Hope
A961
South Ronaldsay
Scrabster
Aberdeen
Burwick
PENTLAND FIRTH
0 5 10 mls
0 5 10 15 kms
a
b
c
d

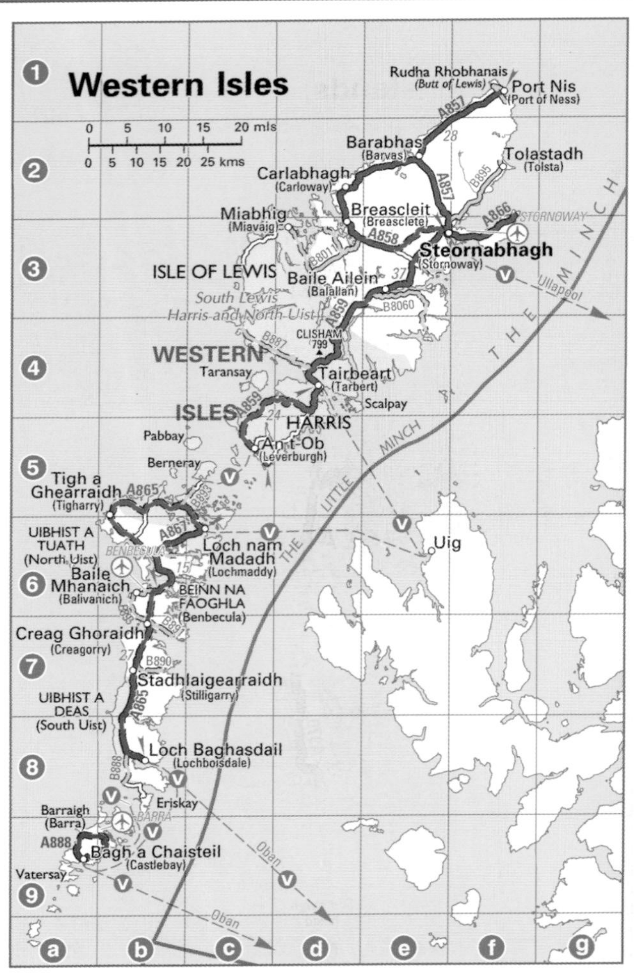
Western Isles
0 5 10 15 20 mls
0 5 10 15 20 25 kms
Rudha Rhobhanais
(Butt of Lewis)
Port Nis
(Port of Ness)
Barabhas
(Barvas)
Tolastadh
(Tolsta)
Carlabhagh
(Carloway)
Miabhig
(Miavaig)
Breascleit
(Breasclete)
STORNOWAY
Steornabhagh
(Stornoway)
ISLE OF LEWIS
Baile Ailein
(Balallan)
South Lewis
Harris and North Uist
CLISHAM
799
WESTERN
ISLES
Taransay
Tairbeart
(Tarbert)
Scalpay
HARRIS
Pabbay
An t-Ob
(Leverburgh)
Berneray
Tigh a
Ghearraidh
(Tigharry)
UIBHIST A
TUATH
(North Uist)
BENBECULA
Loch nam
Madadh
(Lochmaddy)
Uig
Baile
Mhanaich
(Balivanich)
BEINN NA
FAOGHLA
(Benbecula)
Creag Ghoraidh
(Creagorry)
Stadhlaigearraidh
(Stilligarry)
UIBHIST A
DEAS
(South Uist)
Loch Baghasdail
(Lochboisdale)
Eriskay
Barraigh
(Barra)
BARRA
Bagh a Chaisteil
(Castlebay)
Vatersay
Ullapool
Oban
Oban
THE MINCH
THE LITTLE MINCH
A857
A857
A858
A866
A859
A859
A865
A867
A865
A888
B895
B8011
B8060
B887
B893
B888
B891
B890
B888
28
37
24
15
27
1
2
3
4
5
6
7
8
9
a
b
c
d
e
f
g

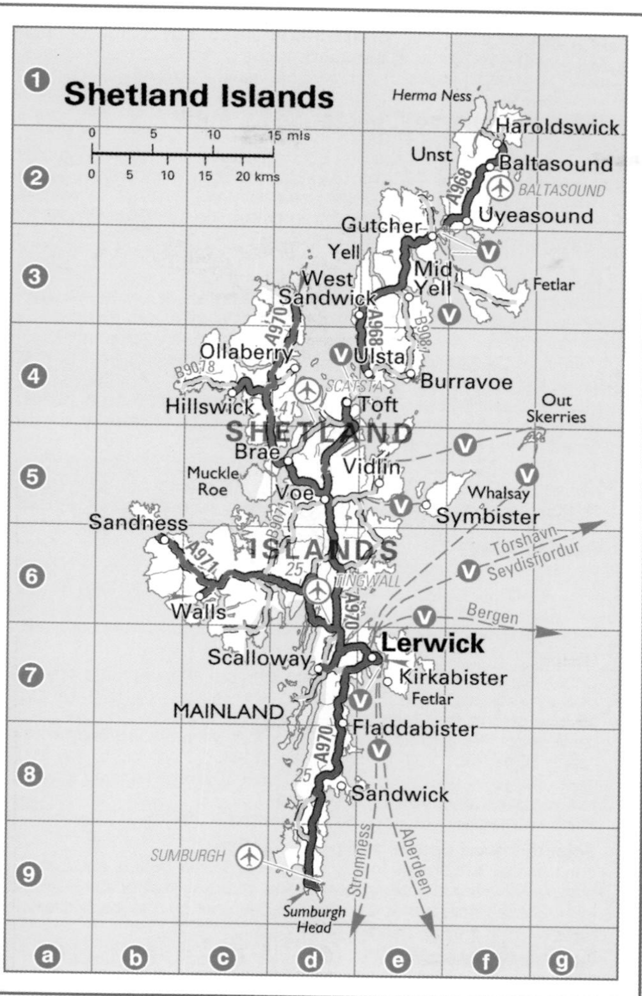
Shetland Islands
0 5 10 15 mls
0 5 10 15 20 kms
1
2
3
4
5
6
7
8
9
a
b
c
d
e
f
g
Herma Ness
Haroldswick
Unst
Baltasound
BALTASOUND
A968
Uyeasound
Gutcher
Yell
Mid Yell
Fetlar
West Sandwick
A968
B9081
A970
Ollaberry
B9078
Ulsta
SCATSTA
Burravoe
Hillswick
Toft
Out Skerries
SHETLAND
Brae
Vidlin
Muckle Roe
Voe
Whalsay
B9071
Symbister
Sandness
A971
ISLANDS
Tórshavn
Seydisfjordur
TINGWALL
Walls
A970
Bergen
Lerwick
Scalloway
Kirkabister
Fetlar
MAINLAND
Fladdabister
A970
Sandwick
SUMBURGH
Stromness
Aberdeen
Sumburgh Head

London Congestion Charging Zone

What is it?
The central London congestion charge is a £5 daily charge for driving or parking a vehicle on public roads in the congestion charging zone during operating hours.

When does it apply?
Since February 2003, anyone (except those exempt or discounted) driving or parking a vehicle on public roads in the congestion charging zone between 7am – 6.30pm Monday to Friday, excluding Public Holidays, is obliged to pay a daily charge of £5. Payment of this charge allows you to enter, drive around, and leave the charging zone as many times as you wish that day.

How does it work?
Motorists driving within the zone during operating hours must have either pre-paid the £5 daily charge or pay before 10pm that day. When you pay, you will be entering your vehicle registration on to a database. Cameras will read your number plate as you enter or drive within the zone and check it against the database. Once the vehicle number plate has been matched, showing that you have paid or are exempt from the charge, the photographic image of your vehicle will be wiped off the database.
At midnight each day, the registered keeper of any vehicle recorded as having been in the zone during charging hours without having paid the charge (or being exempt) will be issued with a Penalty Charge Notice.

How do I pay?
Whichever of the following payment methods you choose, you can pay the congestion charge in advance, or after travelling, so long as you pay by 10pm on the day of travel.
The charge can be paid on a daily, weekly, monthly or annual basis.

Online:
Simply follow the links at *www.cclondon.com* and you'll find paying the charge quick and easy.

Mobile phone text message:
Register for this payment method online at *www.cclondon.com* or by calling 0845 900 1234. Once registered you will be able to pay the £5 daily charge on your day of travel up until 10pm by sending a simple text message from your mobile phone.
Please remember you should never text while driving.

Selected retail outlets and petrol stations:
You can pay the charge in cash at selected retail outlets and petrol stations where you see the congestion charging sign or the PayPoint logo. Some retailers may also accept payment by cheque and credit or debit card at their discretion.

Self Service Machines:
You can pay the charge with certain credit and debit cards at self service machines in major public car parks within the charging zone.

Phone:
Call 0845 900 1234.

Post:

The 'Paying the congestion charge' form can be obtained by writing to Congestion charging, PO Box 2985, Coventry CV7 8ZR or by calling 0845 900 1234. You cannot pay the charge on the day of travel by post.

If you are going to pay the congestion charge often, you may wish to apply online or over the phone for a Fast Track Card - which holds personal and vehicle details - to speed up payments.

Does everyone have to pay?

Certain vehicles or vehicle users are either exempt or receive a discount from the £5 daily charge.

Exemption:

Drivers of exempt vehicles will not have to pay the charge or register with Transport for London. These include:

Motorbikes, mopeds and bicycles
London licensed Taxis and minicabs
Vehicles used by disabled persons that are exempt from Vehicle Excise Duty
Licensed buses with 9 or more seats
Emergency services' vehicles.

90% discount:

Each eligible resident can register with Transport for London for a 90% discount on one private vehicle. The minimum charge payable is one week (five consecutive days) at £2.50.

100% discount:

Some vehicles are eligible for a 100% discount. Users of these vehicles must register with Transport for London to obtain their discount. These include:

Vehicles used by Blue and Orange Badge holders
Alternative fuel vehicles meeting strict emissions standards
Vehicles with 9 or more seats, not licensed as buses.

Under special circumstances, certain NHS staff and patients are eligible for 100% reimbursement of the congestion charge.

What happens if I fail to pay the charge?

If you pay the charge between 10pm and midnight on the day of travel you will need to pay a £5 surcharge on the standard charge (you pay a total of £10).

If you have not paid by midnight on the day of travel an £80 Penalty Charge Notice (PCN) will be sent to the registered keeper of the vehicle. This will be reduced to £40 if paid within 14 days but increased to £120 if not paid within 28 days.

After three or more outstanding congestion charging PCNs, vehicles may be clamped or removed from anywhere in Greater London. The vehicle will only be released on payment of all outstanding charges and related costs.

How can I get more information?

Further information on any of the above can be obtained by visiting *www.cclondon.com* or phoning 0845 900 1234, minicom users can call 0207 649 9121.

Or by writing to:

Congestion Charging London, PO Box 2985, Coventry CV7 8ZR

You can also visit: *www.theAA.com*

CAMDEN TOWN
CAMDEN TOWN
CAMDEN TOWN
CAMDEN TOWN
KING'S CROSS STATION
ST PANCRAS STATION
YORK WAY
ST JOHN'S WOOD
ST JOHN'S WOOD
A40, OXFORD
SHEPHERD'S BUSH
SHEPHERD'S BUSH
HAMMERSMITH
HAMMERSMITH
FULHAM
PUTNEY
PUTNEY
BATTERSEA
REGENT'S PARK
MORNINGTON CRESCENT
EUSTON STATION
EUSTON SQUARE
WARREN STREET
GREAT PORTLAND STREET
REGENT'S PARK
BAKER STREET
MARYLEBONE STATION
MARYLEBONE
EDGWARE ROAD
BLOOMSBURY
GOODGE STREET
TOTTENHAM COURT ROAD
OXFORD CIRCUS
BOND STREET
MARBLE ARCH
SOHO
COVENT GARDEN
LEICESTER SQUARE
PICCADILLY CIRCUS
CHARING CROSS STA
MAYFAIR
ST JAMES
GREEN PARK
HYDE PARK
GREEN PARK
ST JAMES'S PARK
HYDE PARK CORNER
KNIGHTSBRIDGE
KNIGHTSBRIDGE
ST JAMES'S PARK
WESTMINSTER
BELGRAVIA
VICTORIA STATION
SOUTH KENSINGTON
SLOANE SQUARE
PIMLICO
CHELSEA
VAUXHALL
PRINCE ALBERT ROAD
WELLINGTON ROAD
PARK ROAD
MARYLEBONE ROAD
EUSTON ROAD
ALBANY STREET
HAMPSTEAD ROAD
EVERSHOLT STREET
GOWER ST
TOTTENHAM COURT ROAD
BAKER STREET
GLOUCESTER PLACE
PORTLAND PLACE
REGENT STREET
WIGMORE STREET
CAVENDISH SQUARE
OXFORD STREET
NEW OXFORD ST
HIGH HOLBORN
CHARING CROSS RD
SHAFTESBURY AVE
SEYMOUR STREET
EDGWARE ROAD
BAYSWATER ROAD
CUMBERLAND GATE
PARK LANE
PICCADILLY
ST JAMES'S STREET
PALL MALL
WHITEHALL
PARLIAMENT ST
KENSINGTON ROAD
KNIGHTSBRIDGE
BROMPTON ROAD
SLOANE STREET
GROSVENOR PLACE
VICTORIA STREET
BUCKINGHAM PALACE ROAD
ECCLESTON ST
VAUXHALL BRIDGE ROAD
BELGRAVE ROAD
PIMLICO RD
CHELSEA BRIDGE ROAD
KING'S ROAD
FULHAM RD
GROSVENOR ROAD
CHELSEA EMBANKMENT
CHELSEA BRIDGE
VAUXHALL BRIDGE
MILLBANK
ABINGDON ST

Central London
Congestion Charging Zone
Car Parks
500 metres
HOLLOWAY
ISLINGTON
HIGHBURY
STOKE NEWINGTON
BETHNAL GREEN
WHITECHAPEL
GREENWICH
NEW CROSS
CAMBERWELL
CLAPHAM
FARRINGDON
BARBICAN
MOORGATE
LIVERPOOL STREET STATION
CITY
CITY (THAMES-LINK)
FENCHURCH ST STATION
BLACKFRIARS STATION
CANNON STREET STATION
SOUTHWARK
WATERLOO EAST STATION
LONDON BRIDGE STA
BERMONDSEY
ELEPHANT & CASTLE STATION
LAMBETH
NEWINGTON
WALWORTH
River Thames

Distance chart

The mileage chart shows distances in miles between two towns along AA-recommended routes. Using motorways and other main roads this is normally the fastest route, though not necessarily the shortest.

Lincoln - Sheffield = 47 miles

1 mile = 1.6 kilometres

	Aberdeen	Aberystwyth	Barnstaple	Birmingham	Brighton	Bristol	Cambridge	Cardiff	Carlisle	Carmarthen	Dorchester	Dover	Edinburgh	Exeter	Fort William	Glasgow	Gloucester	Guildford	Holyhead	Hull	Inverness	Kendal	Leeds	Lincoln	Liverpool	Maidstone	Manchester	Middlesbrough	Newcastle	Norwich	Nottingham	Oxford	Penzance	Perth	Plymouth	Sheffield	Southampton	Stranraer	Taunton	Wick	York
Aberystwyth	472																																								
Barnstaple	608	214																																							
Birmingham	436	124	180																																						
Brighton	613	288	210	171																																					
Bristol	518	130	100	90	169																																				
Cambridge	463	215	267	97	120	170																																			
Cardiff	537	111	128	109	202	44	203																																		
Carlisle	236	236	371	199	376	281	256	300																																	
Carmarthen	520	48	190	172	264	107	266	68	284																																
Dorchester	600	206	94	172	119	62	184	120	364	182																															
Dover	587	326	272	208	82	205	124	239	381	301	200																														
Edinburgh	126	336	471	299	476	381	333	400	100	386	463	458																													
Exeter	593	198	44	165	178	84	259	113	356	175	57	248	455																												
Fort William	156	435	570	398	576	480	456	499	199	485	562	580	137	554																											
Glasgow	150	332	467	295	472	377	353	396	96	382	459	477	47	451	102																										
Gloucester	484	113	126	56	155	36	150	63	248	125	118	192	346	110	445	343																									
Guildford	571	224	175	128	44	106	96	139	335	201	97	97	433	150	532	430	99																								
Holyhead	464	102	339	167	345	249	259	202	228	150	331	369	326	323	425	323	215	302																							
Hull	376	227	320	139	258	230	138	250	170	311	312	262	247	304	367	266	196	239	218																						
Inverness	106	496	631	459	637	541	517	561	260	546	623	641	157	616	66	176	507	595	488	430																					
Kendal	283	189	324	153	330	234	251	254	47	240	316	354	145	309	245	143	200	288	181	164	307																				
Leeds	329	173	301	120	262	211	146	230	123	224	293	271	200	285	321	219	177	220	165	59	383	110																			
Lincoln	388	199	275	98	216	185	95	205	182	267	246	220	258	260	379	277	151	173	204	44	441	176	74																		
Liverpool	362	110	272	101	278	182	193	202	126	158	264	302	224	257	324	222	148	236	102	128	386	79	74	139																	
Maidstone	545	284	234	166	50	167	82	200	339	262	161	41	416	209	537	435	153	58	327	220	599	313	231	178	261																
Manchester	357	134	261	89	266	171	160	190	120	184	253	290	219	245	318	216	136	224	125	97	380	74	44	85	34	248															
Middlesbrough	276	244	357	176	318	267	197	286	95	294	349	322	146	341	283	190	232	276	235	89	308	84	64	122	145	280	114														
Newcastle	235	275	388	207	349	298	229	317	60	325	380	353	106	372	242	153	264	307	266	142	267	102	95	154	176	311	145	39													
Norwich	488	278	329	160	168	233	63	266	282	328	241	172	359	313	480	378	212	160	321	147	542	276	174	103	240	130	185	223	254												
Nottingham	395	162	232	51	193	142	86	161	189	223	224	210	266	216	387	285	107	151	178	93	449	164	77	39	112	168	71	130	161	119											
Oxford	510	160	170	68	109	73	82	107	274	169	115	146	373	154	472	370	48	67	242	190	534	228	174	132	176	107	164	227	258	146	102										
Penzance	702	308	108	274	287	193	368	222	466	284	167	357	564	109	663	562	220	259	434	415	726	419	403	370	367	318	356	451	482	433	326	265									
Perth	86	388	523	351	529	433	378	453	152	438	515	503	42	507	102	64	399	486	379	291	114	199	245	303	278	461	275	192	150	404	310	426	617								
Plymouth	633	239	62	205	218	124	299	153	397	215	98	288	495	44	594	493	151	190	365	346	657	350	334	301	298	249	287	382	413	364	257	196	78	544							
Sheffield	397	166	272	91	233	182	122	201	161	263	264	247	236	256	359	257	148	191	157	66	421	115	38	47	79	205	39	100	131	148	45	142	366	309	297						
Southampton	578	225	142	135	66	106	136	140	342	201	53	152	440	111	539	437	100	49	309	258	601	295	241	199	243	113	232	294	325	204	169	67	221	489	152	209					
Stranraer	235	342	477	305	482	387	363	406	106	392	469	487	132	461	181	86	352	440	333	276	261	153	229	288	232	445	229	201	163	388	295	380	571	149	502	267	447				
Taunton	560	165	50	132	160	51	226	80	323	142	45	224	422	34	521	419	77	126	291	272	583	277	261	228	225	185	213	309	340	291	184	123	144	471	75	224	94	429			
Wick	207	597	732	560	738	642	618	662	361	647	724	742	258	716	166	277	608	695	588	531	104	408	484	543	487	700	484	409	367	644	550	635	826	215	757	523	702	362	684		
York	323	201	314	133	275	224	154	243	116	251	306	279	193	298	314	212	189	233	192	38	376	91	24	79	102	237	71	51	89	180	87	184	408	239	339	57	251	223	265	477	
LONDON	550	239	216	121	54	120	59	153	314	215	125	78	413	200	512	410	102	31	282	186	574	268	201	143	216	39	204	254	285	118	129	56	310	462	241	169	77	420	167	675	211

Wick
Inverness
Aberdeen
Fort William
Perth
Edinburgh
Glasgow
Newcastle upon Tyne
Stranraer
Carlisle
Middlesbrough
Kendal
York
Leeds
Kingston upon Hull
Holyhead
Liverpool
Manchester
Sheffield
Lincoln
Nottingham
Norwich
Aberystwyth
Birmingham
Cambridge
Gloucester
Carmarthen
Oxford
Cardiff
Bristol
LONDON
Barnstaple
Guildford
Maidstone
Salisbury
Dover
Taunton
Southampton
Exeter
Brighton
Dorchester
Penzance
Plymouth

A

B

C

D

F

G

H

L

S

T

U

V

W